London Recruits

For Rikki, Teigan and Kiera

LONDON RECRUITS
The Secret War against Apartheid

compiled and edited by Ken Keable

with an introduction by Ronnie Kasrils
and a foreword by Z. Pallo Jordan

MERLIN PRESS

Published in the UK in 2012 by
The Merlin Press Ltd
6 Crane Street Chambers
Crane Street
Pontypool
NP4 6ND
Wales

ISBN. 978-0-85036-655-6

British Library Cataloguing in Publication Data is available from the
British Library

Passages from Ronnie Kasril's book *Armed and Dangerous – My
Undercover Struggle Against Apartheid* are quoted by kind permission
of Jonathan Ball Publishers.

The editor wishes to thank the following:
the South African High Commission in London for supporting this
project; Laura Miller for her help and advice; Karen Neal of New
Zealand for the photo of Jo Lewis and Mike Harris (Karen was one
of the tourists on the Africa Hinterland safari); Mavis Cook for the
photo of Bob Condon with herself; Roger O'Hara for the photos of
Gerry Wan and Eric Caddick; all the contributors, who have been an
inspiration.

All royalties from this book will go to The Nelson Mandela Children's
Fund. See www.nelsonmandelachildrensfund.com or www.mandela-
children.org.uk

Printed in the UK by Imprint Digital, Exeter
and in South Africa by Mega Digital, Cape Town

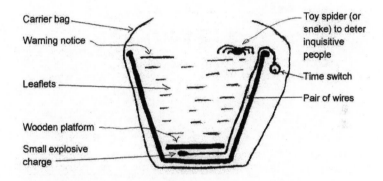

Carrier bag

Warning notice

Leaflets

Wooden platform

Small explosive charge

Toy spider (or snake) to deter inquisitive people

Time switch

Pair of wires

Bucket-type leaflet bomb as used by the London Recruits in South African cities from November 1969 onwards. Prototypes were tested in Bristol, in the Somerset countryside, on Hampstead Heath and in Richmond Park. The devices harmed no one but distributed hundreds of ANC leaflets high into the air. Sketch by Ken Keable.

LEAFLET BOMBS WARN VORSTER: END IS NEAR

From DOUGLAS ALEXANDER

JOHANNESBURG.

TWO BOMBS exploded in Johannesburg today scattering hundreds of leaflets attacking South Africa's government.

One bomb exploded in Diagonal Street, a non-white area in Johannesburg's east side. Another exploded in the great hall at the University of Witwatersrand.

The pamphlets were headlined "The African Nationalist Congress says to (Prime Minister) Vorster and his gang. They said: "Your days are coming to an end . . . we will take back our country."

Earlier similar leaflets were scattered by explosive devices in Durban, Cape Town and Port Elizabeth.

Police believe the incidents were connected with the distribution in Britain of documents threatening police and newspapers in the name of POQO, a militant arm of the African National Congress.

Danger to eyesight

A police expert said charges found in some unexploded bombs averaged about one and a half ounces, enough to inflict burns or damage to the eyesight of anyone close to a blast.

The significance of the "bombing" lies in the precision with which the operation was executed and the relatively sophisticated equipment

CONTENTS

FOREWORD
Z Pallo Jordan

The effectiveness of international solidarity was more than vindicated in the struggle for freedom and democracy in South Africa. What was once remarked as 'the South African Miracle' owes much to the knitting together of a number of interconnected and related threads of that struggle. Among these, the solidarity that the South African liberation movement was able to mobilise, amongst virtually every sector of society, was decisive at a moment when the apartheid regime desperately required credit to survive.

During the 20th century, two movements won virtual universal support among all democrats. The first was the struggle against fascism/Nazism in Europe; the other was the struggle against apartheid/racism in South Africa.

Political figures from across the spectrum, excluding the far-right, found a role and ways in which to relate to these struggles. Conservatives who found racial oppression and racism reprehensible; liberals who regarded racism as a violation of the very basis of their political creed; socialists and Communists who saw racism as a denial of the humanity of other human beings; conscientious religious persons who regarded racism as sacrilege that denied the common fatherhood of God; all could make common cause in an international movement in opposition to apartheid. By the 1980s, cross-party lobbies in a number of European parliaments were able to constitute such a body in the EU Parliament.

After the defeat of fascism/Nazism the international movement for the overthrow and destruction of apartheid was the greatest moral campaign of the century.

This book contains many of the untold stories of South Africa's journey to the democratic breakthrough of 1994. Motivated by a profound commitment to the liberation of humanity, the authors of these narratives were prepared to contribute directly to the reconstruction of the South African political underground. Referred to as the 'London Recruits', they undertook extremely dangerous missions into South Africa, initially to deliver propaganda materials in the form of leaflets, banners and to stage street broadcasts, but later also to transport and store weapons, and to set up secure communications between the ANC leadership and its units operating inside South Africa.

To this effort they brought their time, their skills, their knowledge, but most of all, their undoubted courage.

They were drawn from different backgrounds and political formations on the left. What they shared was a readiness to risk life and limb in the struggle of another country. Working in self-contained cells that were unaware of each other, under the guidance of a small unit operating out of London, these dedicated women and men helped the liberation movement to rebuild its capacity inside South Africa at a time when repression had all but extinguished the embers of resistance. Their contribution to the struggle for South African freedom can at last be told.

They are the continuators of a tradition derived from 19th century Europe and Latin America, when democrats and liberation fighters, regarding the democratic struggle as universal, had shown little regard for national borders. Giuseppe Garibaldi participated in a number of Latin American independence struggles before returning to his native Italy to lead the "Red Shirts" invasion that liberated Naples. Simon Bolivar led and participated in other wars of independence from Spain, in addition to that in his native Venezuela.

When the four rightist generals rose against the Republican government of Spain in 1936, it was the international left who responded to Spain's distress by mobilising the International

Brigades that fought in defence of the republic. The struggle for freedom in South Africa was to benefit from such traditions in a number of ways. The opponents of racism and the apartheid regime who were ready to do more than lend indirect support invariably came from the left wing of the political spectrum.

The Sharpeville massacre of March 1960, the general strikes that it inspired, followed by the banning of the ANC and the PAC, had shocked British public opinion. But it was among the left that it inspired considered efforts to lend assistance. An emissary from the Communist Party of Great Britain (CPGB) arrived in South Africa during May of 1960 to deliver funds for relief and to assist the movement to recover from the repressive onslaught. Members of the Seamen's Union acted as couriers, delivering important messages, documents and funds between London and South Africa.

It was after the racist regime's repression had virtually dismembered the underground, after the Rivonia Trial of 1964, that these tentative international links came into their own as the movement mounted its counter-offensive to reassert its presence in South Africa.

London, Paris and Geneva, where the relative liberalism of the British, French and Swiss political systems offered a degree of security against the repressive regimes of pre-democratic Europe, were the points at which radical political exiles congregated. Twentieth century exiles also gravitated to London, and South Africans were no exception.

By the mid-1960s a sizeable South African exile community had established itself in Britain. Concentrated around London and in a few university towns, the South African exiles actively mobilised support for the struggle back home by becoming involved in the work of the Anti-Apartheid Movement and, more directly, in the work of rebuilding and sustaining the underground movement at home.

London was the centre from which the movement published much of its materials. From April 1967, with assistance from the Socialist Unity Party of East Germany, the ANC produced a monthly journal, *Sechaba*, which served as both an instrument of international mobilisation and an organiser of the South African community in exile. By 1990, when the ANC was legalized in South Africa, it was producing five other publications regularly from London and various points in Africa.

The South African Communist Party (SACP), which had begun producing a quarterly journal, *The African Communist*, from London in late 1959, streamlined its operation by printing and distributing from Berlin in the GDR. By 1990 it was supplementing this with a news sheet, *Umsebenzi*, printed in London.

The regular movement of people between Britain and South Africa made it possible for London to become a staging post for transporting propaganda and other printed materials to South Africa. Soon other possibilities were investigated and implemented.

The radical euphoria of the 1960s inspired many drawn to the international solidarity movement to seek ways of active participation. Demoralised and dispersed, the remnants of the movement that had survived the repression inside South Africa had to be energised and reorganised. The reconstruction of an effective organisation, capable of working and surviving under conditions of severe repression, was the most urgent priority. It was to the reconstitution and reconstruction of that organisation that the London Recruits made a sterling contribution.

At the first consultative conference the ANC held in exile during 1969 it spelt out its overall battle plan. Building on the experience of the past nine years, the movement identified the reconstruction of an effective internal organisation as the *sine qua non* of prosecuting the struggle. Such a reconstructed underground, it held, would be in a position to intervene in large and small local, regional and national struggles and thus stimulate mass mobilisation. In such a more conducive environment, armed units of the liberation army, MK, would thus be in a better position to operate and survive inside South Africa. That would strengthen the underground while stimulating wider mass struggles. For its success, this strategy also needed to be complemented with international solidarity that would help isolate, and so weaken, the apartheid regime by denying it the support it relied on from its allies in western countries.

This four pronged strategy was referred to as the 'four pillars of struggle'.

It was invariably the young and adherents of the Liberal, Labour, various socialist and Communist formations who were at the forefront. It was young people who responded most readily to the message of the Anti-Apartheid Movement (AAM), a broad-based movement, initiated with the active support of leading members of the Labour and the Liberal parties in 1959.

The AAM directed its efforts at changing the policies of the UK government to actively opposing, rather than shielding, Pretoria's apartheid regime, at the United Nations (UN) and in other international bodies.

Historically, South Africa was one of Britain's leading trading partners on the African continent. Indeed, leading British firms had massive investments in South Africa. Many South African goods were sold on the British market; British banks and other financial institutions handled transactions with South Africa on a daily basis; and British institutions – educational, scientific, cultural and sporting – had cultivated and nurtured links with their counterparts in South Africa. The points at which pressure could be exerted were legion.

The strength of the international solidarity movement was that it relied on the cumulative impact of thousands of individual and collective actions. As organised groups of people, in trade unions, teachers' bodies, students' unions, church bodies, pension funds and even a few corporations demanded economic sanctions against the apartheid regime, banks and other financial institutions thought it wiser to distance themselves from it.

By the 1980s the daughter of a prominent South African corporate figure complained to her father that no bookshop, restaurant or other business in the university town of Oxford was prepared to accept a cheque issued by Barclays Bank, which had been specifically targeted for its links to apartheid South Africa.

Sporting events, from the South African favourite, rugby, cricket and other sporting codes were also subjected to disruption as spectators demanded an end to sporting links with apartheid South Africa. The international boycott of racist South Africa was joined by virtually every academic, artists' and sporting body in the world.

After the Soweto Uprising of 1976, the four prongs of the ANC's strategy increasingly converged. It was the coming together of these factors that compelled the apartheid regime and its supporters to seriously consider negotiations.

The role played by these London Recruits is a significant part of that story.

Z. Pallo Jordan.
Cape Town. March 2011

Zweledinga Pallo Jordan was born on May 22 1942 in Kroonstad, Orange Free State, and grew up in Cape Town. He joined the ANC in 1960 and MK in 1975. He has held many leading positions in the ANC (being elected to its NEC in 1985), was elected to parliament in 1994 and held several ministerial positions in the ANC government. In 2004 he was appointed Minister of Arts and Culture. He has since retired from parliament.

INTRODUCTION
Ronnie Kasrils

In possibly the darkest days of apartheid, following the South African security police crackdown of 1963-66 which led to an entire liberation movement leadership being incarcerated in prison or driven into exile, mysterious signs of the existence of the outlawed African National Congress (ANC) began to appear through the distribution of underground leaflets. This baffled the security police who could not believe that the virtually destroyed underground had so soon regained its capacity to act within the country. Beginning with banned literature circulating through the postal system, such propaganda initiatives soon became more and more audacious, ranging from leaflets being showered from city rooftops; banners with the slogan 'ANC FIGHTS!' being unfurled from buildings; firework-type 'bucket-bombs' discharging leaflets at busy public venues; tape-recorded speeches simultaneously blaring-out the call to resistance throughout the major urban centres. These were sensational incidents that managed to pierce the wall of silence established by the authorities, and were given even greater impact when a journalist photographed a 'leaflet bomb' exploding at the very moment a policeman was attempting to de-activate it. The policeman was left embarrassed but unharmed, with the device blackening his uniform. The image was front page news throughout South Africa in 1970.

The impact of those daringly subversive actions on the rush-hour workers who loathed the apartheid system was electric. One eyewitness – a retired policeman from the then Rhodesia – told the press of seeing excited crowds of Africans in his time 'but never anything like this' as people rushed to pick up scattered leaflets and danced in elation as a tape-recorded message was broadcast before the police descended. Indeed, this writer was told by many young guerrilla combatants, after the 1976 Soweto rebellion spread like wildfire throughout the country, that the first time they had encountered an ANC message was through such propaganda coups.

Exactly who was responsible for carrying out those dramatic actions that so inspired the oppressed, angered the authorities and shattered the claim that police action had crushed the ANC-led liberation movement for good? The full story, with the identities of the participants, has never been recounted before (and only sketchily in one or two court cases) and is most deserving of being told both for the historic record and for the educational awareness of current and future generations both within South Africa and abroad, for in this day and age the message of international solidarity is extremely relevant. Indeed this is a story that will enthral the once oppressed South African people, who need to know of such endeavours. At a time when truth was at a premium in apartheid South Africa, and the internal movement was without the capacity to mount organised propaganda actions, young internationalists were willing to step into the breach at a crucial period, at the request of the exiled ANC-SACP (South African Communist Party) alliance that recruited and trained them in London at that time. The period was of short duration for by 1976 the underground movement inside South Africa was well on the way to recovery and had regained much of its former capacity, despite numerous casualties and deaths. Some of those foreign supporters who had participated in the initial propaganda offensive were, however, later utilised on a voluntary basis for more complex and dangerous missions, including the smuggling of weapons and infiltration of guerrilla combatants and cadres in and out of South Africa.[1] The earlier propaganda activities in a sense opened up the road for all the future clandestine operations

1 Much of this later activity has been revealed in various memoirs; for example Conny Braam's 'Operation Vula' and David Brown's documentary film 'Secret Safari' – see Appendix 4.

that utilised courageous internationalists from many different countries, whose stories still need to be told, for this book can provide only a part of the picture. In fact it is hoped that it will serve to encourage others to provide further accounts.

The task of these activists was made easier by the colour of their skin. Apartheid, like any racist doctrine, presumed that all white people were natural allies and hence suspicion was very low with regard to so-called 'Caucasian' visitors from abroad. As long as they refrained from drawing attention to themselves – dressed, spoke and behaved in the approved manner – they could get away with anything. Arriving at customs, booking into hotels, hiring cars, purchasing material, wandering around city streets with shopping bags, was no trouble at all. In fact the pale pigmentation acted as the perfect camouflage – so much so that sometimes at a particularly anxious and dangerous moment, as when a propaganda device was being placed in a public place, a policeman might walk right past and even bid them a good-day. Psychologically programmed to deal with the 'swart gevaar' (the black peril), the racist police might, as often as not, look straight through the activities of a white person.

A fascinating question arises: what drives individuals to engage in struggles for a just cause in distant lands at considerable personal risk? Those contributing to this book provide their own distinct motivations. Certainly the testing of one's own principles and beliefs with perhaps a healthy dose of adventure and romanticism is integral; but certainly the nobility of international solidarity is paramount in the minds of the politically aware, as illustrated from the times of Byron and Bolivar to the International Brigaders in Spain and Che Guevara in more recent times.

The context at the time was the heady days of student and worker occupations and protests around the world; the anti-Vietnam war; the 1968 events in France; the mobilising work of the Anti-Apartheid Movement. All of these formed part of the tapestry. The words of the Persian poet and sage Saadi, prominent on the walls of the United Nations in New York, state: 'If any part of the human body feels pain, even a fingertip, the entire body feels the discomfort; and so with humanity. If one member, no matter how distant, is suffering, the whole human race is in torment.' In South Africa the trade union movement exemplifies this noble statement as 'An injury to one is an injury to all!' And make no mistake: history shows that there are women and men of principle and passion who take such injunctions extremely seriously. In Palestine today the sacrifice of the young American volunteer Rachel Corrie, crushed during an Israeli house demolition in Gaza, represents a milestone of such solidarity.

The internationalist sensibilities of those brave supporters who came to South Africa's aid, and were ready to act and if needs be sacrifice in solidarity with the cause, was exemplary to say the least.

Apart from Tanzania and Zambia, where the ANC was based in the 1960s, London had the greatest concentration of South African exiles, numbering several hundred. Distant from South Africa as Britain was, it was a gateway to the country by ship and air, even though flights in those days took up to 24 hours owing to the need to avoid flying over much of the African continent as a result of the growing boycott call. South African tourists and businessmen and women flocked to the United Kingdom, as did many students who arrived to study in the country. This enabled the liberation movement to multiply contacts with home in a myriad of ways and opened up possibilities of developing and sustaining important links. London, in particular, thus became an important centre of ANC and SACP work. As South Africa's historic and most important trading partner, Britain naturally became the centre of anti-apartheid activities. The political and social space this opened up for the liberation movement was most significant. It did not, however, mean that vigilance could be dropped for a moment, as there was the presence of the British police and security services to take into account as well as the sinister activity of the apartheid spy system. Great stress was therefore placed by the tightly-knit exile community on security, and particularly by those who were responsible for engaging in the new period of clandestine work.

Life in Britain was fortunately pretty sedate back in 1966 when the South African exiles began the first experiments with small explosive devices and the manufacture of false-bottomed suitcases for propaganda and smuggling purposes respectively. That was some time before Irish bombs in Britain began going off again in a renewal of that age-old anti-colonial struggle, and the later 11 September, 2001 attacks on the USA which heralded the outbreak of unprecedented international terrorism that soon reached Britain. If that had occurred earlier it would have made the organisation of efforts geared towards apartheid South Africa well-nigh impossible from any Western shore.

We were a small group in London, joint members of both the ANC and SACP, with the task of reviving clandestine propaganda and underground resistance within South Africa. We were lucky to have got out of the country alive, escaping from the ruthless crack-down by the security police.

We were led by Yusuf Dadoo and Joe Slovo. Another veteran Jack Hodgson, later assisted by Ronnie Press, a South African science teacher living in Bristol, dealt with technical methods. My focus was on recruitment (which is the reason why so many of the contributions refer to me). We were later joined by Aziz Pahad as an additional full-time worker. Rica Hodgson and Stephanie Kemp (then married to Albie Sachs) handled our secret communications, and my wife Eleanor Kasrils helped in obtaining safe houses, safe addresses and general back-up. Dadoo and Slovo linked our work to Oliver Tambo and the ANC leadership in Zambia.

Eleanor and I arrived in London from Tanzania at the end of 1965. I had already undergone training in guerrilla warfare and clandestine work in the Soviet Union. Jack Hodgson had also been trained there but specifically in security measures, forging passports and organising intelligence and counter-intelligence measures. However, we all learnt from one another, and ended up doing a variety of overlapping tasks; especially Aziz and I. As time went by many more comrades were drawn in, but I limit myself here for the purpose of this book to the initial period 1966-76. The command group (Dadoo, Slovo, Hodgson and I) generally met at Dadoo's shabby Goodge Street office, in an area in which the SACP's journal *The African Communist* and offices of the ANC and the Anti-Apartheid Movement were housed. Our command group met twice weekly but much of the work was done from various homes in North London, such as Camden Town, Chalk Farm, Hampstead, Tufnell Park and Golders Green, where most exiles lived. Central London pubs, parks and colleges proved to be suitable rendezvous points with contacts and recruits, and Hampstead Heath was most convenient for early morning or late afternoon experiments with sample leaflet-bombing devices and demonstrating clandestine trade-craft (well known in spy novels) such as methods of counter-surveillance, use of signal systems and DLBs (dead letter boxes) for passing secret material.

One of the first tasks for Eleanor and me was to find a suitable residence, as cheap as possible, where we could live and at the same time create a secret operations room. Eleanor was a most resourceful person and soon found a three-story apartment above a shop in Golders Green High Street which became our home. It had a discreet back entrance in a service lane, at the princely rental of £30 per month. Jack Hodgson was delighted with the space and we proceeded to convert a large top-floor room for clandestine purposes. Jack manufactured a wardrobe (subsequently dubbed 'the magic cupboard' by Aziz Pahad) which replaced the door, thus effectively concealing the room beyond. A back panel in the cupboard, behind coats and boxes, slid open at the touch of a simple mechanism to allow entry and exit. Eleanor furnished the room with worktables and cabinets for topographical maps of Southern Africa which were obtained quietly over many months through her friends in the London book trade. This room (which was kept secret even from our young sons, who were born in London during those years) would have done justice to any professional operations centre. Eleanor, who graduated as a geology technician at a London college, installed a dark room where she developed photographs and stored cine films taken of various locations in South Africa. These locations included the entire east coastline where the ANC hoped to land guerrillas by sea, and others to help orientate the couriers and activists we would in time be sending into the country.

International solidarity has played a significant role in epic struggles for freedom. Apart from World War Two, and the fight against fascism, the 20th Century witnessed popular mobilisation during such conflicts as the Spanish Civil War and the Vietnam War and perhaps gained its greatest and certainly most sustained momentum during the anti-apartheid struggle. In fact so highly valued was international support by the ANC that it was prominently featured in its strategic formulation for victory, referred to as "The Four Pillars of Struggle". These were: the political mass struggle of the people; armed operations; underground organisation (which included the dissemination of propaganda); and international support. These were of course not independent silos, but were interrelated and interactive. Whilst international solidarity with the liberation struggle is generally regarded as the boycott, divestment and sanctions campaign of the world-wide anti-apartheid movement, there was quite another aspect to global solidarity than mass marches and protest demonstrations. In the first place this involved the training of combatants in guerrilla warfare, clandestine operations and provision of arms, principally by the Soviet Union and other socialist countries. It involved also the obtaining of funds from countries like Britain and Sweden. However, solidarity also embraced the activity within South Africa itself of civilian recruits from many Western countries who were willing to risk their security, and even their lives, by directly assisting freedom fighters in smuggling material, and later on providing safe houses and transportation, and carrying out other diverse tasks in their support. 'The Four Pillars' placed the primacy for struggle and ultimate liberation on the popular mass struggle and saw the other pillars as supportive. Whilst the focus, of course, was on our own people's energy and sacrifice as the road to victory, at times the movement lacked capacity in, for example, technical and material means of struggle, training facilities and key rear bases such as in Angola and the other so-called Front Line States. The role of those who assisted with certain propaganda tasks also falls into this framework.

The French left, assisting the Algerian liberation movement in the struggle against French Colonial rule, had a phrase for such activists: *porteurs de valises* – literally 'suitcase carriers'. These were courageous persons, motivated by strong feelings of internationalism, ready, willing and available to contribute in whatever way in supporting the struggle for freedom and justice in foreign lands. As a consequence they were prepared to voluntarily carry funds, false documents and literature in whatever manner of baggage to those involved in the Algerian struggle for national liberation and independence from France. We found that there was no shortage of such volunteers with regards to the southernmost part of Africa. Whilst not equating their actions to the inordinate sacrifices made by the sung and unsung heroes and heroines within the country, their contribution is greatly appreciated. And knowledge of what they did is of enormous interest to those very masses.

The mid-1960s to early 1970s was the most difficult period in the struggle, because of the huge setbacks which saw activity at its lowest ebb. The capture of Nelson Mandela, Walter Sisulu, Govan Mbeki, Ahmed Kathrada, Raymond Mhlaba, Bram Fischer, Wilton Mkwai and numerous other leaders and activists, their sentencing to life imprisonment and some to hanging, certainly spelt the nadir of South Africa's liberation struggle post 1963. The SACP, ANC and PAC had been outlawed; the underground network destroyed; and those leaders and members not in prison had been driven into exile. The disenfranchised, oppressed black masses were demoralised by these enormous setbacks. The apartheid state machine appeared victorious and invincible. Its leaders and security police gloated that the back of black resistance had been broken. White South Africa confidently basked in the glow of race rule and unprecedented wealth and profitability; as did the Western powers that traded at enormous profit with the racist state.

In this bleak period there was the urgent need to counter the lies of the regime with the voice, message and hope of liberation. With the underground presence all but smashed, this was easier said than done. The remnants of the movement that had survived were lying low and seeking to recover. They were not in a position to mount any propaganda offensive. Winnie Mandela, Lilian Ngoyi, John Nkadimeng and a handful of brave patriots attempted to create some form of network but were soon rounded up, as happened in 1969. Others emerging from short sentences in prison were immediately placed under tight restriction and house arrest. Along with Winnie Mandela this was the fate of others like Lilian Ngoyi, Fatima Meer and Helen Joseph. True, the ANC was establishing its rear bases in Tanzania and Zambia, but these were far from home. Certainly guerrilla recruits were receiving military training in the Soviet Union and other socialist countries, and in 1967-68 participated in armed actions with Zimbabwean combatants in then Rhodesia; but such activity was rarely heard of in South Africa, and only then through the distorted propaganda lens of the Pretoria regime. By 1970 black and white students had been registering their first tentative forms of protest activity and an incipient black consciousness movement was emerging. Within a year black workers, first in Namibia and then South Africa, went on strike. The workers, the youth and students, the masses, generally faced the wrath of the security system and craved information about the true state of affairs within South Africa and internationally. They needed guidance and theoretical leadership precisely at a time when the organised presence of the ANC and SACP was minimal. Attempts to establish underground units within the country were extremely difficult and dangerous, as reflected in the arrest and death in detention in 1971 of Ahmed Timol, a young teacher trained in clandestine propaganda work in

London and the Soviet Union. Until such units as he established could survive, and build the necessary capacity, the contribution of foreign assistance had to be relied upon.

The exile leadership had assessed the situation and grappled with the challenge of getting the message across to the people. Indeed, Ahmed Timol was one of an increasing number of South Africans who were recruited and trained in underground work abroad. However, it took time for a comprehensive strategy and operational plan to be articulated and the internal underground capacity to be built and survive; and as is often the case, action preceded theory. Much of the new strategy and tactics emanated from the ANC's 1969 Morogoro Conference in Tanzania which amongst other aspects emphasised the need to re-establish the underground presence within the country. Part of this was the necessity of paying more attention to political organisation and propaganda. The initial success of the London-initiated propaganda activities was influential in this decision.

The very first indication that the voice of liberation was alive after the 1963-66 reversals had previously occurred in 1966 when a printed leaflet from the South African Communist Party circulated by post in South Africa. The leaflets were smuggled into the country by a young South African woman, Vivian Higgs, aged 19, who had been visiting her brother, Barry, a London ANC exile. She travelled home by ship and carried the leaflets into South Africa in two large suitcases with false bottoms designed and made by Jack Hodgson. As a young white woman she aroused no interest as she went sedately through customs control in Cape Town. She lost no time in posting the leaflets to the addresses given to her. It needs to be understood that, in the context of repression and censorship, subversive literature has a far greater qualitative impact than political information in normal times. The appearance of a leaflet or a chalked slogan on a wall in a police state carries a distinct aura of its own. It not only counters the lies of the dictatorship, that everything is under control, but the simple fact of its appearance breathes defiance.

Very soon, in Vivian's footsteps, the special ANC-SACP unit in London began recruiting and training internationalist anti-apartheid supporters to continue with the work, which over the next few years became far more elaborate and daring. This was done side-by-side with, but compartmentalised from, the recruitment of South Africans who would establish themselves back home for what was to be a long, sustained and difficult haul.[2] In time such activities would be taken over by the internal underground but until that became strong and active enough (post-1976) the burden fell to the international activists. They filled a gap at the most important of times with the Soweto student uprising of 1976 proving a decisive turning-point from which time the liberation movement began to regain and surpass its past mass-based strength.

Who exactly were these *porteurs de valise*, who first appeared on the scene in the late 1960s? How were they recruited and trained, what motivated them and how significant were their actions? This unique book answers those questions and tells their story. It is a remarkable account of the direct role of international activists in the struggle against apartheid in their own words. It reveals a picture of what apartheid South Africa was like forty years ago and more, through the eyes of young British, Dutch , Greek, Irish, French, North American leftists of all shades, setting foot in a country that to them was as weird as it was dangerous. Indeed one of them writes that it was like arriving from another planet. This prompted some of us in London to informally refer to those travellers as 'Postmen from Pluto'.

Following the successful once-off work of Vivian Higgs, the London group began to look around for suitable successors. At the London School of Economics, where I had enrolled, we recruited two members of the Socialist Society, Ted Parker and Sarah Griffith, and a New Yorker, Danny Schechter, active in the Vietnam solidarity movement. In June 1967 I had the good

2 Amongst them Anthony Holiday, Ahmed Timol, Raymond Suttner, Sue and David Rabkin, Jeremy Cronin, Tim Jenkin, Steve Lee – all of them were caught which illustrated how difficult long-term survival of such underground propaganda units was.

fortune to meet George Bridges, London District Secretary of the Young Communist League (YCL). He was a friendly, chirpy South Londoner, who struck me as possessing the resilience and wit of the typical class-conscious British worker. He agreed to spot likely talent for the propaganda missions I described and his first recruit was Daniel Ahern, followed in the autumn by Ken Keable. Meanwhile the Communist Party headquarters, via Tony Gilbert, had referred Joe Slovo to one of their members, David King, and we had soon recruited him and his girlfriend[3] Deirdre Drury. Tony Gilbert had fought in the International Brigade in Spain and was a mainstay of Liberation (formerly the Movement for Colonial Freedom). It is fitting that, through Tony, our new project made that great connection with the internationalism of an earlier generation.

Apart from those deployed as two-person teams, none of the recruits knew of each other's existence. We were ready for our first substantive propaganda incursion into South Africa.

Soon the first wave of recruits – three communists and three LSE students – were winging their way to South Africa with thousands of leaflets stuffed into false-bottomed suitcases for simultaneous distribution on a Friday afternoon in August. The mission was totally successful with the recruits involved providing invaluable reports of how easy, if at times stressful, things had been. They were all positive about their achievements and enthusiastic about being prepared to be of future service.

In November David King introduced me to Alex Moumbaris - a tough, dedicated Greek communist. For the next few years David King, Deirdre Drury and Alex were to become virtual full-time couriers for us, although when Alex was arrested for assisting MK infiltrators in 1972, it was no longer safe for Dave and Deirdre to participate in any further activities.

With the success of their mission in 1967 our London command, spurred on by the ANC leadership in Africa, who were delighted by our efforts, decided to step-up the activity

3 The couple left Britain to work abroad and despite Ken Keable's best efforts it has not been possible to trace them. David King is believed to be dead. See also Appendix 1.

and many recruits were to follow in their footsteps. Recruits generally came from two main sources already referred to – the YCL and the LSE, where it was decided I should register as a student. I made many friends there, particularly amongst the dominant Trotskyist aligned International Socialist (IS) group, and in particular John Rose who participated in two missions and became a life-long friend. The communists and the Trots, as they were loosely referred to, loathed each other and it was ironic that they both proved so enthusiastic and effective in working for the South African struggle without being aware of their respective contributions.[4] To be sure, the latter were critical of the 'bourgeois-nationalist' ANC, as they were of me, who they regarded as a 'Stalinist' owing to my readiness to defend the historic role of the Soviet Union. However, there were some members or fellow-travellers of the IS who were less doctrinaire and whom I judged would be willing to strike a blow against apartheid, and these readily agreed to assist. There were also individuals who belonged to neither camp, such as Danny Schechter, who was illustrative of many on the left who did not easily fit into any ready-made political camp, other than being broadly anti-racist, anti-capitalist and decidedly against US domination of the world. It is important to mention here a further dimension to our propaganda efforts which was the placing of leaflets in the cargo and holds of shipping bound from Britain's docks to South Africa. We were greatly dependent in this work on communists such as Jack Coward, Seamen's Union organiser from Liverpool and former Spanish International Brigader, and Danny Lyons, dockworkers leader in London. Contacts made with them were to prove useful for the later ANC attempt to land guerrillas by sea, in which Liverpool seaman Bill McCaig amongst others participated, including Alex Moumbaris, Daniel Ahern and Bob Newland, the latter also from the YCL.

The body of this book belongs to the London Recruits. Their

---

4 This was something they were unaware of until I brought them together at a reception at the South African High Commission in June 2005.

background, motivation, operational experience in South Africa, and reflections, are brilliantly portrayed and it is left to them to convey it in their own words. Their observations and insights as 'white tourists' in the land of apartheid in its heyday form a unique historical record and will intrigue researchers and historians for years to come. Their exploits will in particular appeal to the formerly oppressed people of South Africa who have always generously applauded and appreciated such direct and brave acts of solidarity given at their time of need.

There is a lighter side to the endeavours. Despite being under instruction to keep a low profile, act the typical tourist of the time, and do nothing untoward that might attract attention, actual experience and human behaviour saw not a few risky, hair-raising and sometimes hilarious episodes. Amongst these: the attendance at Chief Albert Luthuli's 1967 funeral in the midst of tight police control; the recruitment in Johannesburg of a Greek uncle anxious to help his visiting nephew; the dating in Cape Town of some attractive young women who, in the midst of a police raid on a supposedly 'whites only' club, turned out to be of 'mixed-race'; a leaflet bomb inadvertently going off in a hotel bedroom in the dead of night; a hotel room attendant interrupting a team packaging leaflets and being won over after being invited to read the ANC message; a British 'tourist' arousing the ire of the police for joining a post office queue for blacks whilst trying to buy postage stamps for his leaflets.

London recruits Sean Hosey and Alex Moumbaris, of Irish and Greek origin respectively, had participated in the earlier propaganda offensive only to be arrested in 1972 on errands to assist MK. They were tortured and sentenced to terms of five and twelve years imprisonment respectively. After their trial, where they were charged with six members of MK including Justice Mpanza and Theophilus Tsholo, whom Moumbaris had helped infiltrate into the country, it was revealed by the press that 'David King slipped through the Republic's security net in 1967, 1968 and 1969 to spread subversion and terror...' Amongst his other activities referred to was the distribution of

MK leaflets, the broadcasting of a tape-recorded ANC speech from an abandoned car in a Johannesburg street, and arranging the dropping-off of suitcases with false bottoms containing money, literature, letters and leaflets at Durban's main railway station. According to the report 'he was responsible for the unfurling of an ANC banner from the top of a parking garage... in Durban in 1968'.[5] Actually Moumbaris had been responsible for the Durban banner.

The idea of unfurling banners and dropping leaflets from rooftops was a continuation of methods the underground had employed during the 1960 State of Emergency in South Africa. In exile in London, and after the success of the initial postings, we discussed how to reach more of our people in the streets, and make the impact as dramatic as possible. Jack Hodgson worked away on a variety of possibilities and came up with the idea of a do-it-yourself banner. A recruit would simply buy a length of white material a metre wide and ten metres in length, and paint on an appropriate slogan. A hem would be sewn at the top and bottom ends of the material through which would be inserted wooden rods, sawn from a broom handle, to give the banner necessary weight and balance. The banner would be rolled up with the leaflets within. This device would then be hung from the roof or window of a building by a wire. A piece of string would be tied around the rolled-up banner to prevent it unfurling and a touch of acid on the string would allow a few minutes getaway time. The acid eating through the string would then free the banner, which would unfurl and the leaflets would float into the street. Another way of releasing the banner was using a timer with a Schick razor attached. The blade would cut through the string. A couple of dummy dynamite sticks (candles wrapped in black or red tape) and a danger sign 'BEWARE EXPLOSIVES' would initially deter anyone from meddling with the banner until a police explosives expert could be summoned. There was nothing we would ask our volunteers to do that we had not proven ourselves. Jack and I duly unfurled a banner from

5 Johannesburg *Sunday Express* 24 June 1973.

a London department store in this way. The slogan we used was 'XMAS SALE' and we dispensed with the need for the fake explosive. Nobody in the store paid the slightest attention to our antics. In time we added the ANC flag to the banners that were unfurled in South Africa.

It was the evolution of the bucket-type leaflet bomb that represented our most dramatic stride forward. It all started from an idea Joe Slovo and Jack had dallied with back in South Africa. At the time of the Congress of the People, where the Freedom Charter had been adopted in 1955, they had filled a huge balloon with helium, aiming to float it out across the meeting area displaying an appropriate slogan. Unfortunately a strong wind had come up and blown the balloon way off course. Jack's idea in London was to shoot leaflets into the air using 'distress signal' rockets as used in shipping. He modified these so that they could carry a 'payload' of leaflets. Aziz Pahad had joined us by then and we met with Jack early one wintry morning on Hampstead Heath hoping for a successful launch. We watched the count-down with growing expectation and the rocket indeed took off, only to suddenly veer off-course straight to where Aziz and I were standing. We just managed to duck behind a tree as the rocket crashed into it. Jack never gave up easily but after many abortive attempts we called in a fellow exile and scientist from Bristol, Ronnie Press, whom we referred to as 'the Professor'. Things sped up from then and before long we were again assembled on Hampstead Heath with our latest model rocket, prototype of what became our leaflet-bomb, otherwise known as the 'bucket-bomb'. This involved filling a bucket with leaflets. At the bottom of the bucket was a small gunpowder charge to which was wired an ignition system, compact battery and clock timing device (we used a small key-ring alarm clock). A small piece of plywood, same diameter as the bucket, divided the explosive charge from the leaflets. The detonation of the charge lifted the wooden platform and leaflets twenty metres into the air with a harmless bang. Modus operandi was to carry the bucket device in a shopping bag and place it in a litter bin or by a bush in a public place such as bus, taxi or railway station. The device was assembled in such a way as to give the person easy access to the timer. At the last moment the timer would be set to whatever time was necessary for a safe get-away.

It always seemed to be cold, misty and wet when we assembled on Hampstead Heath. For our test we chose an early winter morning when we anticipated few people would be about. Indeed the Heath seemed deserted. Jack set the timer and we backed away a safe distance. The five minutes he had allowed appeared endless when suddenly the bucket erupted with a loud bang and the blank sheets of paper we had loaded it with floated perfectly high above our heads. We were elated, but quickly gathered the ruptured bucket and tangled wiring system and timer and made a swift get-away as every inquisitive Englishman and his barking dog seemed to materialise out of the morning mist to investigate what on earth was going on.

The other important item in our propaganda arsenal was the street broadcast apparatus. The idea came to us when we read a news report following the Colonels' coup in Greece in 1967. Activists had booked into an Athens hotel on the central city square. They brought into their room a tape recorder and amplifier which they set up by a balcony window. They played a tape of a rousing speech attacking the dictatorship responsible for criminally seizing power. The first minutes of the tape were blank, allowing for a safe retreat from the hotel. A booby-trap guarded the recording to deter hotel staff from attempting to disarm the device. The action was a great success. The device we instructed David King to place in the rented vehicle was based on this idea. The tape player within the car was wired to an amplifier on the roof with a dummy booby-trap to scare off anyone attempting to dismantle it. The speech that was played was by Robert Resha, ANC leader and powerful orator, attacking the apartheid government and system and assuring the people that the ANC was alive and would never give up the struggle. It had been recorded in London and featured rousing freedom songs. Reports we received indicated that the rented car left outside a busy railway station in Johannesburg in June 1968 was extremely successful. Before long Jack and Ronnie Press had streamlined and miniaturised the system so that everything could fit into a hat box. All the volunteers needed to smuggle into South Africa was a small cassette-tape of the speech, and a small electronic amplifier. We taught them how to assemble a wooden box which would house the latest model cassette player. On one side of the box was a motorcar radio amplifier. The sound would be further magnified by the electronic amplifier Ronnie Press had built. Recruits would need to scout around for buildings and parking garages where these boxes could be chained to railings, preferably above ground level, and left with our trade-mark warning booby-traps.

These devices proved exceptionally successful and were simultaneously activated in November 1969, August 1970 and again in August 1971 in South Africa's biggest cities. 'Hunt on For ANC Bombers'; 'Explosions Scatter Pamphlets;[6] 'ANC Still Active' screamed the 1970 newspaper headlines. The leaflets breathed defiance and declared: 'The ANC SAYS TO VORSTER AND HIS GANG: Your days are coming to an end...We will take back our country!' Several newspapers carried photographs of the leaflets and quoted from them. The banner headlines in the Afrikaans newspaper *The Transvaler* declared: 'ANC Shows it's Teeth Again with Inflammatory Pamphlets. Time Bomb Explodes as Police Sergeant Tries to Remove it. Bombs in Five Cities. State threatened in Leaflet.' Even the London *Guardian* noted the resurgence of activity in an editorial entitled 'Pamphlets from Underground' (15 Aug 1970) and commented:

The ANC have reminded the South African authorities that... in spite of being banned the organisation can still mount a well-coordinated and sophisticated publicity coup. The authorities have shown their anger already by attacking the newspapers for publishing photographs and extracts from the pamphlets,

6 The South African authorities and media tended to use the terms 'pamphlets' and 'leaflets' interchangeably but in fact leaflets were generally what were distributed. – RK.

and thus giving them a wide circulation. In a wider sense the pamphlets are a general reminder to the police but to South Africans as a whole that the nationalists still function. They will encourage Africans and alarm whites.... Once a movement is underground, no white can be sure what the Africans are doing. Are they really passive, or are they waiting and growing stronger? Yesterday's propaganda leaflets are meant to develop this psychological waiting game...'

For the 1970 and 1971 operations five of South Africa's biggest cities were targeted: Cape Town, Durban, East London, Port Elizabeth and Johannesburg. We deployed two-person teams to each city – in some cases even more. Each team was responsible for three or four leaflet bombs. We planned for at least one street broadcast per city. The device that exploded when the policeman attempted to handle it was outside the offices of the *Rand Daily Mail* and the paper carried the photograph on its front page. The following year, in August 1971, the operation was repeated again much to the consternation of the apartheid government and security services. The *Rand Daily Mail* photograph was again given prominence. 'Pamphlet Bombs Blast Again' was the front page headline. At that stage police had no inkling that this was the work of outsiders. It was only with the arrest of Moumbaris and Hosey in 1972 that they learnt, through interrogation and torture, of the propaganda activity the two had previously been involved in. Fortunately, within a few years internal propaganda units were getting the message across to the people of South Africa, reinforced by the ANC's Radio Freedom, which broadcast to South Africa from Lusaka and Luanda.

By the 1980s the ANC came to permanently utilise international volunteers directly from the so-called Front Line States neighbouring South Africa. Additional internationalists from several Western countries – notably the Netherlands and Canada as well as Britain – were recruited. They helped establish safe houses in Swaziland, Lesotho and Botswana, and several expatriates worked from those countries as well as Mozambique,

Zimbabwe and Zambia. By the late 1980s such internationalists had helped establish a sophisticated network within South Africa, providing, for example, a significant contribution to Operation Vula, which was instrumental in establishing an underground leadership structure within South Africa able to use a network of safe houses. Many Dutch citizens were involved in the support aspects and a noteworthy book, 'Operation Vula', has been written by Dutch anti-apartheid activist Conny Braam. Another highly successful project was 'Africa Hinterland', an overland safari agency manned by young British activists and headed by the SACP's Mannie Brown, which succeeded in smuggling forty tonnes of weaponry into South Africa in the late 1980s. A documentary film has been made of this operation. Whilst this book focuses on the earlier, little-known propaganda offensive from London in the late 1960s, there are a few contributions of the later period included, which serve to illustrate the growth, scale and scope of foreign internationalist support. These later activities were certainly far more dramatic, substantive and sustained than the earlier propaganda efforts described and deserve further research and acknowledgement. The arrest in 1986 of a Belgian-Dutch couple, Helene Pastoors and Klaas de Jong, for smuggling weapons into South Africa from Maputo through Swaziland is illustrative of this.

The early efforts which this book generally focuses on were significant in that they were the first initiatives that drew on direct foreign support. Not only did they constitute the nascent signs of a revived underground, but they provided a base of learning and experience for the later more sophisticated operations. Without a shadow of a doubt they played no small part in the ultimate success of the struggle that liberated South Africa from apartheid tyranny. They represent a very significant piece in the kaleidoscope of endeavour, by South Africa's people in the first place, and the supportive international community, that led to the victory over apartheid.

Timeline by Ken Keable

This timeline only refers to people appearing in this book. Some details may not be completely accurate.

May 1967: The recruitment in London begins, at the LSE, with Ted Parker, followed by Sarah Griffith and Danny Schechter.

June 1967: Ronnie meets George Bridges. Shortly afterwards Ronnie Kasrils and Joe Slovo meet the CPGB leadership, who agree to organise recruitment (via G Bridges) and who introduce them to David King.

August 1967: On a Friday at 3pm, the first action by the London Recruits. Leaflets are distributed and banners unfurled. Danny Schechter in Durban, Ted Parker & Sarah Griffith in Johannesburg; Daniel Ahern also in Johannesburg; David King and Deirdre Drury (probably in Port Elizabeth); possibly others in Cape Town.

Autumn 1967: George Bridges recruits Ken Keable.

November 1967: David King recruits Alex Moumbaris.

December 1967: Alex Moumbaris goes on his first mission, posting letters in Durban.

End of 1967: Gerry Cohen, Merseyside Area Secretary of the CPGB, recruits Bill McCaig.

Early in 1968: Bill McCaig begins smuggling leaflets, posting letters and other work whilst a seaman on the Union Castle Line to South Africa.

April 1968: Ken Keable goes to Johannesburg to post letters.

26 June 1968 (South Africa Freedom Day): Sean Edwards (recruited by Kadar Asmal in Dublin) distributes leaflets in Port Elizabeth, Alex Moumbaris in Durban, Daniel Ahern in Cape Town and David King and Deirdre Drury in Johannesburg city centre (with loudspeaker broadcast from a car). Banners are unfurled from high places. This is the first time a loudspeaker broadcast is used and the only time from a car. The leaflets bring news of the Wankie military campaign.

Summer 1969: Bob Allen replaces George Bridges as London District YCL Secretary and inherits, to his surprise, the job of recruiter.

Around August 1969: Alex Moumbaris and Daniel Ahern go on two- or three-month training courses in the Soviet Union in preparation for the *Mother* project (the landing of the *Avventura*). In 1970-71 they reconnoitre the coast for landing sites for the *Avventura*.

Autumn 1969: George Paizis posts hundreds of letters in Johannesburg before teaming up with John Rose and Nella Derrick and helping them with their mission.

14 November 1969: The first use of the bucket-type leaflet bombs. Eddie Adams is in Cape Town, Alice McCarthy & James are in Port Elizabeth, Nella Derrick & John Rose are in Johannesburg, others (names unknown, probably including David King and Deirdre Drury) are in East London and Durban. Loudspeaker devices are also used. All these actions are simultaneous.

6 February 1970: Alice McCarthy and James set off by sea to Cape Town and then Lesotho. Arriving at Cape Town on 20 February they later post hundreds of letters and SACP booklets. Next they go to Maseru, Lesotho.

Jan-March 1970 (approx.): Alex Moumbaris surveys the coast of SA to find a suitable landing site for the *Avventura*. Daniel Ahern does the same around this time.

Summer 1970: Ken Keable recruits Pete Smith to go with him to Durban. Pete goes on to work for the ANC intermittently until 1990.

13 August 1970: Leaflet bombings and loudspeaker broadcasts in five cities: Johannesburg, Durban, Cape Town, Port Elizabeth and East London. We have Eddie Adams and John Simpkins in Johannesburg, Ken Keable and Pete Smith in Durban, John Rose and Mike Milotte also in Durban, Tom and Ron Bell in Cape Town, but we don't know who was in Port Elizabeth or East London. As Phil Greene said he went to PE, alone, in 1970 or 1971, this could fill one of the gaps.

1970-71: Norman Lucas, recruited by Bob Allen, is working as a photographer on the Union Castle Line and smuggles packages which he drops off at agreed places (DLBs) in Cape Town. He was sent by a black ANC comrade – doesn't know who.

January 1971 onwards: Katherine Levine and Laurence Harris fly to Lusaka and then smuggle weapons from Zambia across Botswana over three months.

1971: Alex Moumbaris again surveys the SA coast for the *Avventura* landing. Bob Allen recruits people including Steve Marsling, who recruits Sean Hosey.

Tuesday 10 August 1971 at 5pm: Leaflet bombings by Graeme Whyte and Denis Walshe in Durban, Steve Marsling and Sean Hosey in Cape Town, Pete Smith and Bob Newland in Johannesburg, Gordon Hutchins and Bob Condon in Port Elizabeth, and possibly other teams in Johannesburg and elsewhere. Teams had six leaflet bombs per team. Letters were posted and photos taken by some teams.

1971 or early 1972: CPGB officials in Liverpool recruit seamen for the *Avventura* including Pat Newman, Eric Caddick and George Cartwright, joining Jim Hopwood, Pat McGowan and 'Pat Gallagher' (see p. 121).

Spring 1972: Mary Chamberlain and Carey Harrison (recruited by Katherine Levine) sail for Cape Town where they smuggle in, and post, over 5,000 packages containing ANC and SACP literature.

Aug 1970 to 1972: Bill McCaig works in Durban, including on the *Mother* project.

1972: Bob Newland joins Bill McCaig, Alex Moumbaris and Daniel Ahern in Durban to prepare for the landing of the *Avventura*.

About March 1972: The *Avventura* sets sail from Somalia on its abortive mission.

June 1972: Alex Moumbaris and his wife Marie-José are arrested. Soon afterwards, Bill McCaig senses danger and returns to London.

28 Oct 1972: Sean Hosey is arrested in Durban.

1977-85: June and Michael Stephen are active across Southern Africa.

1981: Two members of the Fire Brigades Union – names unknown – take in leaflet bombs to celebrate the 60th anniversary of the SACP.

1984: Roger Allingham is recruited by Ronnie Kasrils. He is deployed for MK activities until the liberation and settles in South Africa.

1986: Stuart Round is recruited by Ronnie Kasrils - start of the *Africa Hinterland* operation. Lucia Raadschelders goes to Zambia. Start of Operation Vula.

Exploding Buckets by Ken Keable

The worldwide campaign of solidarity against the South African apartheid regime is a wonderful chapter in world history. Through this book I want to tell the story of a little-known, secret British contribution to that campaign. After writing my own story in April 2005 (triggered by reaching my 60th birthday in March) I decided to track down others who took part in this episode and to invite them to write their own stories and to make them into this book. I was amazed at how many there were, and who they were. Some I know about but failed to find; some declined to write anything; some wrote on condition of anonymity. Gathering these stories has been a beautiful experience and I am very grateful to everyone involved.

From the beginning Ronnie Kasrils, the man who sent us all on our amazing, life changing missions, gave this book his full support and it would scarcely have been possible without his help. I am grateful also to the South African High Commissioner in London, Her Excellency Ms Lindiwe Mabuza, who, with Ronnie, hosted a reception for the London Recruits at South Africa House, London, on 9 June 2005. This meeting was a heart-warming occasion for those present, but at that stage there were others yet to be discovered. It was there that I discussed my plans for the book with those I had found and enlisted their support.

I was born in 1945, in London, of communist parents. Most of my aunts and uncles were also communists. Both my parents, and these same aunts and uncles, had taken part in the Battle of Cable Street in October 1936, when the British Union of Fascists (the Blackshirts) were prevented from marching through the Jewish area of London's East End by the mass resistance of Jews, communists and others. Throughout my childhood, Britain was engaged in a long succession of colonial wars, (Malaya, Cyprus, Kenya, Aden etc) and my family read about them in the *Daily Worker* (later renamed the *Morning Star*). We supported the so-called 'terrorists' who were enemies of the British Empire.

My father, Bill Keable, had worked for the Communist Party from 1935 and was the nominal owner of the *Daily Worker* for a period ending in 1946. My mother, Gladys Keable, had been the paper's first cartoonist at its inception in 1930. Our family were all speakers of the international language Esperanto and both my parents were active in the British Labour Esperanto Association and the International of Proletarian Esperantists. So in my boyhood home 'internationalism' was a household word.

My parents also taught me that Britain's immense wealth was obtained by the exploitation of the colonial peoples. They said that the historic weakness of the British working class was its failure to make common cause with the colonial peoples against our common enemy, the British capitalist class. The idea of solidarity with Africans, therefore, was not new to me.

At the age of 13 or 14 I had joined the Young Communist League in Loughton, Essex, and in the autumn of 1967 I was a delegate to the London District Congress of the YCL, representing the Islington Branch. At this congress I was approached by George Bridges, the London District Secretary of the League. He first referred to the fact that my parents were communists, though I am not sure whether he was merely stating the fact or asking me to confirm it. Then he asked me whether I would be willing to 'do something illegal for the YCL', to which I cautiously replied that I would. He said it would involve going to South Africa for a short while 'to help the South African comrades' – I think those were his words. I can't remember him telling me anything more then. I think there was an unspoken assumption between us that no more than the minimum should be said at this stage. I decided at once that I would go, and I felt very honoured and elated that I had been asked. However, I told him I would sleep on it. The next day I told him that I was taking my final exams at City University in January, and I would be willing to go after that.

After graduating, I approached George again and met him at the YCL offices which were in the Morning Star building in Farringdon Road EC1. From there we went to nearby Farringdon Street and he introduced me to my ANC contact, Ronnie Kasrils. It was an almost deserted street and we just talked openly on the pavement. If anyone had been watching us we would have seen them.

Ronnie was the most impressive person I have ever met. He went on to become head of intelligence for MK, the military wing of the African National Congress (when he became known as 'The Red Pimpernel') and then Deputy Defence Minister in the first post-apartheid South African government. In 1968, however, he was part of the ANC exile community in North London and a student at the London School of Economics. He wore a Vietnam solidarity badge, was always smiling, and seemed to enjoy his clandestine work hugely. I always loved meeting him.

From the outset I decided not to ask for any information that I didn't need. I assumed that this would be a principle of our work, and I also thought that it would help to give Ronnie confidence in me. We arranged how we would get in touch in the future. At each meeting, the next meeting place was agreed so that we would never have to mention it on the phone. To avoid suspicion, we always met at places where many other people met, such as outside the Dominion Theatre in Tottenham Court Road. Everything had to look as natural as possible, so that, for example, when he had to hand me a large sum of money to buy my airline ticket, we walked into a bank and did the handover there. We usually talked in the open air, but for the most secret work he took me to a flat near Tottenham Court Road, the owner of which had given Ronnie a key. It was there that he gave me a suitcase with a false bottom containing about 1200 small envelopes, already addressed, which I was to post in Johannesburg. The false bottom was made of fibreglass, neatly covered on the inside of the suitcase so that it didn't look at all suspicious. I arranged to get a few days holiday from work, saying I was going camping. At the time I had returned to live with my parents for a while in their council flat in Portpool

Lane, Holborn. I didn't tell them, or anyone else, what I was doing. I was only to be away for a few days.

At one point I guardedly asked Ronnie where the money had come from. He said 'Where d'you think, mate?' and I took this to mean that it had come from the USSR. The source of the money is confirmed (in general terms) in Ronnie's book *Armed and Dangerous* and in Vladimir Shubin's *The ANC – A view from Moscow* (see Appendix 4). At this stage I was not sure whether I was working for the ANC or for the South African Communist Party. It was clear that Ronnie was a communist, and I didn't ask any more.

I had never flown before. I went to a travel agent and bought a 3-month return ticket to Johannesburg. My cover story was that, having just graduated, I was thinking of emigrating to South Africa and my father had given me some money to go there for up to three months in order to see whether I liked the place and the prospects. This was a very plausible story and enabled me, if necessary, to talk about my plans without having to invent very much.

I flew from London to Johannesburg without difficulty and got through customs and passport control. At this point I had to send a cable, with pre-arranged but innocuous wording, to an address in London. I still remember the name: Lalani.[7] When Ronnie received news that this message had been received, he would know that I had arrived and had safely entered South Africa.

On arrival in the airport, and everywhere I went, the racism and injustice of that society were obvious, not only in the segregation but in the faces of people, in their body language and ways of addressing each other. All the menial jobs were done by black people. I could see how easy it was to be a white person in that country. No one questioned anything I did and there was always a black person to help me, often without my having to ask.

I got a taxi to the hotel that Ronnie had told me to use, in

7 I now know that this was Farida Lalani, a friend of Ronnie's at the LSE. - Editor

the Hillbrow district. A day or so later, after resting and settling in, I explored the city, noting the places where I would post my letters and planning my route. My instructions were to post them in a number of different places, to minimise the risk. I then bought 1200 postage stamps. After breakfast the next day I put a 'do not disturb' notice on my door and set to work for the whole day. First I used the method that Ronnie had told me about (which I shall not describe here) to ensure that I would leave no fingerprints on the letters. Then I removed the false bottom of my suitcase, using a tin-opener that I had brought for the purpose, and took out the 1200 small letters. It took a long time to stick the stamps on the envelopes. With that finished, I put them in a bag and set off on my planned journey round the city, posting the letters in pillar boxes and post offices. I also bought some more South African stamps, as instructed, and posted them to an address in London for future use.

The letter in the envelopes, printed on very thin paper, was from Dr Yusuf Dadoo, Chairman of the South African Indian Congress, and was intended for the Indian community. Most of the letters had therefore been addressed to companies and organisations such as Indian shops, cinemas, restaurants, temples and social clubs, but a few had been addressed to foreign newspapers and news media, including the *Morning Star*.

After checking out of the hotel I sent another cable, with another innocuous pre-arranged message, to inform Ronnie that I had successfully completed the job and was about to return home. Then I boarded the plane for London.

I remember that while on the long return flight I read a novel, *The Death of William Posters* by Alan Sillitoe. It seemed a rather unlikely story about a Nottingham factory worker who had gone to join the Algerian liberation movement, the FLN, to support their fight for freedom from France. During the long flight over the Sahara, in daylight, I looked down, thinking about the story I was reading that was set in the desert over which I was flying, and pondering the parallel between the story and my own situation.

I returned home without having aroused any suspicion at all. A few days later I read a report in the Morning Star about the illegal distribution of the letter in South Africa. I was thrilled, but could say nothing to anyone.

Shortly afterwards I attended a de-briefing with Ronnie. He warmly congratulated me, clearly delighted at my success, and asked me to make a written report, which I did. He discussed this with me at another meeting. He also presented me with a book, *Class and Colour in South Africa, 1850-1950* by Jack and Ray Simons, which I still proudly possess, although there is nothing hand-written in it, of course, to commemorate the occasion. It introduced me to the history of South Africa, and especially to the fact that the apartheid legislation in the South African parliament would not have been possible but for the South Africa Act, 1909, by which Britain set up a South African parliament elected on a racist basis.

I kept absolutely nothing by way of a souvenir of my exploit, or any physical evidence, as I didn't feel safe from the possibility of investigation even at home. This was because Ronnie had told me that the ANC believed that the British Secret Service shared information with the CIA and with BOSS, South Africa's Bureau of State Security, in order to protect the apartheid regime. I also found, to my surprise, that I had a way of putting all memory of the event in a special place in my mind, so that there was no risk that I would mention it accidentally. I never did. I think it is this mental achievement that has made it take so long for me to get round to writing about these events; even after the fall of the apartheid regime I couldn't manage to talk about it for a long time.

I felt very proud to have been part of a team that had outwitted these three powerful organisations and I was determined that nothing I did was going to endanger Ronnie's work of recruiting, in London, white helpers who were unknown to BOSS. Years later, when I saw Woody Allen's film *The Sleeper* I saw an amusing parallel. In a fictional future USA, under a ruthless dictatorship, rebels had to defrost and revive a long-dead, frozen man (played by Woody) to help them because he would be the only person not known to the police.

My visit occurred in April and soon after my return I saw George Bridges at the London May Day march. The march was unusually big that year, being the exciting, amazing year of 1968, and I was marching under an Esperanto banner, playing revolutionary tunes on my melodeon, as I often did on marches in those days. George was watching the march from the pavement and he gave me a huge grin when he saw me. When we were able to speak privately he explained that a plane from London had recently crashed in South Africa, killing many people, and until he saw me he had been afraid that I was on that plane, and that he had, in a sense, sent me to my death.

Sometime in the 1990s I visited the website of the ANC and found, to my delight, the full text of the letter. In June 1968, Dr Dadoo had presented a memorandum to the United Nations Special Committee on Apartheid about the position of Indian people in South Africa. In the memorandum it said, 'Last month a leaflet issued by Dr Yusuf Dadoo was printed and distributed widely within South Africa'. See Appendix 2.

In 1970 Ronnie asked me to go to South Africa again, and said that this trip required two people, so he asked me to find someone. For me there was one obvious choice: my friend Pete Smith, who was active in the Islington branch of the YCL and who had taken the same political side as me in all matters. He came from a communist family background in Southampton. I put the matter to him one Saturday after we finished selling Morning Stars at the Nag's Head, a favourite junction in the Holloway Road. He agreed immediately, and I brought him to meet Ronnie. Little did I know that this was to be the start of something big. Pete turned out to be much better at this than me, and he went on to pursue a long career helping the ANC, travelling to South Africa and its neighbouring countries many times.

During 1970[8] Pete and I met at Heathrow Airport, bound

8 Ronnie Kasrils tells me that this mission was in August 1970, coinciding with the

for Durban via Johannesburg. Panicking when I couldn't find my ticket, I took a taxi back to my parents' flat, leaving my baggage at the airport. On arrival my astonished parents told me that the airline had phoned to say that Mr Keable's ticket for Johannesburg had been found. So my secret was out. They took it very well, accepted my hurried and truthful explanation and awaited my return. Back at the airport I apologised to Pete, who was very tolerant of my behaviour.

Our task this time was much more complicated. There were a few letters to post, as before, but these were to the media. The main job was to play a cassette tape through an amplifier at a very public place, and to distribute hundreds of leaflets using about four 'leaflet bombs' which we were to construct in Durban, mostly using materials bought locally. The leaflet bomb was not a device for hurting people but a plastic bucket full of leaflets with a small explosive charge at the bottom to send the leaflets up into the air. It was set off by a timer of the type that was sold to motorists on a key-ring, to remind them that their parking meter had run out of time. The bucket was concealed in a paper carrier bag, and on top were placed some plastic items bought (in London) from a toy or joke shop. Some looked like snakes, big spiders or turds. Their purpose was to prevent anyone interfering with the leaflet bombs, or standing too close to them, before they went off. The prototype leaflet bomb, Ronnie told us, had been tested on Hampstead Heath! (More information about the origin and development of the leaflet bomb idea is told in Dr Ron Press's autobiography – see Appendix 4).

We were told exactly where to place the sound equipment and the leaflet bombs. On the outskirts of Durban (a "white" city where black people were needed to work but not allowed to live) was a place where black people gathered at the end of the working day to catch buses to take them back to their homes in the townships. There was a 'shebeen' where many people stopped for a beer before boarding their bus. A bike, bearing a recorded message and sound equipment, was to be fixed directly opposite this shebeen. The leaflet bombs were to be placed at points around the bus boarding area. We were to place our devices, set the timers and get away as fast as possible, check out of the hotel (our bags already packed) and get on the plane to Johannesburg and then home to London.

We also had to hire a car (which I drove) and buy a bicycle – the type that has a steel basket at the front for making deliveries. We would order some pieces of wood, cut to our design, and construct, with them, a box to hold an amplifier which was to be fixed in the carrier of the bike along with a cassette player (the first I had ever seen). The sound equipment was covered, but anyone removing the cover would find a bundle of candles underneath, made to look like dynamite, with a hand-written warning sign. This was to give the impression of a booby-trap, thus keeping any inquisitive police away long enough for the message to be heard. The bike was to be padlocked to a post or tree opposite the shebeen and the cassette player started.

Ronnie had played the tape to us in the flat in London. It started with fifteen minutes of silence (this was our get-away time) followed by the striking words 'This is the African National Congress. This is the African National Congress. This is the voice of freedom'. Some militant songs were next, performed by the London-based ANC choir known as *Mayibuye*. I think the first song was the ANC anthem, Nkozi Sikelel' iAfrika, and was followed by a speech. Another song, in an African language, said something like 'Vorster – the black man is coming to get you!'[9]

We had a lot of work to do before the climax. We had to smuggle in, in our suitcases, the leaflets and those items that we wouldn't be able to buy (such as the small explosive charges). We had to find a hotel, hire the car, buy the bike, order the pieces of wood, glue them together to make the mounting for the loudspeaker, and reconnoitre the bus boarding area, which was near a Muslim cemetery.

We had a bit of spare time in Durban, so we explored a little.

9 B J Vorster was then the Prime Minister of South Africa – Editor.

One evening we drove out to Pietermaritzburg, where we had a 'Wimpy' in a Wimpy Bar – a predecessor of McDonalds. We also drove up towards Swaziland, seeing the beauty of the South African countryside, and had a swim in the Indian Ocean.

On the night before the climax of our work I made another bad mistake. We were working late at night in our hotel room, preparing the leaflet bombs. It was about 1.30 in the morning. Somehow I set off the leaflet bomb that I had just prepared. The mechanism was small and very flimsy, and I suppose it was so simple that I hadn't thought about it as much as other details of our task, nor had I practiced on it. With an almighty bang the room was filled with leaflets and there was a mark on the ceiling. My memory of what happened next was that no one came, but a conversation with Pete in 2005 gave a different story. Pete reminded me that it was the end of the Muslim month of Ramadan, and people were letting off fireworks outside. When someone knocked on the door to ask about the bang, I said (without opening the door) that somebody outside had thrown a firework but that there was no harm done. This explanation was accepted and we cleared up the leaflets, though next morning we found, Pete says, that there were still some more to be picked up, as they had been spread everywhere. Once again Pete was remarkably tolerant of my mistake. (Pete also told me recently that the ANC altered the design of the leaflet bombs after this, learning from the experience). We now had one less leaflet bomb. The mistake has haunted me ever since.

Strangely, I can't remember feeling frightened. I was just desperately searching my mind for a way out of our danger. If anyone had entered the room they would have seen the ANC leaflets everywhere – there was no time to hide them and no imaginable excuse for their presence. I can now say a warm 'thank you' to the Muslims of Durban for providing me with cover for the loud bang.

The next afternoon we prepared our baggage for a quick exit, loaded up the equipment in the car and set off for the bus boarding area, which was crowded with black workers. I padlocked the bike to something opposite the shebeen, which was full of people sitting at long tables under a canopy. When I had padlocked the bike, a black man politely offered to guard it for me, but I just as politely declined his offer. We placed the leaflet bombs, got back to the car and drove away. As we drove past the end of the street in which the bike was situated, Pete told me that there was a great disturbance going on. I was relieved to know that the loudspeaker had worked and sorry not be able to witness the event. It was a thrilling moment.

In haste we checked out of the hotel and went to the airport, flying home via Johannesburg again.

The thought had occurred to me that perhaps our action was part of some wider operation, and this proved to be the case. I bought two newspapers on the way home, and found reports of similar events in other cities. The police tried to play them down by saying that the leaflets were old, out-of-date material, which was a lie of course.

When I reached my parents' flat they had gone to bed. I woke them and we had a great time as I told them my story. After the first few days we scarcely mentioned it again.

As before, Ronnie asked for a written report. At the debriefing he told us some astounding news. Not only were similar operations carried out simultaneously in five cities – Durban, Cape Town, Johannesburg, Port Elizabeth and East London – but there was more. By observing the behaviour of police forces generally, the ANC had found that when something highly embarrassing happens, as in this case, they tend to concentrate lots of police into the area where it occurred to avoid the embarrassment (to them) of something happening in the same place again soon afterwards. Hence our action was designed to draw police resources into the cities and away from the townships for a while, thus leaving the townships relatively free for the ANC members there to carry out other activities which would normally be too dangerous.

Soon after my return, Ronnie asked me to produce a report on ways that the ANC might sabotage the South African electricity supply system. I did this, but I'm not sure that it was any use. I learned much later that the ANC blew up electricity pylons using explosives. This is an obvious and effective method if you have the explosives and the expertise, but I had suggested a more low-tech approach which I shall not describe here.

Another job Ronnie gave me was to recruit someone else to go to South Africa alone. I spoke to a young man named Mick about it, but I later learned, to my horror, that he had told his elder brother, who was in the Communist Party, about it and the brother, out of concern, had gone to the CP head office to find out whether the story was true and whether the operation had the Party's approval. Perhaps I had assumed that Mick would understand the need for absolute secrecy without me having to spell it out. I dropped him like a hot brick, without explanation, and with hindsight I think this was rather insensitive of me.

Around this time, also, I learned from Pete that he had recruited our mutual friend and fellow member of Islington branch of the YCL Bob Newland, and that on a return journey from South Africa they had encountered Sean Hosey, also a member of our branch, in the plane. This brings to four the number of members of Islington YCL who went over to help the ANC. Later I heard from Pete that Sean had failed to return from a visit to South Africa, and he pointed out to me, in the 'Metropolitan' pub where we YCL members used to gather at weekends, Sean's girlfriend. He said that she was worried about Sean, as he seemed to have vanished from the face of the earth without explanation or warning. It is a credit to him that he hadn't told his girlfriend what he was doing. I felt very sorry for her, but didn't feel able to do anything to help, which still saddens me.

I remained in contact with Ronnie for a while, during which time I was supposed to be trying to find people who would let the ANC use their address to receive messages from South Africa. I didn't have any success. At some point Ronnie handed me over to another ANC member, Aziz Pahad. (At the time of writing this, in 2005, Aziz is Deputy Foreign Minister of South Africa).

Somehow I lost touch with Aziz. I don't remember when this was, but in 1972 my personal life took all my attention and I was no longer in a position to do clandestine work.

Ronnie Kasrils was part of an ANC exile organisation in north London, of which I was aware. A plaque has been placed on the house in Alexandra Park Road where Oliver Tambo and his family lived for 30 years, and in the nearby Albert Road recreation ground a bust of Oliver Tambo (by Ian Walters) was unveiled by Jack Straw and Ms Zanele Mbeki in October 2007. When Nelson Mandela visited London some time after his release, I saw on TV that he went to Muswell Hill and stood in the street opposite a house (presumably that of the Tambo family), and gave the house the ANC salute. (For this salute the fist is shaped to represent Africa, with the thumb representing the "horn of Africa"). Dr Dadoo was part of that community. He was elected Chairman of the South African Communist Party in 1974 after the death of his predecessor, J B Marks. Throughout his life he had played an outstanding role in the ANC, being a member of its Revolutionary Council for some years. He died in 1983 and is buried in Highgate Cemetery.

I met several members of this exile community over the years, though I never told them of my own ANC work. My first wife worked in the accounts office of the *Morning Star* when I met her, and working in the same office was Sarah Carneson. I met her and her husband Fred several times over the years. They returned to South Africa in 1993. This white couple had both suffered enormously for their opposition to the apartheid regime and they impressed me very much.

Throughout the years in question, and later, I was active in the Muswell Hill district organisation of the Woodcraft Folk (a secular, anti-establishment, national children's organisation sponsored by the co-operative movement) and there I met other members of the ANC exile community, including Steve and Thelma Nel, Ghairu Hussey, Bessie White and Esme Goldberg, and their children. Because of the internationalist and anti-racist character of the Woodcraft Folk it was natural that these people should join and send their children to it, and I often camped with them. Meeting people like these has been one of the greatest rewards of my life of activity in the labour movement.

I have since thought about what effect the whole experience had on me, especially on my political thinking. Because of my family background I was already inclined to take the pro-Soviet side in political matters, and with hindsight I think that this experience reinforced that tendency. It was partly because, as the money for my visits to South Africa came from a Soviet source, I felt as though I was, in a sense, part of the Soviet team in the world-wide, bi-polar struggle. It was also because I had seen one of the most oppressive regimes in the world at first hand, knowing that the USSR was opposing it so resolutely whilst the capitalist world, including Britain, was defending it and doing everything possible to thwart the world-wide boycott campaign. I was also aware, from my own observation, that South Africa was full of well-known British companies, all participating in the super-exploitation of the South African people, and I knew that the finance houses of the City of London were raking in the profits of investment in South Africa, inflated by artificially cheap labour. The whole British economy was therefore subsidised by the underpaid black people of South Africa. All this made me rather impervious to the hypocritical concerns of the British media about the lack of freedom in the communist world. It also strengthened my resolve to fight the capitalist system, and I felt that loyalty to the Soviet Union, its main opponent, was essential to that.

I remember having a cathartic moment. I think it was on my second mission. Standing in the street, surveying the scene in which the oppression was so obvious, I thought to myself that, if I lived here, I would give up all trivial activities and devote myself to fighting this injustice. Then I thought, why only if I lived here? I knew that the apartheid regime was dependent on the support it received from the British government, the City of London and British businesses. I think that this moment ensured that I would become a life-long political activist, fighting the capitalist system in my own country and thereby assisting the liberation of South Africa and all peoples oppressed by British imperialism worldwide.

Of course, I now see the USSR in a somewhat different light since its collapse, but that hasn't made me a supporter of the capitalist system. I think that anyone who thinks that we human beings should find a better way of managing the world must study the history of the communist movement, its successes and failures, in order to learn from this vast fund of experience. Admitting that I ought to have been more critical of the Soviet Union does not mean that I in any way regret what I have done. I am proud of my life of struggle against the capitalist system, and especially my work for the ANC. In the 1990s my dismay and disillusionment at the collapse of the USSR was allayed by my delight at the release of Mandela, the victory of the ANC and the arrival of democracy in South Africa. In retirement now, my struggle for a better world continues. After leaving the Communist Party of Britain for a number of years I returned to it with renewed enthusiasm in 2006.

Sometime in the late 1980s I helped to organise a well-attended 'fringe meeting' on apartheid at the Annual Delegate Conference of my trade union, the Electrical Power Engineers' Association. In 1989 I was elected to the union's National Executive Council. When the NEC met Robert Malpas, the Chairman-designate of the newly-created and privatised power generating company Powergen, I asked him about his policy on using South African coal, produced by cheap labour with no political rights. He sneeringly replied that he had 'no ideological objection' to using South African coal. But it was 1989, and the end of the apartheid regime was not far off.

The previous year had seen the battle of Cuito Cuanavale in Angola, in which Cuban forces played the decisive role in defeating the forces of the apartheid regime and its surrogates. Fidel Castro said, 'The history of Africa will be written as before and after Cuito Cuanavale'. Mandela called it 'a turning point for the liberation of our continent and my people'. As I put the finishing touches to this story twenty years later, in 2008, South Africa's national-democratic revolution, despite many problems, continues apace. Solidarity forever!

Memories of Ronnie Kasrils at LSE

John Rose and Martin Tomkinson were at the London School of Economics when Ronnie Kasrils was there. John went on a mission to Johannesburg with 'Nella Derrick' in November 1969 and to Durban with Mike Milotte in August 1970. Both were involved in the revolutionary student movement there in 1967-8 and Martin Tomkinson became a leading spokesperson for the students. – Editor.

John Rose

Ronnie Kasrils was one of a number of very remarkable students I met when I began my first year as an undergraduate at the London School of Economics in 1966. I was a naïve 20 year old from the very middle-class town of Harrogate in Yorkshire. I had just returned from a summer hitch hiking around Israel and working on a kibbutz. He was rather older and he had spent his summer, and most of the rest of his adult years, plotting how the ANC would finally overthrow the Apartheid regime in South Africa – though that only became clear later. Our lives to that point had been rather different....

For an excellent thumbnail sketch of Ronnie in those days, see the attached note from former LSE student leader Martin Tomkinson.

I first met Ronnie in the first year Sociology class. He was cursing the conservative sociologist Max Weber. 'Why do we have to bother with this rubbish?' he said, or something like it. 'We should concentrate on Marx'. Another remarkable student, Ted Parker, a very working-class blond-haired young man, agreed. Ted, also destined to become one of Ronnie's recruits, had been dishonourably discharged from the RAF for helping to form a CND cell. I was in awe of these two – but also I was beginning to agree about Weber and Marx.

Such debates were constantly on the agenda in the Three Tuns Bar from 5.30 pm onwards where other equally impressive students – many of whom went on to form the cadre of IS, the International Socialists (forerunner of the Socialist Workers Party) in the early 1970s – held forth on a vast range of topics including Weber, Marx, dialectics, philosophy and the meaning of working-class politics. A major and often (over) heated argument concerned the differences between Trotsky and Stalin and the implications for Mao, Castro, Nasser, Ho Chi Minh and of course Che Guevara, and other contemporary revolutionary leaders in the developing world. I had begun as a fascinated, but nervous, onlooker on the sidelines – but I was slowly becoming intoxicated – and it wasn't the beer (alone) – it was the prospects of revolution.

Because these students didn't just talk, they acted. Within months they were leading Britain's first militant student sit-in. They were joining with Tariq Ali in building a mass student movement against the Vietnam War and rioting in Grosvenor Square outside the US Embassy. They even recruited LSE students for picket duty to help the building workers on strike confront strike-breaking, police protected, 'scab' workers at the Barbican Centre, then in the process of construction.

Ted Parker had an early claim to student revolutionary fame when he ran as LSE Socialist Society's candidate for student President on the unambiguous platform: Smash Capitalism! Vote Parker!

Professor Meghnad Desai, now Lord Desai, then one of the very few LSE lecturers to support the students, recalls those early days of the 'student revolution'. 'These were not mindless activists. The level of debate in the bar and in the canteen, corridors and streets outside was often far superior than the seminars in the classroom.'

In truth a new Marxism was being fashioned: or new marxisms. The IS students played a key part, but they weren't the only ones. There were more anarchic varieties; but they had one thing in common. They wanted to liberate Marxism from its Stalinist straightjacket.

Here Ronnie Kasrils stuck out like a sore thumb. He was

impervious to all attacks on Stalin and 'Stalinist' policies.

I had become more and more friendly with him. I visited his London home and met Eleanor, his wife and partner, also an ANC comrade, and children Andrew and Christopher. We argued Trotsky Stalin incessantly. I wasn't convinced about either of them, but I would test IS arguments on Ronnie. On one occasion Ronnie reached to his bookshelves. He was and remains the only person I ever met who not only owned Stalin's Collected Works but would quote directly from them.

Looking back on those years now, how much, in retrospect, I admire Ronnie's patience with the LSE 'revolutionary' students.

Ronnie was already a highly trained professional revolutionary. He had helped blow up the electricity supply lines to the South African city of Durban, and help put MK (Umkhonto we Sizwe, 'Spear of the Nation'), the ANC military wing, very much on the political map. He and Eleanor had made a sensational escape from South Africa and from the clutches of the South African police. He had been trained in the Soviet Union in both partisan and regular warfare. His instructors included some of the toughest soldiers in the world, Red Army veterans, no less, who had defeated Hitler in the Second World War. He had also met Che and Malcolm X.

It wasn't even true that Ronnie was an uncritical Stalinist 'hack'. In Armed & Dangerous, his autobiography, he writes particularly sympathetically about his political instructor, the Armenian, Major Chubinikyan. Ronnie didn't need the LSE Trotskyists to raise doubts about Stalin. He heard it first from Comrade Chubinikyan, though I like to think we helped deepen those doubts.

If we did, then we should all thank Tony Cliff.

Tony Cliff was by far the most remarkable person I came across at the LSE – only he wasn't a student. At a pivotal moment, Tony Cliff and Ronnie Kasrils would propel me on a life-time commitment to socialist revolution.

Born in British-occupied Palestine into a Zionist Jewish family, Cliff was jailed by Britain during the Second World

War for advocating resistance to British Imperialism. Uncompromisingly hostile to the Zionist colonisation of Palestine, and following the Zionists' victory in 1948, he came to Britain and founded the IS group.

Cliff was a Trotskyist but he had refined Trotsky's original criticism of the failure of socialism in the Soviet Union. Like Trotsky, he agreed that socialism in one country, especially a developing country, was impossible. But he added a crucial argument. The world market traps developing countries. Even if the state can control the internal market, the external market – today we call it the global market – is so powerful that it imposes itself on the developing country. This leads inevitably to the restoration of capitalism whatever the revolutionary and socialist intentions of the leadership. If the state continues to dominate the internal market then a new variety of capitalism emerges which Cliff called State Capitalism. We now know the difficulties faced by state capitalism in protecting even the internal market from global pressures.

In the 1950s and 1960s this argument had profound implications for revolutionary nationalist movements in the developing world challenging imperialism and colonialism.

Cliff argued that there was only one way these 'third world nationalist' movements could avoid being trapped by wider global capitalist pressures. That was by workers and peasants in these countries maintaining their independence and being ready constantly to act in their own interests. Ideally they should take power directly. But even then there was no guarantee against being overwhelmed by outside forces. Only revolution in the heartlands of capitalism could provide such a guarantee. But at least if workers maintained strong independent trade unions, peasants their own land-based independent organizations; if they demanded democratic control insisting, not just free and fair and regular elections, but all important government decisions subjected to vigorous debate in the factories, offices and fields, with vetoes, the worst excesses of global capitalism could be kept at bay.

It's the difference between the 'Communist' Government in China, today, openly embracing global capitalism whilst using Stalinist tyranny to break internal opposition to the ever-widening inequalities; and Hugo Chavez in Venezuela using the country's oil revenues to close the gap between rich and poor and openly encouraging the poor to form their own independent mass-based organisations.

As I write about all of this now I may give the impression that I was clear about these arguments at the time. I was not. But they did come to a spectacular climax, in my mind at least, when what has become known as the Six Day War broke out between Israel and Egypt, and the rest of the Arab world, in June 1967. The two protagonists invited to argue publicly about the line that socialists should take were Ronnie Kasrils and Tony Cliff.

Ronnie had resisted the temptation to play a significant role in the celebrated LSE student sit-in and occupation in the earlier part of 1967, the first of its kind in the UK. But he did impress with his message of support for the student rebels from Bertrand Russell, the veteran philosopher and peace campaigner.

The atmosphere in the university that summer sparkled with political debate. The Six Day War confronted those Jewish students, enthused with all the revolutionary ideas spinning around, with a potential nemesis. We could not claim to be revolutionary socialists and support Israel at the same time.

The LSE student Socialist Society sponsored a teach-in on the war. The argument between Cliff and Kasrils boiled down to Nasser's role in the war, and his wider part in developing 'Arab socialism' in the Middle East. They both agreed that socialists must support the Arab side. In the jargon of the day, Cliff supported Nasser 'unconditionally but critically', Kasrils, 'unconditionally and uncritically'.

There was a third speaker, Mike McKenna, a highly respected philosophy student, like Ted Parker dishonourably discharged from the RAF for forming a CND cell. McKenna had initiated it. McKenna argued a neutralist 'plague on both their houses' line - ie don't take sides either with Israel or Egypt. I began by supporting McKenna. Maybe I couldn't support Israel, but I certainly couldn't support Egypt.

This teach-in, for me, operated at two levels. There was the open political argument about Nasser's revolutionary credentials, thrown into doubt by Cliff's argument that Nasser's Egypt was caught between the capitalist West and the state capitalist East. Hadn't he executed workers' strike leaders and jailed members of the Egyptian Communist Party? Cliff even argued that Nasser could not prosecute the war with Israel as forcefully as he should because he would not mobilize the mass of workers and peasants, across the Middle East, for a wider revolutionary struggle.

By contrast, Ronnie pointed to Nasser's undoubted achievements at land reform and closing the gap between rich and poor. He hailed Nasser's standing throughout the Arab world as an outstanding anti-imperialist leader, proven by his nationalisation of the Suez Canal in 1956 in the teeth of opposition from Britain, France and Israel.

Important though this argument was, I was hearing and seeing something in addition. I saw two fearless revolutionaries, both of Jewish origin, both of whom felt completely at ease with their Jewish identities. They both took for granted that the creation of the state of Israel was a catastrophic mistake; that it was, first and foremost, a creature of Imperialism. Its intense hostility to the Arab world, induced by the very act of its creation in its expulsion of nearly one million of the original Palestinian Arab inhabitants, served imperialism's interests very well. It turned it into a gendarme protecting Western interests, above all, the free flow of cheap oil.

Years later I read an essay by Isaac Deutscher called *The Non Jewish Jew*. He was talking about Spinoza, Freud, Marx; Jewish heretics who 'transcend Jewry but who belong to the Jewish tradition… (who) dwelt on the borders of various civilizations…this enabled them to rise above their…times… and strike out mentally to wide new horizons.'

Cliff and Kasrils were non-Jewish Jews. And during those six days I learned from them both that Zionism and Internationalism were incompatible. I have never looked back.

That, though, should not overshadow the argument about Nasser.

This was not about the Egyptian leader's integrity. It is about his room for maneouvre in a world dominated by capitalism, East and West. It was also about a vision of socialism which, in the tradition of Stalin, is essentially elitist. It sees the masses to be mobilised for specific causes from above, rather than the creation of leadership amongst the masses from below, the workers and peasants, so that they can act directly in their own interests.

I can hear Cliff and Ronnie arguing about South Africa in the corridors of the LSE even now. 'Ronnie, even if the ANC takes power with the backing of the South African Communist Party and you get rid of apartheid, aren't you still going to end up managing capitalism?'

Yet an LSE revolutionary student could still work for Ronnie Kasrils. We had all learned to support the Arab side in the Six Day War, irrespective of our views of Nasser. And there was absolutely no doubt that we all wanted the revolutionary overthrow of the apartheid state.

But there was something else. LSE students, who began secret discussions with Ronnie in 1969 about ANC funded 'missions' to South Africa, were about to leave the university. We had had the time of our lives. It really had been like a laboratory of revolution. Only the revolution had failed. The high point had been May '68 in France. We had exaggerated the role of the 'revolutionary students'. And we were unprepared for the sudden collapse of the student struggle. Cliff put it very well: 'The students had gone off like a rocket but had come down like a stick.' Ronnie, probably, would have agreed with him.

Those of us who had by now joined the IS were under extreme pressure to, as Cliff, put it, 'throw away your books and get down to the factory gates'. This was 'IS-speak' meaning 'you bloody students are now ex-students: if you are serious about socialism, you'll make the effort to relate to working-class people, especially workers in struggle.' Cliff correctly anticipated the rise in rank and file trade union struggle across Britain in the early 1970s and he wanted the students to build IS branches in working-class areas.

Politically, Cliff's case was unanswerable and, two years later, I did exactly what he suggested. But in 1969 and 1970, it seemed far too tame. Ronnie was offering something far more exciting....

****

In June 2005, Ronnie, now Minister for Intelligence Services in the ANC South African Government, together with the South African High Commissioner, held a reception at South Africa House in the Strand, for many of us who had been recruited for the ANC missions. This was where the decision for this book was finally agreed upon.

For the first time I met many former members of the London Young Communist League from the late 1960s, who had formed the major base for Ronnie's recruits.

It was the first occasion that Ronnie's 'Trots' and' Stalinists' had ever met. When Ronnie pressed me to speak I made two points. I pointed to the irony that Ronnie, the isolated 'Stalinist' revolutionary at the LSE, was in reality the most successful of the LSE revolutionary students. He had actually helped make a real revolution. I also acknowledged the little known co-operation between 'Stalinists' and 'Trots' and how it anticipated the very high level of co-operation between former Communists and members of the Socialist Workers Party in Britain's fastest growing left-wing movement, George Galloway's Respect.[10]

What I didn't say then, because I judged it to be far too undiplomatic, but would like to say now, is this:

10 Alas Respect imploded. Nevertheless I stand by the principle that co-operation between former Communists and Trotsky-influenced members of the '1968 generation', ageing though we all are, is a vital ingredient for any serious twenty first century mass based left-wing movement.

'Ronnie, I never for one moment doubted your revolutionary integrity and courage. You were just as much an inspiration as any one I ever met in the IS & SWP. But, Ronnie, is there not a danger of an ANC government merely managing capitalism? And doesn't it point to a disaster in the future?'

Martin Tomkinson

My chief memory of Ronnie at LSE was his unfailing enthusiasm and good nature. He was in the SACP and we were varying shades of 'Trot' but Ronnie was always the supportive and helpful comrade in the best sense of the word. He was of course older than most of us and inevitably less involved in the social life of the university which centred around the bar.

Ronnie had bigger fish to fry and his dedication to the revolution was 100 per cent. However this did not make him dull or boring. I seem to recollect that. He was a keen Arsenal supporter (like myself) and he could get almost as heated talking about football as about politics.

I had enough sense never to question Ronnie too closely about his involvement with South African liberation politics. Given the egregious nature of the long arm of BOSS it was clearly important not to actually know too much. (In the 1960s Boss, the South African secret police, ran an extensive student infiltration programme and one could never really be too sure who one was talking to - even at the LSE). Ronnie's committed politics were never hidden but on things like demonstrations he had to be more careful than the rest of us. This did not stop him from breaking many of the windows of South Africa House in Trafalgar Square on one particularly violent demonstration against the apartheid regime. That of course was personal for Ronnie.

Several years later I met and later married Audelia – universally known as Mickey Peake. Mickey was the daughter of George Peake, the first political prisoner to serve time on the infamous Robben Island. According to Mickey, Ronnie had always been a favourite of her mother Lulu and she remembered him well from the early 1960s in South Africa. George and the family were effectively deported from South Africa and he became active in the labour movement in England, serving as a Labour councillor in Slough.

Tragically, his experiences in South Africa could never be forgotten and he committed suicide in 1982, one of the countless victims of apartheid's inhuman practice.

As everyone knows, Ronnie went on to higher things and he will I am sure be pleased to know that since his time his beloved 'Gunners' have played some of the best football seen in the UK. I send my warmest greetings to a staunch and generous comrade.

VENCEREMOS

THE DAY I JOINED THE REVOLUTION
Danny Schechter

I was 25 years old. I was righteous and identified with the need for a revolution in my own country and around the world. I had not yet completed my lifelong journey from activist to journalist. I was political. I was passionate. I was part of a generation that wanted change and was determined to be part of the struggle to achieve it. We were living in the 1960s, revolutionary times in 'Swinging London' no less, and of course were shaped by its fashions, hopes, and even some of its illusions. We loved the Beatles and fancied ourselves Street Fighting Men á la The Rolling Stones. We wanted to be Che Guevaras (who was killed in 1967). We were engaged and ready to rock. We wanted the war in Vietnam to end and the apartheid system to end with it.

Many of us were available to serve our values and join the fight for justice. Few were chosen. My opportunity to join a real revolution soon came in the form of a furtive and hushed invitation from a charismatic friend in the African National Congress to secretly slip in to apartheid South Africa, to 'help'. It was also a concrete challenge to someone who talked about revolution to put up or shut up, a concrete chance to put my own life on the line for a cause I believed in and to support a movement I admired. It was hard to say 'no' even though I was scared shitless. There, I said it. Scared shitless.

Before I came to the London School of Economics and started running with some South Africans, I had been deeply immersed in the struggle for racial justice in the American civil rights movement, and soon became a full time civil rights worker.

I became a student activist who dropped out of college to organize in Harlem. I had worked on voter registration campaigns in Mississippi. I knew fear and saw the ugliness of repression and segregation. I met Martin Luther King, I bantered with Malcolm X. I could sing all the songs. I helped organize the great 1963 March on Washington. I was part of what we called the 'movement'. It defined me and educated me and helped me transcend my Jewish roots in a Bronx housing project. I was not a 'red diaper' baby[11] but the whiff of socialism, and family history in the labour movement, shaped my values. I was the white boy who thought he got it, and who could dance and get down. I also knew about apartheid. My first encounter was through the pages of *Life* Magazine. I had read Alan Paton's *Cry the Beloved Country* in High School. At college, I met some South Africans and was outraged by the realities they described. I learned more about the 'winds of change' transforming Africa. I saw a connection between racism in the USA and the RSA. I also knew that my own country was on the wrong side of the issue even though Bobby Kennedy went there, and some Americans rallied against apartheid. Like Che, I believed in 1-2-3 Vietnams and saw South Africa as a domino in the great global conflict between imperialism and democracy. And then, in London, I met Ruth First, the brave South African journalist and activist and now a heroine/legend of the first order. She was in my class at the LSE. Perhaps because we were both outsiders in an often parochial English academic culture, we became friends. She made South Africa vivid and personal for me. She was a journalist too and a marvellous storyteller. And what a story she had. One of her daughters, Shawn, would later write a fabulous dramatic movie about one chapter of her life called *A World Apart*. Another daughter later wrote a book complaining that her parents had more time for the revolution than for them. They all loved her and, like me, miss her. She was married to a leader of the ANC's revolution, Joe Slovo, who the press described as 'the white man who led a black revolution'. They were not part of some academic debating society, but immersed in a real revolution, a war with serious risks and high costs. Many of their comrades were in prison, others in their graves.

There she was, forced into exile, bringing up three girls who, I am sure, resented her political priorities, but always tied to a struggle far away that consumed so much of her time and

---

11 i.e. not the child of communists –Editor.

energy.

I was more of a New Leftist. She came from an old left tradition but was breaking away, in her own way, towards feminism and a stance critical of Stalinism. Through constant battling she pushed her husband Joe, a Communist Party of South Africa stalwart, in the same direction. He would later become the head of the armed struggle, a chief negotiator and Minister in the Mandela government. He would also acknowledge her influence in the evolution of his thinking.

She would later be assassinated by a South African spy who sent a book bomb to her in Mozambique on 17 August 1982. She became a revolutionary martyr. I visited her graveside in 1986 while on a TV reporting assignment in Maputo, Mozambique. Ruth and Joe were not directly associated with my decision to 'go south' when recruited by Ronnie Kasrils, a fellow student at the LSE and a bundle of determination to transform South Africa through the ANC. (He too would become a minister.) Their movement, like many, was compartmentalised, so I don't know if they even knew. I didn't tell them because I was warned to stay silent for security reasons. I was never meant to be a secret agent – I am too affable and talky for that – but I mostly kept my decision to go on this unpaid 'mission' to myself. That was the first challenge – learning how I thought a secret 'operative' (which I really wasn't) was supposed to act. I was anxious to share my fears with others and seek reassurance, but I couldn't.

Next, even though the 'operation' was not 'heavy' (to use a term much overused at the time – I was not, for example, armed, so couldn't claim to be part of the 'armed struggle') yet I came to understand its importance. The ANC was fighting a life and death battle. Many of its leaders were in prison or forced into exile. They had to communicate with their base in the country and keep the spirit of resistance alive, or at least its appearance, while they regrouped and reorganised.

Sending letters to activists from inside the country and creating a stir that would be relayed by word of mouth and generate a 'buzz' was worth the exercise. Guerrilla warfare is often about propaganda spread by the deed. My task was to help deliver some messages, post some mail, and send some political flyers flying in a public place to keep the then-banned ANC's capacity to communicate visible and alive in one of the darkest days of apartheid. I was given piles of letters and told how to get stamps for them and then mail them in a main post office, assuring they would get a postmark. Some of the letters went to addresses in London so that my 'handler' could confirm that that part of the job was done. When I went to the post office, I noticed South African soldiers going in. I freaked out, but they were probably sending packages to their aunties. I summoned up the courage to be brazen, to act as if I belonged there.

I had become an underground 'postman' from another world. The mail was sent. The next part of the mission involved creating what amounted to poster bombs. They were simple devices but they worked. It involved attaching the clock mechanism of a parking meter to a bundle of ANC flyers.

I was assigned to go to Durban. I took the night train down from Jo'burg. I was on the lookout for people following me and tried not to be obvious – I probably tried too hard and was very obvious. I was convinced I was under surveillance. I walked around and around the streets and looked at where the police cars congregated, and what people wore. I noticed that a lot of the whites wore short pants, and I bought myself a pair in an attempt to 'blend in'. I realized that while what I was doing was minor to me, it wouldn't be if the police snatched an American with a poster bomb[12] in a satchel, and hundreds of letters addressed to ANC sympathizers. A wrong move, I realized, and the very people I came to help would be put at risk.

I fiddled with the poster bomb mechanism. It kept slipping. Unlike my dad, I was not 'handy'. It took a real effort to get it right. I had to place it in the appropriate location which would

12 No explosives were used for leaflet distribution until 1969. - Editor.

give the very subversive (and certainly illegal) flyers the most public visibility. That required reconnoitring and finding a point of entry and egress. I found a parking structure over a busy street. I watched it. I was sure people were watching me. They probably weren't. I was just another white person in what was then a white city with 'non-Europeans' restricted as to where they could live, and even sit. As much as I hated to admit it, I blended in as just another 'whitey'.

I seem to recall that others who I didn't know were doing the same and that we were all going to set them off at the same time in different cities. I was conscious of the time and timing, and worried that someone might interfere or that I would screw up. I was as scared to abort the mission as to complete it. Once I found the right place, I had to arrange the device, set the time, turn the clock-like meter, and then disappear. In short order the leaflets would be dumped out in a public street, picked up by some, noticed by pedestrians and probably the police and demonstrate that the ANC was in the country and appealing for anti-apartheid activism and denunciations of the government. It was an ingenious idea and I think I pulled off my 'bombing' well. (How innocent this all seems now in a world where serious bombings are a daily occurrence in scores of countries.) It was hardly a heroic guerrilla mission, but the risks were real. If anything happened, I was told to send a postcard to a mail drop in London with the stamp upside down. I never figured out how any cops that caught me would allow me to send a last postcard or how that would get me out of jail. I actually put that thought out of my mind. I did my 'job'. I have a feeling that if captured and connected with a banned organization considered terrorists of the highest order, my 'vacation' in sunny South Africa would have been a prolonged one. I thought of that years later, when I visited Robben Island prison. I would not have liked 'living' in that hellhole.

The reasoning for my recruitment made sense: South Africans in exile were too high profile to go 'home'. They would be arrested on sight. American and English students were not known and so could, it was hoped, slip in as tourists. We were also disposable, as I later realized. The ANC would not suffer a big loss if we were captured. The seriousness of what I had gotten myself into only hit me later. I was keeping a scrapbook during my years in London. On June 27 1967, I turned 25 and a girlfriend wrote me a note which partially speaks to my mental state and the culture I was then part of.

'For your birthday, she wrote, 'I give you permanent immunity from the army, more time in which to do your things, lots of beautiful weather, good food and wine, US withdrawal from Vietnam, a secret map of the Pentagon's security system, luscious girls falling in love with you helplessly, tact, subtlety and sexuality forever.' My dad sent his hope 'that in your lifetime you should know only happiness and peace'.

Going to a war zone was a funny way of finding peace, but go I did, by plane, BOAC I think, through Kenya and on to Johannesburg. I remember flying into the city of gold. I was sure I would be caught, along with my suitcase and its hidden compartment. I was sure they knew I was coming. I didn't realize what a small fish I was. I breezed through with a 'Welcome to South Africa'. It was a terrifying moment. The border police I had feared couldn't be friendlier.

Afterwards, I would tell myself how stupid I had been, how dangerous it would have been had I been busted as an agent of a 'terrorist movement'. (Yes, Nelson Mandela's movement had been outlawed as terrorist under South Africa's draconian Suppression of Communism Act). South Africans then were like some Americans today, fearing terrorists under every bed. Robben Island was a segregated jail but I am sure they had an empty cell for me and my ilk elsewhere. (I had known about Ruth's incarceration as well as the jailing of other whites.)

I was supposed to keep to myself, talk to no one, blend in, stick to the routine and rely on my white skin privilege. I had rehearsed and reviewed the itinerary that was planned for me. I did what I went to do but I couldn't just do that. It was just not my style. I was more of an adventurer on what was the ultimate adventure. I just wasn't disciplined enough. I had to see the country and get a sense of the larger movement which was, I later learned, well underground.

What I didn't know then would be how that trip, and the encounter it gave me with South Africa, would change my life forever, would involve me in that struggle for the next 30 years, would lead me to write countless articles, help produce a hit record and organise concerts, make five films with Nelson Mandela and produce 156 weeks of a TV Series called *South Africa Now*.

I went to South Africa in 'the summer of love' but in some ways never left. In fact, I fell in love with the country and its promise; something I, unlike others, lived to see. Before I took the trip, I tried to make it sound as if I was just fulfilling an obligation and then would quickly move on to other pursuits after I did my 'duty'. I actually wrote that in the form of a poem of sorts under the heading of *23 July 67* and tucked it away.

I am surprised now about its anti-political tone, as I re-read it, and how ambivalent I really was. Maybe I was just posturing, as if this was no big thing. In fact this small sojourn would turn out to be a very big thing, although I have avoided talking about it because it was also clearly a case of a journalist crossing the line from a supposed 'objectivity' to advocacy. Remember, I was still a student.

Even now, I fear that this story might end up in the CIA file that I know the government has on me. I have seen an earlier incarnation, all blacked out, documenting my days in London. (It was as screwed up then as intelligence is today from Iraq – some things never change). I actually have a picture of Dick Cheney in my mind (who I met and quarrelled with bitterly in 1966), getting the CIA file with this article added to it with a note that says, 'You were right, he always was a terrorist!' Recall that this Dick refused to support a Congressional motion calling for the freedom of

Nelson Mandela. But I digress.

My hesitations then were honest and naïve and expressed this way in a poetic journal entry written on the very day I left London for South Africa. Can you believe I saved it?

23 July 67

This trip that I make,
In fear,
With hope
Is my response to language.
I am overstuffed with
Declamations and admonitions,
Exclamation points!
Let's be done with it
Already & move on
There are bigger
Things, more important

Matters
The personal mystery
The joy of construction
The fever for creation
All of these things make politics a lesser concern
And its destructiveness
An absurd disposition.
So I will pitch in,
'Do my Bit'
And speed the moment
When larger
Visions can be pursued.

We have to start somewhere.

At the bottom of the page, I later noted, 'On 12 September I returned alive & wiser.'

Wiser indeed. Issues and problems can be abstractions until you see them for yourself, until you go there. I have been back to South Africa many times but I will never forget the first time. (We always remember the first time in our personal pursuits, don't we? Smile). I have written about the experience (sans the "secret stuff") in my book *The More You Watch The Less You Know*, about my later career in big media.

I 'went out to South Africa' then, as I told my friends, for a three-week holiday on a student fare. In some ways, I've never come back. I'm not sure what it is about that country that exerts such a pull but I'm not the only journalist to whom it has happened. Joe Llelyveld, now the editor of The New York Times, won a Pulitzer for a book about South Africa. In it he wrote that no country he'd ever covered had the same personal impact on him.

For many years, when people ask me when I was last there, I tend to say "this morning", because for so many years I have been deeply immersed in reading about, researching, reporting on and in effect living with South Africa. It is as if some South African gene had gotten mixed up in my DNA. Some South Africans were sure I grew up there, perhaps because one of their most famous race car drivers is Jody Schecter. But I didn't. No relation he. I developed a passion for the country's people and their struggle from a distance and it wouldn't let me go. I realize now that the relationship has been unequal: I have received far more from the transaction than I have given.

South Africa is a special place, an eerie mix of the familiar and unfamiliar set against a landscape that is magical in its beauty. Every contrast there is pointed; every contradiction, revealing. Squatter camps perch in fancy neighbourhoods. Horrible racial oppression co-exists with enough relaxed moments of racial interaction to make New York seem far more tense and polarized. Almost every white South African has been raised by a black nanny, and yet every black has been united by a history of oppressive laws and attitudes. At the same time, for many there is an interracial intimacy that has always conflicted with the reality of apartheid.

When I first visited in 1967 during the 'summer of love' in America, South Africa was firmly in the grip of its first State of Emergency. There were few visible indications of black protest. As a civil rights worker in the US, I looked for such signs and thought that I, of all people, would be able to sniff them out if they were there. In Mississippi, at the height of the anti-segregation confrontation back in '64, white 'nawthin' college kids like myself had no problem getting black people to express their feelings or talk about 'the man'.[13] That was my experience at home, but not here.

South Africa was not the American South, and apartheid was never another name for segregation. We could at least appeal to a constitution that theoretically guaranteed everyone's rights. In South Africa, the law upheld racism and there was no constitution. Apartheid was as much a labour system as a racial one, and blatant economic exploitation was as much the problem as racial separation.

Ironically, the first thing I saw when the airport bus deposited me at the Jo'burg train station was a newspaper headline 'Detroit Riot: 37 Dead'. A year earlier I had worked in Detroit for Mayor Jerry Cavanagh, whose claim to fame was that he had prevented a Watts-type riot. His luck had run out in 1967. The Motor City was in flames, and I was reading about it in, of all places, South Africa, where a police state had been established to make sure rebellions like that didn't occur. At that moment, America's racial problems seemed worse. Our civil rights movement was disintegrating in the bitterness of insurrection and internecine racial division; South Africa's movement was on hold, but poised to erupt again.

It was hard for me to meet black people there. Attempts to even make eye contact with black workers guarding white property in Durban were unsuccessful. They stared past me and spoke to each other in Zulu. I felt frozen out, however much I

---

13 A term used then by US civil rights activists to mean white racists or people in the power structure. – Editor.

naively wanted them to think of me as a brother, as an ally in the liberation struggle. I was white, therefore one of their oppressors. I later realized that I had reduced the problem to one of race when it was far more layered and complex. Those Zulu workers most likely didn't speak English and, if so, couldn't understand me. Many had also been taught as children that eye contact with strangers is impolite.

I found the unextinguished flames of the South African struggle quite by accident, after I drew a bath at a small Durban beach hotel. I started reading the paper, noticing an announcement that the next day a funeral would be held not far away for Chief Albert Luthuli, then President-General of the African National Congress and a Nobel Peace Prize winner. He had died mysteriously, allegedly in a train accident in the rural area to which the government had banished him. I was thinking about going to the funeral when I noticed that I hadn't been watching the tub. It had overflowed, with water spilling over into the hall. I jumped up, unplugged the bath and raced one floor down to the lobby to find a mop. The Indian man behind the desk said, 'No, no, I'll send the boy up,' referring to the African man sitting to his right. I didn't see any boys. I shot back: 'No, no, just give me a mop. I made the mess. I'll clean it up.'

He and the 'boy' came upstairs with me, and we all dried the small flood. I asked them to please not call me baas. He smiled. The Indian guy told me that I was the first white man there who had ever cleaned up after himself. That broke the ice. I then asked how I could get a ride to Luthuli's funeral. At first he said it wasn't safe, then disclosed that he and a cousin were going to see their family in a nearby Indian township and that they would take me if I chipped in a few Rand for gas.

Sure enough, the next day, a brilliant Sunday morning alongside the Indian Ocean, I piled into a crowded jalopy with a few other Indian passengers who were also paying for the ride. As we passed through Natal's rolling hills and vast sugar plantations, we noticed several planes flying close to the ground, circling up ahead. They were monitoring the funeral site. 'That is the church where the funeral is taking place,' I was told. 'It's not safe to take you there directly.'

Instead he dropped me off about 300 yards away, on a dusty side road. 'We will pick you up exactly here in one hour, sharp,' I was told. 'Be here because it is not safe to wait.' This man seemed to have a fixation with the words 'not safe'. He knew something I didn't.

As I started toward the church, camera in hand, I noticed about a hundred black people in khaki uniforms lining up for what looked like a parade and carrying black, gold and green flags. I recognized them from pictures as the flag and uniforms of the ANC. But the ANC was banned, their leader, Nelson Mandela locked away for life on Robben Island near Cape Town, clear across the country. This wasn't supposed to be happening. I couldn't believe what I was seeing, and started taking pictures, walking with them as they marched up to and into the church.

It must have been a strange sight, that small army of chanting black militants with a skinny, long-haired white kid tagging along. (Yup, I was skinny once.) They marched right past a larger army of police who had the place totally surrounded. They weren't stopped, I was told later, because much of the western diplomatic corps, led by the Swedish Ambassador, were there along with some western reporters. Some white policemen started taking pictures of us. I was told that some of the demonstrators were quietly picked up later.

The place was inundated with plainclothes as well as uniformed cops. A few started pointing at me as if to ask, 'Who is that guy and where did he come from?' They probably had all the whites accounted for. Most had been brought into this closed African area, with permission, under escort. I had just shown up on my own. Suddenly the words 'not safe' took on a real meaning.

Inside the church, the ANC folks took up positions in front of their chief's coffin and unfurled their flag. One small, uniformed black man put his right thumb in the air in the ANC salute, keeping it there for almost the whole ceremony. I kept staring at him, not believing his strength and fortitude in a heroic gesture of defiance.

And then the singing started, hymns that reminded me of many a hot night in Mississippi when freedom songs were the movement's first line of solidarity against the cops and the Klan. South Africa's church music and freedom hymns were even more vibrant, rich with call-and-response rhythms. The sound made you ache with its beauty. That's when I first heard Nkosi Sikelel' iAfrika (Lord Bless Africa), then banned, now a national anthem.

The speeches were electric in their intensity, including one by a young student, president of the National Union of South African Students or NUSAS. Her name was Margaret Marshall, and she was as gorgeous as she was eloquent. I was not prepared for someone who was so white and blond to also be so articulate and uncompromising in her denunciation of apartheid. At that time in South Africa, it was dangerous to speak or write about such things. Her words were received with great warmth by Luthuli's family. The late writer Alan Paton also spoke well, but Margie's remarks were more memorable. We would become friends when she moved to Boston as part of an outflow of white liberals. She later married Anthony Lewis of The New York Times, who had covered South Africa for years, and is today a Chief Judge on the highest court in Massachusetts.

After spending some time in the Natal area, I travelled on to Cape Town, the 'mother city', a place that might have been in England if it wasn't for the beautiful Table Mountain and the vast African townships that surrounded it. I remember visiting the Parliament buildings and watching a group of liberal whites hold a vigil. I think I may have brought them a flower or two, as a symbol of the hippie-yippie counterculture I was also very much part of. It sounds stupid when I write about it now.

An American friend put me up in a quiet suburban community near the beach. Her beau, a white jazz musician, an excellent bass player, who played in one of the country's few interracial bands, took me on a tour of Guguletu, a nearby township. We went without the proper pass, were intercepted by the police and asked to leave. I was there long enough to see the great gap that existed then, and exists now, between white wealth and black poverty. It remains one of the biggest such gaps in the world.

In Johannesburg, I toured Soweto on a government tourist bus that cost about 25 cents and included a stop for tea at an official tourist centre that would be burned to the ground years later in the Soweto uprising. I wrote about that trip anonymously for the *Village Voice*. The bus stopped at government-backed workshops for the disabled, took in a model creche or nursery school, stopped at the weirdly named Uncle Tom's Hall (a community centre) and also toured that section of Soweto where the handful of black millionaires lived. If you could imagine a German sightseeing trip through 'Auschwitz-Land', that's what it felt like.

On April 27, 1994, I found myself back at Uncle Tom's, which hadn't changed very much, to film something that had: South Africa's first democratic and interracial elections. On that day, vast lines stretched in front of the hall while thousands waited patiently for voter cards.

One of the things I saw was how the texture of their struggle was not being reported well in my own country. For years now, through articles, on the radio, television and films, I've tried to report on what's missing, to fill in some gaps. I am sure that similar problems exist in the coverage of other countries, as well as my own, but South Africa has unique characteristics, and became a prism through which to view, and judge, the world of power and the world of journalism.

When I first went there, there was no hope. On my last trip, there was nothing but. Did my original 'mission' make a difference? Maybe a small one at first, but, I would like to think, a larger one later as I used what skills I had with musical projects like ('Don't Play) Sun City' and TV series like *South Africa Now* to try to wake up America to the truth about South Africa.

Back in 1967, none of us would have believed how long it would take to win the country back and how much misery, heartbreak, murder, and madness was yet to come. The Soweto uprising was years away, as were the township uprisings. The idea of a peaceful change occurred to only a few. Many dismissed it as an unachievable dream.

And yet it happened. History happened. South Africa became the rainbow nation, a world 'miracle' at a time of so few miracles. Many in that world credit Nelson Mandela, but he, and all of us who became involved, and stayed involved, know it was much more than one man – it was the powers of super dedicated leaders with integrity, men like Oliver Tambo, and the Sisulus and Chris Hani, Thabo Mbeki, Ruth and Joe and Ronnie and Pallo and so many others, who sparked and led the ANC and its people's movement.

It was the determination of millions that made a difference, with songs to lift our hearts, toyi- toyis to move our feet and slogans like *Amandla Ngawethu* and *Viva* to free Mandela and move the movement forward. And I am sure there were many more secret 'missions' that we still can't talk about yet, that helped, or, in my words then, 'did their bit'.

The activists who invited me into their movement back in the 1960s believed they could liberate their country, and fought with dogged determination through all the dark times. They also believed in me, a person they really didn't know but came to trust, who cared, from a far-away land and a culture that was not their own. I say *Viva* for that. They didn't give up, and neither have I.

Yes, I know problems remain. The contradictions are still everywhere, now as then. We have not achieved nirvana, there or here, but I was proud to be asked and prouder to serve in the small way I did. Doctors pledge to 'do no harm'. I did none, and maybe did some good. As my friend Abbie Hoffman would later say of our student movement in 1960s America that fights for real democracy still, 'We were young. We were foolish, naïve and made mistakes.

But we were right.'

Now known as The News Dissector, *Danny Schechter is an American writer and filmmaker with 8 books and 15 documentaries to his credit. As a journalist he reported on South Africa for 30 years. He created the* South Africa Now *series seen in 40 countries and he has directed five documentaries on and with Nelson Mandela. He was co-producer of the anti-apartheid hit record* Sun City. *He edits Mediachannel.org, a global media website. His latest film* WMD (Weapons of Mass Deception), *protesting at the media coverage of the Iraq War, won the documentary prize at the Durban Film Festival in 2005. It was aired on South African Broadcasting's Channel 1 in 2006. - Editor.*

Sarah Griffith and Ted Parker

Sarah Griffith

I have been trying to recall details about a trip I was asked to make 40 years ago. In 1967 I was a second year sociology student at LSE who spent most of her available free time travelling. My first year was a rather desultory effort on my part, but that was all changed by the appointment of Walter Adams from a university in what was then Rhodesia as the new Director of LSE. This sparked off the first student protest and sit-ins in the UK and my and lots of my fellow students' political education was truly underway.

Towards the end of the summer term I was approached by one of the South African students at LSE with what was, to me, a remarkable proposition. I should go with another student, Ted Parker, to Johannesburg, carrying fake bottomed suitcases containing hundreds of hidden ANC leaflets which would then be distributed by a timing device from the roofs of three different hotels. I had a very short time to make up my mind whether to accept or not. I obviously couldn't discuss this with anyone and I was told as little as possible about the details. I have to say that I was amazed, excited, proud but mostly terrified all at once, and also totally baffled as to why I had been asked. I knew Ted as a pretty serious student, a leftwing member of Soc Soc (the LSE Socialist Society), whereas I inhabited the dilettante hippy fringe, with liberal leanings. The only thing in my favour, I supposed, was that I had done a lot of travelling and was likely to agree to go. After all, how could you be offered an opportunity like this and turn it down? I had seen myself as someone who took risks and had adventures and here was the perfect opportunity to do both and hopefully even be of some use. I decided to go.

The story concocted was that Ted and I were a recently engaged couple (I hoped his girlfriend never found out) who were thinking of emigrating to South Africa and so were having a bit of a recce. The trip was to take about three weeks, about ten days in Jo'burg followed by a week or so in Durban (a 'real' holiday). We therefore needed suitcases for three weeks clothes (and leaflets). The only problem I could see was clothes for me, (a bit of a beatnik). I was dispatched with a wad of cash to the King's Road and Biba where I bought suitable outfits for a nice fiancée going to stay in a fairly posh hotel. This seemed to me to be the most bizarre aspect of the whole plan. Within a couple of weeks we were off. Ted (I hope) knew what was going on, while I was essentially along for the ride, providing convincing cover for his assignment.

The flight in those days was about 22 hours long with a stop for refuelling in Rhodesia in the middle of the night. I remember the extraordinary heat coming off the runway at 3 a.m., my first introduction to the southern end of the African continent. I remember how afraid I was in the last couple of hours before touchdown in Jo'burg. I knew that the risk of the leaflets being discovered was minimal, but also that the repercussions would be great. I was very scared of being arrested, as two years earlier I had been detained overnight in police cells in Athens (for wearing jeans: this was just pre the military junta) and had been roughed up by the police a bit; and, whilst righteous fury had carried me through that experience, I was understandably terrified of anything like that happening again. We went through Customs separately so as not to incriminate each other and I remember having to carry my heavy suitcase nonchalantly past the officials, praying that no one would offer to take it off me and wonder how a few clothes could weigh so much.

Of course we sailed through without difficulty but the rest of our stay in Jo'burg passed by in a blur. I remember going out on one occasion with Ted, both of us carrying leaflets in carrier bags. We arrived at the appointed hotel and Ted disappeared up the stairs at a side entrance which led to the roof. I waited, terrified, for an eternity (probably about 5 minutes) during which time he found the right spot on the roof, set up the timing device next to the stack of leaflets and ran back down again without being seen. He did this twice more and then after a couple of days we were free to leave. I don't think I have ever spent so many days in abject terror as I did in Jo'burg.

At the end of our time there we took a train to Durban, which was fantastic and colourful and relaxed, a completely different atmosphere, by the sea, where the inhabitants, mostly of Indian descent, looked us in the eyes and treated us and themselves almost as equals - completely opposite to the fear which seemed to be emanating from everyone in Jo'burg, myself included.

Even so, we were keen to get home and cut short our holiday in Durban and flew back a few days early, arriving at Heathrow with relief.

It was over 30 years later that I returned to South Africa, this time for a bargain holiday in Cape Town which, on the surface, appeared to be a lively, joyful city to visit, as long as you stayed in the tourist part of town. I insisted that we did the tourist trip to Robben Island where you are shown round by an ex-prisoner and where you cannot fail to be affected by the almost palpable atmosphere of the decades of prison life and death. My tears shed on the catamaran back to the harbour were, I hope, not entirely sentimental. I felt I finally understood a small part of what I had been involved in as a naïve student in the 1960s.

Ted Parker

A lot happened during my three years (1966-69) at the London School of Economics. I've got mixed feelings about what we got up to but I'm proud of the South African episode.

LSE welcomed mature students from across the globe, many of whom had extraordinary tales to tell. In the mid-1960s these included Americans avoiding military service in Vietnam and exiled members of opposition movements in Rhodesia and South Africa.

My own story was far less exotic. My dad died in 1950 at the age of thirty-two having got home from the army in 1948 after being garrisoned in Berlin. I was only six but my mother impressed on me my dad's horror at what the Allied soldiers had found in Nazi concentration camps. I think my lifelong hatred of racism stems from my early exposure to images of the holocaust.

I left school at fifteen determined to join the Royal Air Force but, with mediocre academic results, I concluded that I could not become a pilot. The next best thing seemed to be an electronics apprenticeship which I began at RAF Locking in Somerset in January 1960 soon after my sixteenth birthday.

For the next three years I was a member of the 94th Entry of RAF apprentices – among whom I developed friendships which have lasted, with the help of annual reunions, until the present day.

In the 1960s anyone becoming an apprentice had to commit themselves, by getting their parents to sign the appropriate documentation, to serve in the RAF until the age of thirty. However, during the final year of my apprenticeship something happened which would transform my life. Another apprentice, Mike McKenna, a lad from a tough estate in Manchester, became involved in the Campaign for Nuclear Disarmament (CND). This was clearly unthinkable for anyone in the RAF. Indeed, both of us happened to be training specifically to work on the top secret radio and radar equipment installed in the British nuclear bomber fleet – the V bombers.

McKenna and I argued bitterly for months, the disagreements becoming increasingly public as groups of supporters coalesced around each of us as we sought more and more sophisticated evidence for our own points of view.

McKenna eventually convinced me that British nuclear weapons could not, on their own, deter an attack from the Soviet Union and that if the USA and the USSR could achieve a 'balance of terror' there was no justification for a third country maintaining a nuclear force, thereby creating a precedent for greater nuclear proliferation.

In January 1963 McKenna and I both sent a letter outlining our views to the pacifist newspaper *Peace News*, giving our names, service ranks and numbers, and inviting other likeminded servicemen and women to join us in setting up a 'forces branch of CND'.

Shortly after this we were both sentenced to eight months imprisonment (later commuted to four months detention) in the military prison at Shepton Mallet in Somerset and discharged from the RAF for 'conduct to the prejudice of good order and air force discipline' contrary to Section 69 of the Air Force Act. It could have been much, much worse and I later found out that far more serious charges had been considered and eventually rejected.

On my release from prison I worked as a TV engineer whilst McKenna pursued his ambition to gain a university education, entering LSE as a Sociology student in 1964.

He then encouraged me to sit in on a lecture on one of my days off – thus instigating another life changing event! I was so impressed by the lecture that I turned to him and said, 'How do you get into a university?' The insights he gave me were so perceptive that, by October 1966, I too had enrolled as a Sociology undergraduate at LSE, having first obtained 'A' levels at Wandsworth Technical College, during which time, incidentally, I managed to get arrested on an LSE-organised demonstration against the Unilateral Declaration of Independence (UDI) by the white minority government of Ian Smith in Rhodesia.

By the time I got to LSE I was therefore already familiar with the political groups into which the students had organized themselves. I had also been developing my own political ideas independently, finding myself drawn towards rank-and-file struggle based in the workplace. A pamphlet about the student occupation of the University of California at Berkeley in the USA had a powerful effect on me. I gravitated towards the LSE Socialist Society (Soc. Soc.) which was leading an increasingly militant campaign against the appointment of Dr. Walter Adams as the new LSE Director because of his alleged collaboration with the Smith regime in Rhodesia.

Events, punctuated at one point by the deeply tragic death

of an LSE porter who suffered a heart attack following his deployment by the administration to keep students out of a meeting hall, spiralled into a major student occupation of LSE – one of many as it turned out – in the spring of 1967. This signalled the beginning of a nationwide wave of student occupations which became global news. Like many other students I joined the International Socialists (later the Socialist Workers Party – SWP), thinking that it provided radical political solutions to the issues we had identified.

In May 1967, in the immediate aftermath of the LSE occupation, I was approached by another LSE student, Ronnie Kasrils, a South African forced into exile by his membership of the banned African National Congress (ANC). Ronnie was an old-style Communist Party member who cheerfully disregarded the factional differences which preoccupied most of the far-left groups. He said, 'You've been very vocal in your opposition to racial oppression in southern Africa. Would you be prepared to go undercover to South Africa to help black people in their struggle?'

Faced by this moral pressure – and indeed by the intriguing opportunity of going abroad for the first time in my life – I said that I would go, depending on precisely what I would be expected to do. Thus began a period during which I was briefed, trained and equipped by the ANC through Ronnie.

His own history was amazing and included narrowly evading arrest through all kinds of subterfuge whilst in South Africa. He still feared surveillance by the South African security forces whilst in the UK so we held our initial discussions in open parkland and our later training – on things such as how to avoid leaving fingerprints, how to disguise your appearance, how to avoid pursuit and how to assemble primitive timing devices – in safe accommodation unconnected to either of us.

Ronnie also suggested that the chances of avoiding notice in South Africa would be increased by travelling as a couple. I considered asking my own girlfriend but she was considerably younger than me and was not involved in politics. I felt I could not justify the risks involved to myself or her family if things went wrong.

Ronnie and I discussed various options from among other LSE students known to us and settled on Sarah Griffith, daughter of renowned LSE law professor John Griffith. Sarah had been involved in events throughout the recent student protest and had always been calm and self-assured in the face of fast-moving developments. It was agreed that Ronnie would explain the situation to her. She agreed to go. It is perhaps worth noting at this stage that despite our 'engaged couple' cover story – to say nothing of the colourful reputation of 1960s students - our relationship was chaste and businesslike throughout, both of us having long-term attachments back home.

The mission was to get ANC propaganda material into Johannesburg and to deploy it in various ways. The material was to be transported in the false bottoms of our suitcases and then we were to post two hundred leaflets to known ANC sympathizers and release ANC banners and more leaflets at a pre-determined time in the city centre. Ronnie made clear that we were not to speak about the mission before, during or afterwards. 'You should only do so', he said with his usual confidence 'once South Africa is liberated'. To do otherwise, he said, would endanger others involved in similar operations.

Ronnie showed us the suitcases to be used. They had been fitted with a checkerboard internal lining intended to confuse the eye if opened by customs officers. A false lining in the same material was to hide thousands of leaflets, two ANC flags ('black for the people, green for the land and gold for the wealth') and two timing devices. We memorized a list of other items to purchase locally at an 'OK Bazaar' chain store.

We were to fly out with South African Airways (reputed to be subject to less scrutiny than other airlines by South African customs and security officers) checking in separately to increase the chances of one of us getting through if the other was arrested.

When I was given my suitcase containing its hidden cargo it seemed very heavy. Even with my modest belongings it greatly exceeded the baggage allowance. However, I opted to pay a surcharge rather than to transfer anything to hand luggage which would have left the suitcase looking absurdly empty if opened at customs.

The flight south was a revelation. Looking back forty years later it is amazing to reflect on just how dramatically the world has changed in terms of politics and air travel. We took off from Heathrow as dusk was falling. Our first stop was during early evening in the Portuguese capital Lisbon – then ruled by the fascist government of Antonio Salazar. In the early hours we sweltered in Angola – held in a cruel colonial grip by Portugal as part of its African empire. By early morning we had touched down in Salisbury, capital of Rhodesia, ruled by Ian Smith's white racist government in defiance of Britain and the United Nations.

It was at Salisbury airport that I began to get really alarmed. Rhodesian airport magazines had headline warnings about the need for vigilance against 'red plots'. It struck me that if the South African intelligence services were as good as its opponents feared they might have got advance notice of a visitor whose recent past included internment in a military prison followed by playing a prominent role in a well publicized student revolt. It also occurred to me that the arrest of such a person would not be treated as an example of naïve idealism. This, after all, was three years into Nelson Mandela's life sentence for 'terrorism'.

Our final destination was Jan Smuts airport in Johannesburg. The differences in treatment on grounds of race became evident immediately. African porters were shouted at to carry the heavy bags, including mine. The white travellers were treated with courtesy and deference although the customs officer appeared to think seriously about asking me to open my bulging case before waving me through.

Once on the airport bus Sarah and I linked up and made our way to a part of town recommended by Ronnie Kasrils as likely to have accommodation readily available. The various manifestations of apartheid became immediately evident.

Separate buses for whites and non-whites. Public toilets in groups of four – white-only men, white-only women, non-white men and non-white women. Non-whites were only to be seen in menial positions. Only non-white waiters served in restaurants with white-only diners.

We soon secured two rooms in a guest house. This became our base for the next several days. After getting our bearings we cut the false bottoms out of the suitcases, taking care to minimize damage so that we could safely reuse the cases for our return journey. We stuffed leaflets into the pre-addressed envelopes and posted them from city centre postboxes well away from where we were staying.

During the next few days we obtained the additional equipment we required including such items as wooden battens from which to suspend the flags and varnish to paint on our fingers to avoid leaving fingerprints.

Next we began our reconnaissance to locate tall city centre buildings from which the leaflets and banners could be dropped. A minor concern during this period was the heightened security arising from the presence in Johannesburg of a serial arsonist nicknamed the 'Jo'burg Firebug'. A photofit prominently featured in the press looked uncannily like me and the description of 'ruddy complexion' fitted someone recently arrived from an English summer for a couple of weeks in a mild Johannesburg winter!

The procedure was for me to wander into various suitable buildings carrying a camera so that if challenged I could claim to be a tourist looking for somewhere to take photos.

Few places seemed quite right but I eventually found two – the first was the City Treasurer's Department, one of the most prominent public buildings in town about five stories high and with a flat roof, and the second was a domestic block of flats where the dwelling at the far end of one of the balconies afforded a degree of privacy from neighbouring flats. Both met the key requirement that they were in highly visible and busy locations where the ANC flags would be seen by hundreds of passers-by before the security forces were able to respond.

We had originally hoped to identify three locations – two for the banners and another for the leaflets – but in view of our difficulty in finding suitable buildings we decided to use two only, wrapping the leaflets into the rolled-up banners so that leaflets falling into the crowded streets would cause people to look up and see the banners.

We had been instructed to get the banners to drop at precisely 3 pm on a specified Friday. This necessitated packing the banners and leaflets beforehand, fitting but not setting the timing devices – these were simple clockwork alarms to which razor blades could be attached which would, in turn, cut a thread, releasing the cord fastened round the banners. We then wrapped everything up in brown paper, creating two bulky parcels about four feet long.

I approached the City Treasurer's Department first and walked up the stairs with my large parcel to the top floor without encountering anyone. A particularly anxious moment was going up the final set of stairs to the roof, which was clearly unused with debris scattered around. A stranger going up there would be likely to cause suspicion. However, I reached the roof without incident and went over to an upturned bench, identified on my previous visit, close to the side of the building nearest to the busy main street below.

The next few minutes were the most dangerous – if anyone saw me assembling the device there would be no mistaking what I was up to. My heart was racing. First I removed the brown paper packaging, putting it into my pockets. Next I set the timer to go off about half an hour later at 3 pm. Finally, I secured a cord to the bench and carefully positioned the package over the wall hanging down over the street where there would be no obstruction when the banner was unfurled and the leaflets went cascading down.

Whilst going down from the roof to the floor below I had a scare. Someone looking like a senior manager emerged from an office and looked directly at me whilst I was halfway down the stairs. I was by then holding my camera and I made sure he saw it as I gave him my broadest smile and proceeded briskly to the next stairwell. He smiled back and went into a neighbouring office as I left the building.

I rejoined Sarah and we proceeded to the second building, but here I hit trouble. The secluded area of the balcony I had chosen had previously seemed suitable because the only nearby door was closed and I had concluded that the occupants were unlikely to interrupt me during the vital few minutes I needed. In the event the door opened just as I was about to unwrap the parcel and a middle-aged woman challenged me with an inquisitorial "Hello?" Having no ready alibi I responded with an incomprehensible grunt and wandered away.

On getting back to Sarah I admitted that I had no fall-back plan and we had to dump the parcel in an alley. This was clearly a disappointment but on balance I think the outcome was worthwhile. Ronnie had made clear we should walk away if we felt threatened. The one successful drop would have been spectacular and to have compromised the whole ANC operation by improvising something without proper preparation would have been inappropriate.

Immediately after the drop we followed our instructions to get a late afternoon train travelling overnight to Durban and to lie low for a week before travelling back to the UK.

On our return Ronnie showed us newspaper reports which indicated that the whole operation had fully achieved its objectives. Similar banners and leaflets had appeared all across South Africa, the security forces were caught completely by surprise and, above all, the ANC had demonstrated to supporters and opponents alike that it could still operate in South Africa despite the draconian measures in place to ban it.

On reflection, although our role at the time was both frightening and exhilarating, what we did was insignificant compared with the enormous heroism shown by those standing up against township massacres and involved in the Soweto risings - as well as the unimaginable individual courage of people such as Steve Biko, Nelson Mandela and countless others.

Despite this I am proud that LSE students had, quite literally, helped to keep the flag of freedom flying in apartheid South Africa during some of its bleakest moments. With Ronnie's permission I did tell my friend and fellow student John Rose, who carried out further missions as they gained in sophistication during the following years.

I did not go back and have never been to Africa since, though I would like to now. I stayed involved with the SWP for several years, notably playing a key role in organizing opposition to the National Front in the so-called 'Lewisham riots' of 13 August 1977 which prevented the NF from marching through Lewisham and were of considerable significance in the NF's subsequent political decline.

I retired in 2008 at the age of 65 having spent the last 17 years of my working life as Principal of Barking College in East London. During 2006 I was unexpectedly propelled back into limited political action when the neo-Nazi British National Party gained 13 seats on Barking & Dagenham Council and I took to the streets with *Unite against Fascism* in protest. I also opened up the college to 'Love Music Hate Racism', attracting the vocal hostility of the BNP but providing our 13,000 students with a focus for action in line with college diversity policies which are enthusiastically implemented to ensure equal treatment but seldom tested under the fire of organized racism.

The South African episode afforded me the chance to play a very small role in the fight for racial equality which has been the major global issue throughout my lifetime and which such major world figures as Nelson Mandela and Barack Obama have crystallised. Much has changed – Ian Smith's white rule in Rhodesia has been replaced by Robert Mugabe's black rule in Zimbabwe – but political tyranny and racial/religious intolerance remain. I hope that my own children and erstwhile students find themselves on the right side in the shifting battles to come.

'Nella Derrick' and John Rose

The name Nella Derrick is a pseudonym, as the author of this story wishes to remain anonymous for professional reasons. – Editor.

'Having a wonderful time here in Geneva'. So read the postcards that dropped through my parents' letterbox during a three week period in November 1969. They were deceived. Wrong country; wrong continent. But how could I tell this Conservative couple that I was, in fact, in South Africa on a mission for the African National Congress. And that our aim was to use our own home-made explosive devices to shower information leaflets on the unsuspecting black population of the townships surrounding the fringes of Johannesburg. Hence the deception. It was to be another thirty years before I would eventually visit Geneva, and give those postcards a belated reality. At the time of this – for me – momentous expedition I had just left the London School of Economics. My years there had been some of the most eventful in the School's history: events in which I took an enthusiastic part. As with many others, the experience politicised me. It was the time of the war in Vietnam. Along with the political situation in South-East Asia, the vile and oppressive regimes in South Africa and Rhodesia were prominent among the issues forming the core of our political concern and actions. And LSE had its own internal disputes; the directorship of Sir Walter Adams, a Rhodesian, had generated fierce controversy. The manner in which he had performed in his previous post as Director at the University of Rhodesia was the focus of much criticism by the more radical elements of the student body at LSE. He was said to have complied too freely with the discriminatory system operating in his country. Like most students attracted to LSE, I was well aware of its radical tradition – and perhaps drawn by it.

For the first time I found myself in an environment where politics – real politics, as I saw them – were being discussed. Not by everyone, of course: there were those students who profoundly disagreed with the left-wing analysis of political events; others who were apolitical and simply wanted to be allowed to complete their studies quietly and peacefully. For still others, talk – however critical and fiery – was not enough. There had to be action.

I certainly wanted to graduate. But also to take part in the meetings, the demos, and the various other goings-on intended to draw attention to inequities and injustices on the global scene. The School's Socialist Society, a leading promoter of activism, was an obvious vehicle through which to get involved. I became a regular at its meetings.

I find it difficult to remember, but it was probably through the Socialist Society that I first met Ronnie Kasrils. In the autumn of 1969 it was he who approached me to see if I would be interested in going to South Africa on a mission for the African National Congress. It was an offer I couldn't refuse. Apart from anything else, it seemed like an enormous privilege to be given an opportunity to do something positive instead of just talk about the horrors perpetrated against the black and coloured communities there.

It is also difficult, after the passing of so many years and when so much has since happened, to recall my feelings at the time. In some sense the whole affair seems almost unreal. But the evidence is there: I have an old passport stamp to remind me that I really did make the trip. And many memories do still remain vivid. I don't recall any uncertainty about making the decision to take part. I do know I seriously considered that, if we were caught, our fate would be to end up on Robben Island in the company of the likes of Nelson Mandela! But one of the benefits of youth is a willingness to take risks and act in accordance with one's beliefs; the baggage that comes to weigh so heavily in later life has not yet been accumulated. The cause was so obviously important and worthwhile that any perceived risk seemed, if not inconsequential, then well worth taking.

It was more than 20 years before I discovered that a number of my contemporaries had signed up for similar trips. But, of course, in the interests of security, we all kept our missions a secret. Just in case anything should go wrong I told one close friend what I was intending to do. It was she who organised the postcards that arrived from Switzerland during my absence.

The plan was that I would travel to South Africa with John Rose in November 1969. With us we were to take leaflets, printed in the UK by the ANC, to Johannesburg. These were to be distributed to the blacks in the early evening as they left the major railway stations to return to their satellite townships after a day of work in the city. But of course you couldn't simply turn up at a South African railway station and hand out leaflets as you might do on the Strand in London. Ingenuity and technology were required. Hence the need for a device offering an explosive boost to send the leaflets on their way. Bizarrely, as it now seems, the chosen instrument of political support was to be a plastic bucket kitted out with a small explosive charge and a battery-operated timing device.

First, of course, we had to be trained in making basic explosive mechanisms. John and I went with Ronnie on several occasions to a small attic room somewhere off Oxford Street. Here he showed us how to make the device from various easily obtainable components. Technology not being among my principal life skills, I can't imagine how I ever mastered the necessary arts. Nor indeed do I now have even the glimmering of a recollection of the mechanism or how it was constructed and operated. But, surprisingly, the devices worked – as we discovered when we went trawling over Hampstead Heath to find suitably private places in which to test one of them.

Before our departure we were each given a large, false-bottomed suitcase in which had been packed the vast numbers of leaflets we were taking out with us. The idea was that John and I would pass for just another couple travelling on holiday to South Africa to see the sights and wholly indifferent to the political situation. In an attempt to add credence to this endeavour I even abandoned my jeans and, for the first time in years, put on a dress.

We left England on a bleak November day and arrived at Jan
Smuts Airport. This was the first dose of reality: the immediate
and all too apparent evidence of the apartheid system in words
and deeds. There for all to see – no shame or embarrassment –
the total segregation of black and white.

Nervously carrying our loaded cases we passed through
customs. First hurdle negotiated; no problems. Then on to
Johannesburg where we checked into our hotel. We were met by
Costas Paizes. He was the uncle of George, a fellow student from
the LSE, who had arrived separately in South Africa. Costas had
been living in South Africa for many years but was a staunch
and active critic of the regime. He knew why we were there, and
was to help us during our stay.

Our first task was to locate the places where we intended
to set off the three devices. These were to be the busy railway
stations used by the blacks returning from their day's work in
the city. Then we went shopping: not for souvenirs, but for
the components of our explosive devices. We had the sense
to realise that we shouldn't get everything from the same
shop; this might have led an astute vendor to appreciate the
nature of the complete object. So we made our purchases
in several different places. And what would the reception
staff of the hotel make of its guests returning to their rooms
carrying plastic buckets? We tried somehow to disguise them
as we entered the building and crossed the lobby. Safely back
inside the hotel we began the assembly process. Again my
memory of the technical details is a complete void, but after
three or four days we had succeeded. We were ready for action.
Once again we had to conceal the buckets, this time as we carried
them out of the hotel to the car. We put them in the boot, and
covered them with newspapers. George's uncle drove us to each
in turn of the pre-selected railway stations. This, obviously,
was the riskiest part of the mission – not least because whites
like us could hardly merge invisibly into the predominantly
black travellers crowding the vicinity of the stations. We had
chosen late afternoon: a time when the maximum number of

blacks could be expected to pass through the stations on their way home to the townships. At each location we placed one of the plastic buckets, packed with leaflets and, of course, our homemade explosive devices. We had set the timers to give us what we hoped would be sufficient opportunity to make our getaway before the detonator was activated and sent the leaflets high into the sky, before they rained down on possibly bemused passers-by. Then it was on to the next station to repeat the process – and finally to our third destination.

The leaflets were published by the ANC. They told black Africans who read them that their plight had not been forgotten. They reminded them that each man and woman had their own part to play in the struggle, that the African National Congress was the voice of their freedom, and that the time had come to remove their government. The ANC called upon the people, black and coloured, not to give up, not to submit to white oppression, but to organise and fight the unjust laws and to support their freedom fighters in the war of liberation. Having successfully placed our three buckets we planned to escape the city as quickly as possible. No time to wait or wonder. It was clear that the authorities would be looking for the perpetrators. Our destination was Durban.

The four of us – John, George, George's uncle, and me - drove from Johannesburg through the night. For me, this car journey provided what turned out to be the most scary moment of the whole trip – and it had nothing to do with our clandestine activities, or with the South African Government. It was a swarm of locusts. The memory remains vivid to this day. We were in the car completely surrounded by the wretched creatures, their faces pressed to the windscreen, their enormous eyes staring in at us. At one point we were critically low on petrol and had to stop to fill up. The insects clung persistently to the vehicle. Indeed they were stuck all over the car, and most particularly to the windscreen.

We arrived in Durban and spent a few days relaxing – just as any genuine tourists might do. Then it was back to Johannesburg, and time to part company.

I had decided to travel home via Rhodesia, as it then was. On the aeroplane I got talking to a South African pilot who invited me to stay with his family in the suburbs of Salisbury. To them I presented myself as a wholly non-political tourist interested in seeing their beautiful country. I had the opportunity to experience their way of life first hand, and to gain a real insight into their feelings about the black majority population. It reinforced what I had, of course, already known: that their view of their fellow black countrymen as an innately inferior form of being was deeply entrenched.

Our mission, as I later found out, had been a success. The head of the local Security Police reported that 'subversive ANC pamphlets were released by exploding devices at the Railway Station at Johannesburg used mainly by Africans'. He said they were investigating the incidents. What, if anything, that investigation revealed I have no idea. Very little, I would imagine. We'd got away with it.

Looking back, all these years later, the affair does seem slightly unreal, even comical. Rather like something from a schoolgirl adventure comic! But it did happen, and I think I can be proud that my commitment extended beyond words and into deeds. Like most great changes in human society, the downfall of apartheid government in South Africa was not the result of a single action by a single individual at a single moment, but the culmination of deeds – some heroic, many quite pedestrian – performed by hundreds of thousands of people over decades. In my very small way I am happy to have been among them.

HOW I SERVED THE ANC STRUGGLE AND LET DOWN MY FAMILY
George Paizis

I had just finished my Law degree at the LSE in the summer of '69. It had been an interesting three years, what with the anti-Vietnam demos, the occupations, the Socialist Society. But it had all begun with Rhodesia. The Governors of the LSE had appointed Walter Adams, ex-Chancellor of the University of Rhodesia, to be the next Director of the LSE. Our reasoned protests had met a blank wall. Protests over Adams's appointment led to the first occupation. Two years later – January 1969 – we found ourselves protesting outside Rhodesia House. Predictably, it was protected by an eight-deep cordon of police and we could not get anywhere near the building. In the middle of the hopeless pushing and shoving somebody's political brain made the connection between Ian Smith's regime and his staunchest supporters and life-line. The shout went out: 'South Africa House!' We all ran along the Strand, leaving the impenetrable cordon of police in place and arrived at our new target to find one solitary policeman. We failed to get in. However, somebody managed to pull a phone out of one of the ground floor offices and we took it in turns to swing it on its long flex to smash the upper floor windows. Ronnie Kasrils was flinging himself against a very solid side door, trying to bash it in. By the time police reinforcements arrived, most of the first and ground floor windows on the front had been 'done in'.

The summer of '69: a holiday in Yugoslavia with my hippy-anarchist friend Geoff J. The '60s was not only about protests; it was also about breaking other barriers. After a vivid two weeks, I left for Athens by train and thence to my village of Kioni, in Ithaca. That's where my grandmother Milia lived. At the time, Greece was enjoying the dictatorship of the pro-US Colonels who had announced the dawning of a revived Greek civilisation. They banned 'degeneracy', the dropping of litter and imposed short hair and respect for the army. I sent a rude letter to my friends back in England reporting what these CIA trainees were up to and what people thought of them. For security, on the back of the envelope I put my grandmother's name as a 'sender'.

Having finished my degree, it had been decided that I should go to meet the South African branch of the family. They were paying my fares. Inexplicably, I insisted that I had to go back to London prior to leaving for Johannesburg. My first formal meeting with Ronnie was outside the Dominion Theatre, Tottenham Court Road and we went to talk round the corner in Russell Square. He told me the risks involved and what I would have to do. Even today, every time I pass that theatre my mind still flips back to that meeting. My job was to take some propaganda material, unpack the double-bottomed suitcase when I arrived, post the material from certain designated post-boxes and get rid of the case. We also worked out a story if I was stopped by customs. He also told me that my friend John Rose was to come out later with more dangerous materials, but he never got round to giving me training for that.

My family in South Africa consisted of my father's elder sister, Katerini, who had emigrated there in the 1930s and now owned the Ellis Park Hotel. After the Greek Civil War, my father's younger brother, Costas, had also fled there. He had taken an active part in the war-time Resistance and that had now made him a marked man. The victorious Allies in post-war Greece – first Britain and then the US – presided over and assisted in the killing, persecution and intimidation of those associated with anti-nazi activities because they were suspected of Communist sympathies. So Costas had to get out and South Africa seemed an obvious choice, since his sister was already there. By the late 1960s my Auntie Katerini had two daughters – Emily, respectably married and living in London and Marie, newly re-married, and that was crucial. That summer of '69, my elder cousin Marie had come on honeymoon to London with her new husband. But they did a lot of shopping, what with being rich, newly wed and in Europe. Their baggage became overweight.

The day before my departure, Emily asked me to take some

stuff that her sister had left behind. I produced a normal suitcase, in which we weighed my own stuff and she gave me items that would put the weight at just below the limit – some children's clothes, a box of new electric hair curlers and a new, beautifully heavy, bespoke, Saville Row pin-stripe woollen three-piece suit freshly made for the new husband, Solon. So I took the stuff and placed it in the false bottom suitcase that I was really taking, which was now made much heavier than the other one by the concealed propaganda material. With the optimism of youth, I thought that I could get away with a few kilos over the limit. I set off to Cromwell Road air terminal, to check in and board the bus that took you to Heathrow, accompanied by my friend Geoff J. At the check in, the staff proved less tractable than I had imagined. I could not or would not pay the excess, so I had to shed the heaviest stuff – my cousin's husband's new suit and the electric hair curlers; the children's clothes I kept.

The journey to Jo'burg was uneventful. The sunrise over the African plains was memorable, enhanced by the mescaline tab that Geoff had given me. Passage through customs was simple. I was met by my family at the airport, taken to my auntie Katerini's hotel and installed in a small residential apartment that I was to share for the next four months with my uncle Costas. I delivered the children's clothes and explained that the other stuff was too heavy, that my friend Geoff had taken charge of it and it could be picked up from the address where I had been living.

I said nothing to my uncle Costas about the clandestine materials I had to distribute, because my instructions were clear. One day, soon after my arrival, when the flat was empty, I ripped open the double bottom of the case and saw that I was carrying nothing more exciting than hundreds of brown sealed envelopes, containing letters or leaflets or perhaps some money. But I never knew, and this, too was part of the plan in case I was caught at customs. Packing the stuff in carrier bags, I went to different post-boxes in the centre of town, and tried to post hundreds of letters as casually as I could. On returning home, however, the problem was to dispose of the suitcase in a safe way. Somehow, my uncle noticed the wrecked interior of the case and at this point he became involved. To protect me, he told me that he would deal with it all and took charge of the case; I never found out what he did with it. But it was not the end of the matter.

Back in London, my cousin Emily had received a very frosty and evasive reception when she went to recover the new brother-in-law's suit. Apparently, my friends pretended they knew nothing about anything. My cousin, feeling outraged by the rudeness of my friends and feeling mocked and insulted, returned with her husband. This time they were told more forcefully to go away, and aspersions were cast on them with respect to their country of origin. I knew nothing of all this till a call of complaint came through from London. Uncomprehendingly, I insisted that all was due to some misunderstanding and wrote and rang to get some sense out of my London friends. They were curiously evasive over the expensive suit and the hair curlers. Given the hostile behaviour of my friends and my inability to provide any explanations, my cousins concluded that we had sold the suit of the new son-in-law and spent the money on drugs. I was outraged, and protested that my friends all had degrees, were honourable, self-sacrificing revolutionaries. But then, they asked, why had I taken out the most valuable items and brought only the kiddies' clothing? My uncle Costas was supportive, but where was the suit?

It got worse. The family in South Africa got a call from my parents in Athens asking them to find out what I had done to implicate my grandmother in anti-government activities. Apparently the Greek Secret Police (KYP) had visited my parents' flat late one night. They had a warrant for my arrest and they wanted to take my grandmother in for questioning. Now, my grandmother was not just a-political; she hated politics with the passion of a woman who had suffered all her life in entertaining monarchists and other right-wing dignitaries who visited my grandfather, the long-time mayor of our village. Worse still, she had a profound contempt for politics since my grandfather had never gained anything from his long-time allegiance to the Crown and its supporters. To save her from their clutches, my father had to go to the security offices and managed to convince them that his seventy-five year old mother was as innocent as an old woman can be. Again, thousands of miles away, I protested my innocence of any wrongdoing, but suspicions lingered, for my family remembered that I had been involved in anti-government protests in London. And anyway, why had I insisted on going to South Africa via London instead of going direct from Athens?

As it turned out, the family had a contact in the HQ of the Greek KYP (secret police). Risking his career, he looked at my file to find out what I was wanted for and why they were after my granny. For a start, there was the letter I had written in the summer with her name and address on the back that had been intercepted. Even worse, however, the family learnt, to their horror, that the Greek government suspected me of unspecified illegal and violent activities in South Africa. When the family got to learn this in South Africa, this information somehow became entangled with the fact of the missing hair curlers and suit. I was shamed and exposed: there seemed to be no limits to which I would not sink. The rest of my stay in Johannesburg remained under a dark cloud. However, my uncle Costas stuck by me through all the suspicion.

Then in early winter, John Rose and Nella Derrick[14] arrived, pretending to be a newly wed English couple. Now, they had brought the real stuff – in two large double-bottomed cases. They had with them not only propaganda material but also the wherewithal to distribute it to the South African workers – explosive devices and timers. They had also brought money for our mission and for our escape. Unlike me, they had also undergone extensive training.

I took them round to meet my uncle Costas, and he realised that more suitcases would have to be disposed of. He asked no questions, and within a few days was stoically undertaking the task. This time, our preparation was more elaborate. We had to

14 I have inserted her nom-de-plume here at her request. – Editor.

paint our fingers with nail varnish so as not to leave any finger prints. We had to assemble the explosive devices (which each used a 12 bore cartridge) – and attach the timers: key ring timers made in Switzerland. We had to assemble the plastic buckets in which the leaflets would sit and place these on a cross of sticks, so that the explosions would propel them into the air just when the crowd of workers was its densest at five o'clock at the gates of the stations to the townships. We also had another device, a cassette recorder and speaker that we concealed in a cardboard box. Here the delay mechanism was that the first twenty minutes of the tape was covered with silver foil, to give us time to get away. Apparently, it could not be left blank, as it would have hissed and attracted attention.

All went according to plan. We placed the material; we did not think we had been spotted. We got in the hired car and followed instructions to leave in the early evening for Durban. Bits of the journey linger in my mind: the loud rock music, the open windows of a big American car, the dope we smoked all night, the long and straight road. Above all there was the euphoria that we had done something against apartheid and got away with it.

Arriving at Durban at six in the morning, we drove down to the seafront. There we found a fish and chip café and I had the best fish of my life: a huge fresh sole. Again, we had been given money to book into a hotel and stay a few days till the police had stopped actively looking for us. After about a week, we went back to Johannesburg and John and Nella left with new suitcases. I stayed for another few months, returning to London in January 1970. I remember what we did with joy but not so the rest of my stay in South Africa.

Back in London, when I became involved again in activities against the Greek Colonels, they tried to issue a warrant for my arrest with Interpol – for drug running and gun running. Who would believe them? As for the suit and the hair curlers, my friend Geoff J. had indeed taken them that same day to Notting Hill Gate street market and sold them for £3.50. The price of my shame.

Contribution of my uncle Costas Paizis

It's with gratitude and thankfulness that I face the mention of my name in the description of these very daring, revolutionary and philanthropic acts of three courageous young men:[15] Rose, Mike Milotte and Paizis. I am sorry that a high degree of amnesia that I suffer from lately (I am now 82) prevents me from participating in the narration of those acts such a long time after they were carried out, and which I used to know and remember.

The fact that in spite of my forgetfulness I can mention one act, which the above mentioned three do not, shows that the more people cooperate in writing down the history of the South Africans' struggle against apartheid the more details would be retained. I do remember the following:

In the winter of 1969 George Paizis, my nephew, called me and 'instructed' me to be prepared to go to a railway station close to Soweto at a certain time late at night to place an explosive device to scatter leaflets containing messages that would not only encourage the black and oppressed people to fight the domination of the whites, but would also remind the governing dictators that the liberation of the 'native' (a term which the black South Africans hated) is an inevitable, natural and approaching event. I am sorry, again, that I don't remember the actual contents of the leaflets. The 'bomb' exploded, the leaflets were scattered and the newspapers, the following day, published the event.

The participation of the whites in the black people's struggle against apartheid was very limited but effective. It is natural that, belonging to the part of society with industrial and educational advancement, they would contribute efficiently. They really did, and a number of them are considered heroes today. Their names are often written next to the names of the real heroes, like Mandela, Sisulu etc.

That the three young men came to South Africa from England with the exclusive purpose of adding a nail to the structure of

15 Costas Paizis has forgotten to mention Nella Derrick – Editor.

LIBERTY, setting aside the possibility of being caught and not caring about the consequences, is to be appreciated not only by the people who can now live now like ordinary humans but by everyone who knows what oppression means.

WORKING FOR RONNIE
Mike Milotte

In the spring of 1967, while I was still studying for my 'A' Levels in Northern Ireland, I was asked to attend for an interview at the University of Kent in Canterbury where I had applied to study politics. But my first choice of University was the London School of Economics, so, while passing through London *en route* to Canterbury, I detoured to the Aldwych to have a look at the LSE. The famous student 'sit-in' – the first in a British university – was then in full swing, provoked by the appointment of Walter Adams as Director of the college. Adams had come from University College Rhodesia, where he had failed abysmally to support his students when they were savagely victimised by the illegal Smith regime. One of those students, Basker Vashee, was then studying at the LSE and was the main inspiration of the anti-Adams revolt. As I walked down Houghton Street I observed the sit-in in progress – banners and placards everywhere, crowds of students gathered in the main foyer, and someone – whom I later discovered to be Ted Parker, later to be another of Ronnie's London recruits – playing the guitar while protest songs were belted out.

I was smitten. After that the interview at Kent was of no great concern to me. I knew it had to be the LSE or nothing. Back at school I redoubled my efforts, became an out and out swat, determined to get the higher grades I needed to secure the place I had been offered at the LSE. It paid off.

By October 1967, there I was, a student at the LSE and a card carrying member of the Socialist Society. Northern Ireland was an unlikely breeding ground for socialist politics. Where I grew up you were either a Protestant or a Catholic, a Unionist or a Nationalist. The Labour Party was tiny, the Communist Party smaller still, and groups to the left of the CP microscopic. It was, in its own way, an apartheid state with strict, if unofficial segregation. Catholics were very much second-class citizens, excluded from many areas of employment, discriminated against in housing allocation, gerrymandered into electoral constituencies that ensured their vote would never change anything. But in 1967, the Civil Rights Movement that a year later was to change for ever the political landscape in Northern Ireland was still just in embryo.

I suppose I was one of the fortunate few in Northern Ireland. My family background was very much on the left, and crossed the sectarian divide, with a Catholic grandfather and Protestant grandmother. My grandfather had been a trade union activist and early member of the Labour Party. In the 1930s he had been one of the leaders of the unemployed movement that momentarily united workers across the sectarian divide. Those on the Protestant side of my family, too, were Labour supporters. I had an aunt and uncle who were fervent members of the Communist Party. My mother was an active Labour Party member during my childhood, and I joined Labour Youth in the mid-1960s and was very active in electoral politics.

The Labour Party presented itself as non-sectarian, but in reality that meant the party avoided talking about the issue of sectarianism as that was seen as divisive. It certainly did not confront the underlying causes of the problem – the imperialist legacy and the partition of the country under two near-mirror-image capitalist regimes. But then, without warning, our Labour Youth branch was suddenly dissolved by the party leadership. I only found out afterwards that it was shut down because it had been 'infiltrated' by Trotskyists – the hardest working, and to my mind clearest thinking member of the branch turned out to be a member of the dreaded Militant Group. It was that experience – at the age of 15 – that led me to reject Labour reformism and join the International Socialists once I had arrived in London a couple of years later. Before long I was actually sharing a flat with Basker Vashee and other leading figures from the LSE sit-in. Over the following years we engaged in countless protests over the Apartheid regimes in South Africa and 'Rhodesia', and Ronnie Kasrils was never more than a stone's throw away. And many stones were thrown.

It was in 1970, after I had secured my degree, that I was persuaded - without the slightest difficulty - to become one of the London recruits.

We were to work in pairs in South Africa, and my partner was John Rose, a fellow LSE student, and a close friend and comrade since 1967. First of all we had to be trained. Ronnie's kitchen in his small Hampstead flat seemed an unlikely place to learn how to make pipe-bombs and micro-amplifiers, how to use distracting disguises and evade 'tails'. Compared to the level of struggle that was to follow, the sort of stuff we were training for was extremely small beer. But it was politically very significant as it was designed to provoke a new wave of struggle when things were at a low ebb. While we studied wiring and soldering, timing devices and explosive mixes, we argued all the while with Ronnie about the ANC's use of 'substitutes' like us in place of genuine mass activity. Yet despite our sharp, if good natured political exchanges, we were happy enough to take on Ronnie's mission – paid for, I have no doubt, by 'Moscow gold'.

It was going to be an unimaginable adventure, although Ronnie's parting message certainly dispelled any notion that we were setting off for an all-expenses-paid holiday in the sun. 'If you get caught,' he told us, 'you'll be severely and repeatedly tortured.' It was absolutely vital that we didn't reveal his name under torture, as that would jeopardise the safety of other current recruits as well as all future operations. He told us we would probably be charged with treason, which, on conviction, carried a lengthy prison term. If possible, he asked, would we please make political speeches from the dock, denouncing apartheid and praising Nelson Mandela, before being carted off to our stinking rat-infested cells.

The day before we set off for South Africa, we collected money, tickets and suitcases from Ronnie. The cases looked perfectly normal, but they had false bottoms. The concealed compartment was stuffed full of leaflets, thousands of them, printed on the lightest of paper, with a message from Nelson Mandela on one side and instructions for making Molotov cocktails[16] on the other. These were to be showered into the air using small explosive devices hidden in plastic buckets left at pre-selected locations around the Indian Ocean city of Durban. Our false-bottomed suitcases also carried the powdered explosive and the little pre-formed pipes into which it would be packed. The buckets we would buy when we got there, along with cheap watches, pins and soldering irons to make timing devices. In our cases we also carried little band-aid tins containing micro-amplifiers that we would attach to tape cassette players with booster speakers to blare out a speech from Nelson Mandela himself, recorded before he was jailed.

There was a final, mysterious item in our suitcases: a bottle containing large capsules, too big to swallow, and containing a yellowish-brown powder. Ronnie wouldn't tell us what it was, but he said if we got caught with it we were to say we suffered from sore feet and the capsules, dissolved in hot water, provided relief. He probably reckoned that if we knew what it was we wouldn't carry it! This mystery bottle was for a separate mission: when we had finished planting our 'leaflet bombs' and cassette players, we were to drive to Swaziland, take a room in a small motel, and, after ensuring that we hadn't aroused any suspicion, deliver the strange bottle to an ANC contact along with an equally mysterious coded message.

We travelled as wealthy tourists, not scruffy students. I had bought a white linen suit and white Fedora for the purpose. Of course the only thing that really mattered when we got to Durban was that we were white. I cannot recall any black person we encountered who wasn't completely subservient. Bowing and scraping was endemic. Every black person we had face to face business with – I can't say 'met' as that implies a level of familiarity that was totally absent - addressed us as 'baas' – boss. The hotel porter who carried our subversively laden suitcases to our room even walked out backwards, as royal servants must do so as not to show their backs to their monarch. It was grotesque and depressing, but we had to behave as if we took all this as

16 i.e. petrol bombs – Editor.

natural and normal, as if we were happy to belong to the master race. We couldn't react in any way that might attract attention. Very shortly our hotel room was turned into what the tabloid press would probably describe as a 'bomb factory'. We had hired a car and used it to transport our purchases: half a dozen cheap plastic buckets; a sheet of thin plywood for making circular platforms to fit inside the buckets for the leaflets to sit on; a length of doweling to fit the platforms into the pipe bombs; a small saw; a soldering iron and solder; cassette players and loud speakers; cheap watches for timing devices; plastic snakes and scorpions that might just delay the police from picking up and turning off the cassette players for a minute or two longer. We had also acquired fancy hats and brightly coloured scarves to act as decoys and distract attention when we were planting our devices. If the police found eye-witnesses after the devices had gone off, hopefully they would remember and describe only our bizarre outfits which would, of course, have long since been destroyed.

It wasn't long before we had our 'bombs' assembled and our cassette players wired up to amplifiers and speakers. They were kept hidden in our suitcases, locked and stowed away on top of wardrobes. In the meantime we had been reconnoitring Durban to find suitable locations for our devices. The bus station and railway station were obvious choices. We had to figure out where within them was the most suitable place. Then there were a couple of busy intersections, and a market. The cassette players would be located at factories with timing devices that would turn them on at lunchtime when the workers were outside.

I don't remember being nervous during our preparations, and if we were we didn't reveal our concerns to one another. We went about our days as tourists would: sightseeing and swimming in the Indian Ocean. Then the day arrived for our mission. We loaded our equipment into the car and drove to a disused quarry we had reconnoitred earlier on the outskirts of town. There we set the timing devices, giving ourselves half an hour to get everything in place. We put the ticking buckets and the cassette players in big brown paper carrier bags and lined them up on the back seat. The drive back to town was uneventful and we made our way to a marketplace where the first device was to be planted. But just as we parked the car and were about to don our disguises, we were suddenly surrounded by four or five burly white men, well dressed in jackets and slacks. One knocked on the driver's window, and as he leant across to do so I saw the gun and holster strapped beneath his left arm. We both realised immediately that these were plain-clothes policemen. It looked like the game was up with just twenty minutes to go before those fiendish devices in the back of the car would go off with a boom.

John was in the driver's seat. He rolled the window down. 'What have we here?' said the cop as he reached his hand in the window, straight towards the brown paper bags in the back. It seemed to me the ticking of the timing devices was so loud that anyone passing on the street could have heard it. TICK TICK TICK TICK. Every detail of that moment is etched clearly in my memory. I saw the manicured fingernails of my nemesis, the reddish-blond hairs on the back of his freckled hand, a gold signet ring and expensive watch beneath the cuff of his sleeve – all this as his hand moved inexorably towards the ticking bags. TICK TICK TICK. Several people, Asian and African, had gathered on the sidewalk to watch the spectacle. I was wondering would any of them come to our assistance, rescue us from the hated forces of the state before we were hauled off to the inevitable torture Ronnie had promised us if – which had now become 'when' – we were caught. But in a flash John brought his elbow down sharply on the cop's forearm, pinning it to the window frame. 'We're British tourists.' John's voice was imperious and angry. It was a stroke of genius. The cop froze. He looked from John to me. I tried to smile and nod, but can't imagine what it came out as. 'I'm sorry sir,' came the cop's humble response. 'It's just that we get a lot of thieves around this market trying to shift stolen goods, and as most of them come from Johannesburg, and as you are driving a Johannesburg car, we had to check you out.

But if you could just show us your passports, we won't trouble you any longer.' Now normally if a cop asked John or me for ID we'd get into an argument about why they wanted it, what authority they were acting on, and so on – the usual Bolshie stuff. But on this occasion we were only too happy to oblige. Here's our passports, officer. Would you like me to open it for you at the right page? Thank you very much officer. What a beautiful country you have. No, we certainly aren't offended. You have a very important job to do. Have a nice day. TICK TICK TICK TICK. Reverse away from the kerb, drive ever so nonchalantly around the corner and find somewhere to conduct an instant post mortem. Fifteen minutes to blast off.

Can the mission go ahead or are we compromised beyond redemption? The cops have seen our passports. They didn't write anything down, but did the one who saw our passports memorise our names? Did they note the car number before approaching us? If we plant the devices, will they quickly put two and two together and realise they had us and let us go? Is capture inevitable – if not now, then when we try to leave the country? TICK TICK TICK. Ten minutes left.

It didn't take long for us to agree that, as we had come so far, we had to finish the job. We agreed we would figure some way of escaping from South Africa after the event, maybe through Mozambique. There wasn't time to think too long or too hard. The silly hats and coloured scarves were donned. The ticking bags were dropped in rapid succession, the last one with just a couple of minutes left before it exploded. We raced to the industrial zone and dropped off the cassette recorders, not forgetting to scatter the plastic snakes and scorpions around. That was it. Mission accomplished.[17] Without wasting a second we headed for the road north and soon were on our way to Swaziland.

I have only two recollections of that journey. The first was when we stopped to dump our disguises along with a couple of rolls of exposed film that I had used to record various moments

17 Mike has established that this occurred on 13 August 1970 – Ed.

and locations from the preceding couple of weeks. The second was when we left the road to look for water. We drove up to a remote farmhouse and were greeted by a family of Afrikaners. They invited us in and offered tea. We were seated at a huge bare wooden table. From a cupboard a huge cake was produced, rich fruit cake like Christmas cake. It was delicious and we ate slice after slice. They were so friendly, and quite astonished to see two 'English' tourists in such a remote and uninviting location. We left with bottles of water and a supply of cake.

When we finally reached the Swaziland border we found it closed – literally. There was a huge iron gate firmly locked shut, a high wire mesh fence stretching off into the distance on either side. There was no one there, not even a guard's hut. But a sign on the gate let us know it would reopen in the morning. We settled down and finished off our cake. It was a hot night and we decided to sleep on the sandy road-side verge, beneath the stars. Shortly after we stretched out I leapt up again with a start. Just yards from us a tree had spontaneously burst into fire. It must have been smouldering slowly before sunset, until the balmy breeze caught it and whipped it into flame. It was a surreal end to a wacky day.

Next morning we drove through to Mbabane, capital of Swaziland, and booked our rooms in a small inn. Because of our night in the open we were fairly certain no one had followed us to the border. And there was no reason whatever to think our arrival here had attracted any unwanted attention. We lounged around all day and then in the evening decided to visit our ANC contact, a butcher by trade. He was expecting us. We handed over the bottle of mysterious capsules and the coded message. He left the room to conceal them and when he came back he was carrying a bottle of brandy. We each had a glass and were talking about the ANC's prospects when he suddenly bade us be quiet. A car was approaching. He recognised the engine noise as that of the local cops. It looked like we were in deep shit, rumbled after all. We were ushered rapidly into the meat chiller, the heavy door slamming shut behind us. It was totally dark and very cold. As well as the sound of our hearts pumping rapidly, we could hear muffled voices outside as our contact dealt with his unwanted visitors. After a few minutes an outside door banged shut, a car engine started up and drove off. A few minutes more passed before the chiller door swung open and we were released back into the company of our beaming host. It had been some routine police matter, totally unconnected with us. But while it lasted it had been unnerving. A second glass of brandy was followed quickly by a third and a fourth. Later, much comradely hugging accompanied our departure for the short stagger back to the inn and bed.

Next day we faced the long drive back to Jo'burg where we had decided to take our chances by flying out on a scheduled flight to Lusaka. We figured that if they were looking for us they would be more likely to concentrate their attention on flights to London. But we were concerned too that if our suitcases were searched while we were leaving the country, even just in random checks, the fact that they had had false bottoms would be immediately apparent from the damage that had been done ripping them out. We needed to change them.

Fortunately we had someone to turn to in Jo'burg, unknown to Ronnie but completely sympathetic and totally trustworthy: Costa[18] Paizis, the émigré uncle of our indefatigable Greek comrade George. John had met Costa on an earlier trip. He ran a small hotel called the Ellis Park. We told him everything and he found us a couple of old cases in the attic and gave us dinner and a bed for the night. He didn't think they would be waiting for us at the airport, and agreed that our decision to fly to Lusaka was sensible. Reassured, we set out next morning for the airport and, without a hitch, boarded the plane for Zambia.

It wasn't possible in those days to fly directly to Lusaka. Our plane landed on a small airstrip close to the Victoria Falls in what was still 'Rhodesia'. We crossed the border on a bus and boarded another small plane on the Zambian side to fly on to Lusaka. So far so good, but on arrival in Lusaka we discovered that our

18 A form of 'Costas' – Editor.

bags had not accompanied us. Our first thought was that they had been intercepted by South African security services, and we congratulated ourselves on the foresight that had led us to swap our false-bottomed cases for innocent ones. We had planned to stay in Lusaka for a couple of weeks, visiting John's cousin who was at university there and who later carried out ANC missions herself. A couple of weeks later, the bags finally turned up again. We never did find out what had happened to them, but by then my white linen suit had turned several shades of pink from the ubiquitous red dust on the streets of the Zambian capital.

From Zambia we travelled on to Tanzania, hitchhiking all the way from Lusaka to Dar es Salaam. I think we covered the 1000 odd miles with just one 'lift' – a petrol tanker whose driver was rather too fond of his Chibuku. He stopped several times along the road to drink large plastic buckets of the thick brew that reminded me of porridge. After that we weaved our way along the empty highway where the only other vehicles were petrol tankers. We spent the nights – three of them, I think – in roadside huts constructed for these long distance lorry drivers, and equipped with army-style cots and blankets. Just before crossing the border into Tanzania, a navy-blue Land Rover passed us and screeched to a halt in front of the lorry. Several burly police men got out. It was clear that they too had been imbibing, but they still berated our driver for his erratic weaving. When their commander spotted us his attitude changed from stern and angry to avuncular and excessively jolly. Big slaps on the back followed and beery inquiries about life in Dear Old Blighty. He was a great admirer of Winston Churchill and wanted to know if we had ever met him. It was a bizarre encounter – like so much else on this journey.

In Dar es Salaam we were put up by an old friend from London – Dorothy Mbeki, wife of Moeletsi Mbeki. Dorothy was then living in Tanzania with her young son who, back in London in later years, went to school with my daughter. I never knew Moeletsi, although I had encountered his brother

Thabo[19] from time to time in London and remember on one occasion having a whispered discussion with him about the application of Marxist economics to Third World development – a discussion that took place, fittingly, in the reading room of the British Library.

After our eventual return to London – via Djibouti and Cairo – we found out from contemporary South African newspapers, supplied by Ronnie, that our mission had been a complete success – at least in terms of the number of leaflet devices that had exploded as intended. Much harder to gauge was the effect it had on those at whom it was directed – the African workers of Durban. We didn't know at the time just how extensive Ronnie's missions were, that we were rather small cogs in a sizeable wheel. Perhaps the small contribution we all made in those long distant days played a part in the ultimate triumph of the ANC, and that may indeed be something to be proud of. For myself, I would still maintain the point of view we used to argue with Ronnie nearly four decades ago: that ending apartheid and capturing state power would not, in itself, bring freedom for the 'toiling masses'. For that the complete destruction of capitalism – black, white, national and international – and the triumph of socialism – from below and beyond the frontiers of individual countries – was, and remains, absolutely necessary.

19 Thabo Mbeki, later to be South Africa's president – Editor.

Katherine Levine

January 1970. My cousin John Rose and his friend are sprawled on the fine white sand of a palm-fringed Indian Ocean beach near Dar es Salaam, fervently discussing revolutionary politics and explaining the finer distinctions of British Trotskyist parties to me. They are on their way back from a trip to southern Africa, the nature of which I only find out later, and which is recounted elsewhere in this book. I am 24 years old. I have been living in Tanzania for nearly two years; I rent a room in a Swahili house shared with 20 other people, in a poor part of Dar es Salaam, where I am researching local politics for a doctorate in anthropology. I also spend a lot of time at the university and in town, absorbing revolutionary politics wherever I can find it. I learn it from Vietnamese diplomats and southern African liberation activists, from African-American and other political exiles and radical academics who populate Dar es Salaam at that time, when it is the political heart of Africa.

Unlike many Europeans who were drawn to the Third World, I had no history of family connections there, and Africa did not feature much in my upbringing. Racism and discrimination did, on the other hand. I grew up in a Labour household with the News Chronicle and the New Statesman. My mother claimed that on their honeymoon she had to share my father with *Ten Days that Shook the World*. Family values were a curious combination of socialism and snobbery. As secular Jews in the north-east of England, we were oddities who didn't fit easily into any category, a tiny sub-group of an upwardly mobile ethnic minority in the class-ridden, racist, industrial city of 1950s Newcastle upon Tyne. My father's immigrant parents hoped he would find a career as a carpenter. Instead he became a businessman, who went to anti-fascist meetings, voted Labour all his life, was proud of paying his employees better than most, and in time embarrassed to find that he resented them for not appreciating his generosity. My mother, a highly intelligent woman from a more middle-class Jewish background, wanted the very best of British education for her daughters. And so at 13 I was sent to a progressive, co-educational but nevertheless very privileged boarding school in Hampshire. Staff proudly went on CND marches and the maths teacher was an avowed atheist and member of the Communist Party, yet we called the kitchen staff 'the plebs', mocked the local schoolboys, and I was encouraged to hide my father's occupation ('trade').

By 1960 South Africa began to feature more and more prominently in our conversations. I joined the Anti-Apartheid Movement at 14, soon after it was set up. My first attempt at political activism was getting the school kitchen to boycott South African marmalade, the easiest victory with the least opposition I have ever faced. In 1963, as I was doing my A levels and looking for exciting things to do in the months between leaving school and starting university, a visitor from South Africa came to give a talk. Michael Stern was a former teacher at our school who had left to work with Trevor Huddleston in Sophiatown, Johannesburg, until the school which they ran was closed down under the apartheid laws for being 'a black spot in a white area'. An inspirational teacher and a deeply moral man, he drummed up support among liberal whites to help set up a multiracial boarding school, mainly for South Africans, in the British protectorate of Swaziland.

Waterford School opened its doors to 60 boys, many of them Stern's former Sophiatown pupils, who learned Latin one moment and built classrooms the next. I volunteered with a friend to work there during its second term. This was 1964, during the Rivonia trial that sent Nelson Mandela to gaol for 27 years, a time of tortures and murders in South African police stations, vivid tales of escapes, and a steady stream of reports on the daily humiliations and injustices borne by black South Africans. Swaziland was both a haven for South African exiles who managed to cross the border, and an open prison for them to rot in, with nothing to do and nowhere to go once they got there, surrounded as it was by racist states.

There I met Ashby Mpama, who was the Zulu teacher at

the school and an ANC supporter. In his company I met other South Africans, including the former *Drum* journalist Can Themba and his wife. A day in the company of Can Themba was an education like no other in the intricacies of South African oppression and resistance. This vibrant, witty man later drank himself to death in Swaziland. When we were leaving Swaziland Ashby put me in touch with the ANC office in London, headed at that time by Mazise (then known as Raymond) Kunene, where on my return I volunteered for a short while before going to university.

Some of the students at Waterford school, tough boys from the Johannesburg townships, talked of newly independent Tanzania as the place to be, a sanctuary for the southern African liberation movements, an African country liberated from the oppression of colonialism. Several boys used the Swaziland school as a stepping-stone to get to Tanzania. In a way I did the same. I went back home, and four years later headed back to Africa, this time to Tanzania.

Meanwhile, I went to Cambridge University to study social anthropology. Archie Mafeje, an outstanding scholar from the University of Cape Town, was doing his PhD in the same department. Reserved and critical, Archie was nevertheless a brilliant teacher for those like me who cared to listen. Our friendship continued until his recent death. In my last year at Cambridge I became friends with other South Africans. Together we attended talks and conferences about African liberation, and took part in demonstrations against apartheid, UDI, and the Vietnam War.

The first person I met on arrival in Dar es Salaam was Eduardo Mondlane, the founder of Mozambique's liberation movement, Frelimo, whom I had previously encountered at a conference in Oxford a few months earlier. As we sipped fresh lime juice together at the New Africa Hotel and talked about anthropology and liberation, I was aware that I had come to the political centre not only of Africa but of many of the world's major struggles against oppression. North Vietnam and the Southern Vietnamese Liberation Front had their joint mission there, African-American and Caribbean activists took refuge there, left-wing Western academics taught there, and remarkably I had the opportunity to mix with them.

A few months later, Mondlane was blown up by a parcel bomb in his Dar es Salaam house. So Dar es Salaam was not such a 'haven of peace' after all, the racist enemies of liberation had a long, deadly reach. I had ever-increasing doubts about the academic research I was meant to be doing. Marcelino dos Santos, Vice-President of Frelimo and for a time my neighbour, told me that the diplomats at the North Vietnamese embassy were looking for someone to teach them English and suggested I did it in my spare time. I also taught English to one of the Frelimo cadres.

Dos Santos' wife Pamela was South African and a member of the ANC. On 1 January 1970, at an Independence Day party at the Cuban Embassy, she introduced me to Jimmy Khoza, another South African exile who lived in an ANC camp outside Dar es Salaam. I fell for him immediately. Jimmy was a working-class guy from Durban, an amazing footballer, stunningly good-looking, and, as I only learned much later, a member of Umkhonto we Sizwe. He had a close group of comrades whom I came to love too. Mostly when we met it was to relax and have fun. I only had glimpses of what they had come from and were up against. Once Jimmy needed to collect something from his camp, so I gave him a lift in my old VW. He told me gently that it was better I stayed out of sight while he went in. 'We're a non-racial movement. It's just some people here have had such terrible experiences at the hands of the whites, it's easier for them not to see you.'

Until meeting Jimmy I had only mixed with the radical intellectuals at the university and the leaders of the movements, who were frequent visitors to the campus. Through my friendship with Jimmy I got to know some of the ordinary cadres. They made a profound and lasting impression on me. Working-class women and men, they had left South Africa to train as guerrillas in the Soviet Union, and had then been sent to Tanzania 'to wait for the call'. They were in limbo, frustrated at being inactive and so far from home. I have no idea what happened to any of them.

Jimmy never talked to me about his political work. I like to think he would not have broken under torture. There was an unspoken understanding that our relationship, although important to both of us, came a long way second to the struggle. I didn't expect to see him again after I left Tanzania in August 1970, but he and his comrades were uppermost in my mind when my cousin John told me that a friend of his, Ronnie Kasrils, wanted to talk to me about undertaking a mission for the ANC. I was scared and exhilarated in equal measure. I had a privileged life that belied my political beliefs, and I relished the opportunity at last for action rather than words.

The mission was to last three months. Two of us were to carry arms from Zambia to Botswana. In Botswana we were to map a track from the northern border with Zambia down to Francistown, which could then be used as the African Ho Chi Minh trail by ANC guerrillas aiming to infiltrate South Africa, some of whom we would transport. Ronnie introduced me to my prospective travelling companion, Laurence Harris. In preparation for the trip we bought maps from Stanford's in Covent Garden. Laurence mugged up on his car mechanics for the Land Rover we would pick up in Francistown. We had to pose as a honeymoon couple who were taking an extended holiday exploring northern Botswana and southern Zambia. For reasons we were fortunately not asked, since there could be no innocent explanation, we preferred to repeat the same route several times rather than travel further afield.

We flew into Lusaka in January 1971, conveniently leaving behind an extended postal strike in the UK which for several weeks helped cover my tracks from a deeply suspicious mother. As part of the preparations in London she and my father had met Laurence, an academic whose research assistant I was pretending to be, but she was far too canny to be taken in by our cover story of an economics research trip to Zambia. Ronnie had given us training in how to check if we were being followed, how to do secret writing, and the way to meet undercover contacts without being detected. We had a pre-arranged meeting in Lusaka with the comrade who would instruct us on the next stages of our mission. Although Zambia had been independent for six years, it was reputedly rife with South African agents, and the colour bar was still strong. We knew we had to be very careful not to arouse suspicions. Laurence and I went over the arrangements several times. We would meet on the steps of the central post office at midday. We were to walk up the stairs while our contact walked down. We would know each other by something, I forget what, that we would be carrying. We would pass each other without acknowledgement and continue up the stairs; then after a few minutes retrace our steps and discreetly join our contact in his car.

At the appointed hour we duly climbed the stairs, to be greeted loudly half-way up with a friendly handshake and a big smile. 'Hello, I've been waiting for you. Welcome to Africa. Let's go to my car.' In shock, we followed him. He took us to a small house in an African residential area of Lusaka, where our hosts briefed us. During our three months' stay we would need to cross the Zambezi several times at the only point where it was possible, on the small pontoon ferry from Kazungula on the Zambian side over to Kasane in Botswana. The 400m crossing was disputed territory, with Southern Rhodesia to the east and the Caprivi Strip to the west, both white ruled and deeply hostile to independent Zambia and Botswana. Rhodesian patrol boats had been known to take pot shots at the ferry on occasion.

The post office steps meeting was the first of several horrific blunders. The second came a couple of days later, in Botswana. We flew from Lusaka to Francistown in a small local plane, landing on a grass strip runway, where we were met by the British expatriate manager of the firm from which we had pre-ordered the Land Rover. As Laurence did the negotiations and paperwork, the manager's tight-faced wife made small talk to me, 'I used to live in London. Which part are you in?' she asked. 'I'm in South-West London and Laurence lives in ...' I began, then turned beetroot in horror at my mistake. 'At least, we did before we got married', I stammered, sure that our cover was already blown before we began.

We stayed in Francistown for a few days to stock up with supplies for our first trip while the final touches were made to the shiny new Land Rover. We would drive from Francistown to Chobe in the far north of Botswana, mapping the route on the way. The ever-attentive manager invited his rich young honeymooners to lunch at the Francistown Club. It was Laurence's first experience of colonial British expatriate social life in Africa, which I had been forced to experience briefly in Tanzania before promising myself never to set foot in the Dar es Salaam Yacht Club, Gymkhana Club or Little Theatre. I had fun observing his heroic efforts to conceal his horror.

These days the journey from Francistown to Kasane has a 'good tarred road... [and is] a straight and easy drive' (Botswana, the Bradt Travel Guide). In 1971 after a few miles there was no road at all, just an overgrown track that no one had used for years. Our London-bought maps, the best ones available on Botswana, turned out to be based on a very old survey. We soon discovered that the bush was effectively unmapped. Still, we knew we had a compass, plenty of petrol and water, and Laurence was a reasonable car mechanic.

After a very short distance the Land Rover shuddered to a halt. The radiator had overheated alarmingly. The cause of the problem was easy to detect. The long grasses along the faint memory of a track that we were following were catching on the radiator grille and clogging it up. We were relieved that it was something we could deal with, sometimes using the spade we had stowed in the Land Rover. From then on we stopped every ten minutes to clear the grasses. We drove over fallen tree trunks and into ditches, found ourselves at dead ends and had to retrace our steps to try other tracks that might or might not be the one we needed.

In my previous experience travelling in Africa, even in what seemed to me the most remote and desolate areas, as soon as the car stopped people would appear. Not so here. It seemed to be uninhabited by humans, though full of animals and birds, and we knew that if we broke down we would be on our own. Our small magnetic compass turned out to be useless; our orienteering skills were not much better. We kept getting lost and were beginning to worry about dwindling supplies of fuel and water when we surprisingly found ourselves close to a border post with Rhodesia. After the initial shock we debated which risk was preferable, to struggle on through the bush, or to go to Chobe via Rhodesia and the Victoria Falls. Reluctantly, we decided it was more practical to cross the border.

At the Botswana border post a guard asked us whether we would give a lift to a young man who was hanging around there and wanted to go into Rhodesia. We decided to refuse because we didn't want any complications that could arouse Rhodesian suspicions. Later Laurence told me he suspected the man might have been a ZAPU freedom fighter. Definitely the right decision then, although we felt bad about leaving him behind.

Chobe River Lodge was an idyllic holiday place, if you were white. It was owned by a white racist South African, full of oppressive bonhomie towards us. Almost the hardest part of the whole mission was the friendly façade we had to maintain towards him. His assumption that we would obviously agree with his vile opinions served to provide me with a sharp daily reminder of the grossness of apartheid, and probably helped to firm my resolve to complete our mission in support of Umkhonto we Sizwe.

After a couple of days we set off to cross the ferry for the first time. We had a rendezvous in Livingstone, as pre-arranged at our briefing in Lusaka. The Land Rover needed to be fitted with an extra petrol tank with a false compartment, where the contraband cargo was to be hidden. Sure enough the vehicle was mysteriously picked up from our hotel car park and mysteriously returned to the car park with the work done.

On our next trip through the bush we were to take two men, and a pile of weapons. The men would be dropped off in the vicinity of Francistown, while we would drive down further south towards Gaborone. We were to stop and camp some way outside Gaborone, where we needed to find a suitable spot to bury the weapons.

It was thought to be too risky for us to smuggle our contraband over the pontoon ferry, which could only take four cars and a load of foot passengers. Somehow arms and men would be taken over the river separately, for us to collect on the Botswana side before heading off towards Francistown. When the work on the vehicle was completed we were told to go back to Chobe. We had to drive along the river at a certain time each morning looking out for a comrade who would contact us en route.

The morning drive was delightful, through a beautiful game park full of monkeys, elephants and the occasional lion. But when no one had made contact after more than a week, we decided to drive to Livingstone and contact our handler there. There we learned that the first plan had failed. Instead we had the arms loaded in Livingstone and drove them back over the ferry, with instructions to pick up our two passengers on the other side. We crossed without incident and went to the agreed pick-up point. There waiting for us was one man, not two. He was blind drunk; his companion apparently had passed out before the secret journey over the river, and had to be left behind. It was a disheartening start.

The second journey through the bush was less hair-raising than the first, and we reached Francistown after two days with no hitch. Our passenger left us there, while we drove on towards Gaborone. Finding a promising-looking spot near a bridge, we set up camp and waited for night. Then we took our spade and the package of arms under the bridge and started digging. The ground was unyieldingly hard. Try as we might, we could make no impact. We chose another spot and tried again. After hours of digging all we had achieved was a shallow depression in the parched ground. Frustrated and flustered, we gathered up sticks, grasses and any other detritus we could lay our hands on, put the arms in the hollow and simply covered them up, marking the spot on our map as best we could.

We made other trips between Chobe and Gaborone, but after all these years I don't remember the details. I have a memory of endless days of waiting, lying in the sun reading at Chobe River Lodge, and watching monkeys and elephants. It was a surreal experience pretending to be a rich tourist, living a luxury lifestyle, wondering whether the men we had helped get within striking distance of South Africa would actually make it. Mostly I remember a continual sense of anger that a regime so vile could continue to exist, with such confidence and complacency.

Finally the three months were up. We headed to Lusaka, to dispose of the Land Rover and visit the ANC office for a debriefing. Thabo Mbeki, recently posted there from London, opened the door to us. I think he and I were both surprised to see each other. We had friends in common, but our paths had only ever crossed before at South African exile gigs in London.

Afterwards, I wished I could say for sure that our mission played a significant part in the struggle against apartheid. I was honoured to have been trusted to carry out what was, although I didn't fully realise it at the time, a dangerous mission. I preferred not to think about the consequences of being caught, and fortunately never had to. Did Ronnie give me back the letter I had left with him for my parents, just in case we didn't come back? I don't remember.

While I was away, Jimmy was sent back to the Soviet Union for further training. He was excited to be on the move again after stagnating in Tanzania. We corresponded briefly on my return to London, and then he vanished. Ronnie let me know that he was on his way down south. Perhaps he used our mapped trail to get back inside South Africa; I'll never know. One of the bleakest conversations of my life was in a London street some months later, when Ronnie told me 'Whoever invented the phrase "No news is good news" had no idea what they were talking about.'

Two or three times during the next couple of years I made

other short trips for the ANC, crossing the Channel with false-bottomed suitcases whose contents I never knew and never asked about. The suitcases had to be delivered to various addresses in Paris, with Joe Slovo as intermediary and occasional dinner companion. I stayed in run-down hotels and delivered the suitcases to nondescript apartment buildings. Gradually the missions dried up as the rest of my life took over.

What struck me then with Joe and with Ronnie, as with Jimmy and his comrades, with Joe's wife Ruth First, with the Vietnamese diplomats in Dar es Salaam, with Eduardo Mondlane and the Frelimo cadres, was the dogged determination to keep struggling against the oppression that had forced them out of the countries they loved so deeply. Regardless of all the political debates that went on about the end of apartheid in South Africa, the independence struggle in Mozambique, and the defeat of the Americans in Vietnam, whatever reservations and caveats there may be, nothing alters that sense of admiration and awe I have for the extraordinary and ordinary people who made it happen. For me personally, three South Africans who had profound influence on my life deserve my lasting gratitude: Zulu teacher Ashby Mpama, who introduced me to black South African life and the ANC; revolutionary intellectual Archie Mafeje, who challenged and questioned yet always had the patience to teach me more; and my beloved, beautiful freedom fighter Jimmy Khoza.

(With many thanks to Laurence Harris for all his help in filling the memory gaps)

Seán Edwards

Seán Edwards of Dublin, after some reluctance, submitted the following brief story. Seán is a leading member of the Communist Party of Ireland. His father, Frank Edwards, was an International Brigader in the Anti-fascist War in Spain – Editor.

I went to South Africa in 1968. Kadar Asmal[20] asked me to go. I went to London where I met Joe Slovo, who explained the mission. I was given a suitcase prepared by Ronnie Kasrils, with materials packed in the lining. I went to Port Elizabeth, where I used the materials from the lining of the suitcase to prepare a banner with the words 'ANC fights', which I rolled up, putting lots of leaflets inside. I hung the rolled up banner from a tall building, with a crude timer involving copper wire and acid to give me time to get away. The banner opened up and the leaflets were scattered in the street. I also posted lots of leaflets. That's it.

---

20 Kadar Asmal left South Africa in the late 1950s, was a founding member of the British Anti-Apartheid Movement in 1960 and of the Irish Anti-Apartheid Movement and its Chairman 1964-90. From 1994 he served as a minister in the ANC government. – Editor.

Roger O'Hara

Early in 1970 I became the Merseyside Area Secretary of the Communist Party of Great Britain. I lived in a two-up-and-down terraced house in Crump Street, Liverpool; it was situated close to the city centre and near what is now known as China Town.

I had been a seagoing engineer who had come ashore and started to work on various construction sites. During the latter period I had been very active as a trade union convenor and shop steward, and due to involvement in a number of high profile disputes and anti-government campaigns I was blacklisted as a militant prior to moving into the position of CP secretary.

A few years after taking up the full-time post, I was visited at home one evening by a small delegation with an unusual request. The group was made up of Frank Cartwright and two others. Frank was the North West District Organiser of the CP, who I knew well. He had a very humorous but slightly cynical personality and would never pass the opportunity, as we say, to try to 'Take the Mickey'. Another visitor was his brother George, whom I had never met before. I was informed he was a seaman who had come up from London. He was a large guy, unlike Frank who was lightly built. I could immediately see he had similar characteristics but more of a good `teller of tales' about him. The Cartwrights were a large family with only one of their lads not a CP member. The third person was Eric Caddick. Eric was a former work colleague and a personal friend. He was an ex-professional boxer and a self-educated expert on English literature; he was also an ex-seaman and a local black member of the CP.

Frank Cartwright informed me they were looking to recruit a seagoing engineer to go on a trip that was being organised. He then asked if I would go with them to persuade my brother-in-law, Pat Newman, to join them as he was a qualified engineer. I questioned them, in an attempt to get more details, but they became very evasive. Both Frank and George kept pressing me to agree, but I told them I wouldn't until I knew what I was letting Pat in for. Eventually, they reluctantly decided to tell me, provided I swore to keep the matter secret. They gave me the impression this was official CP business, which I later was to find out was not quite correct. Because of the heated debate and due to the house being so small, my wife had joined us. She had heard most of the discussion, so she had also to agree to keep the matter strictly confidential.

Frank explained that George was collecting a crew to go out to join a ship, which would be carrying out work for the African Nation Congress.

Once we heard this, both Lily and I were acutely aware of what this could possibly mean. Over a long period we had, in our house, parcels of small ANC propaganda booklets. These we had been passing on to CP dockers to hide within the ships' cargo as it was loaded into holds of those vessels sailing to South Africa. Also, the propaganda materials were given to the Party branch members at the Ford Halewood and the Vauxhall factories. They secreted them beneath and behind the seats of any cars being exported to South Africa. So, we knew the dangerous situation that the people in South Africa faced, in picking up these documents and attempting to take them off the ships.

I reasoned with them, making the point that Pat had only recently been married and did not, in my opinion, have the temperament for such dangerous work. I made the recommendation that I, as an engineer, should go instead and stressed I was both better qualified and more experienced than Pat. They said it was impossible for a CP official to become involved because if things did go wrong it would be catastrophic for the ANC.

After another long and at times acrimonious debate, I finally and reluctantly agreed to take them to Pat's home, situated in a small street off Lark Lane in Liverpool. When we arrived, the house was still in a state of refurbishment and redecoration. They outlined to Pat the proposal, he listened very thoughtfully, as was his wont, and asked a number of questions. He then said, 'I cannot make this decision on my own; it must involve Frances' (his new wife). He then turned to her (both she and her sister were Party members) and said, 'Do you want me to go?' and she replied, 'I will accept whatever you decide'. He then agreed to go on the trip.

Within a couple of days, all three – George Cartwright, Eric Caddick and Pat Newman – had virtually disappeared and were not heard from until Pat returned home some three to four months later.

The story he told me, in the strictest confidence, was as follows. They had travelled down to London where they met a Greek guy called Alex[21] (I think) and were joined by other crew members; these were a 'Pat Gallagher' [see p. 121] from Glasgow and another seaman, Jim Hopwood, who, I later found out, came from Queens Ferry in North Wales.

Shortly after this they were flown out to Mogadishu in Somalia. Here they were met by vehicles of Somalia's President's bodyguard and taken to a hotel where they stayed the night. The following morning they were informed they were to take over as the crew of a yacht. They later learned the vessel was the yacht that had been used by President Roosevelt. They were told they had been brought over to carry out a highly important mission on behalf of the ANC. They were also informed that there had already been an attempt to start the project, but it had had to be aborted. In addition, they learned that the ship had previously been manned by a Greek crew, and these men, as they were suspected of sabotaging the vessel, were all now in jail in Mogadishu.

After spending some considerable time making repairs they eventually set sail down the East Coast of Africa. Just prior to sailing they had taken on board five young African men.[22] This group had apparently recently returned from the Soviet Union where they had been trained as freedom fighters; they were also

21 This was not Alex Moumbaris – Editor.
22 'Pat Gallagher' says there were 20. – Editor.

accompanied by Joe Slovo, who was at the time, I think, General Secretary of the SACP.

Pat informed me that, during the voyage, they were made aware that they were being shadowed, some miles further out to sea, by a Russian cruiser. They had also started to get to know the five young men, who they thought were really great people, and had long discussions with Joe Slovo.

Just off the coast of Kenya, unfortunately, the vessel broke down again. On opening up the main engine it was discovered there were faults in the cooling system which had allowed sand to penetrate the system and contaminate the main engine's lubricating oil. The sand in the oil, in turn, had created a situation where the engine bearings were overheating and were getting to the stage where they would seize up the main engines, so they had to put in to Mombasa to allow for repairs.

They informed the ANC representative and suggested this meant the Greek seamen, in Mogadishu, had not sabotaged the ship and, therefore, could be released. But, they were informed, this would only happen after the project was completed to ensure secrecy was maintained.

Then Pat and the crew attempted to repair the engine, but soon they discovered there were no spare bearings. Apparently the previous crew, in their attempt to keep the vessel moving, had used up the spares. Then attempts were made to source them from where the ship had been built, in the United States. It was at this stage, Pat said, that he had become frustrated over what was now a couple of months' delay, and criticisms of the behaviour of the other comrades, and decided he'd had enough and asked if he could come home. The others stayed, while attempts were made to obtain the spare parts in order to repair the engines.

It was within twelve months, and before the others returned, that Pat, at the age of 45, died of cancer of the lungs.

His funeral was attended by hundreds of family, friends and Party members, most of whom knew nothing of his sacrifice, other than his wife, me, my wife and the representative from the

ANC who came up from London.

It was over twelve months later that Eric Caddick returned. He confirmed the general thrust of Pat's tale, without of course the latter's criticism. He in turn made criticisms of Pat, arguing that Pat was a super-conservative engineer and would not attempt anything unless it was completely 'by the book'. He also suggested he did not have the skills and expertise to carry out the type of repairs that were needed. He said they were still awaiting delivery of the spare bearing, which had had to be manufactured. He suggested the organisers wanted to return the ship to working condition so that the funds invested could be recouped and reinvested.

He also related the terrible news that when it had become clear the ship would be out of commission, other ways of completing the mission were looked for. It had, therefore, been decided that the young men should attempt to enter South Africa over land. This was organised but, unfortunately, they were eventually captured and, tragically, were all shot by the security forces.

A few days after he returned, Eric asked me to visit a person (I think his name was George or Alex) who had been involved, who lived with his wife in a very small house in Vale Road, Woolton, Liverpool. He was from Greece and I think had been part of the original crew or had some connection to it.

He also took me to the house of the parents of Jim Hopwood, who were quite old and lived in Queens Ferry, North Wales. He gave them news of their son, who was still out with the vessel in Mombasa, and some letters and money.

Eric Caddick was born and brought up in the old China Town area of Liverpool. His father was from Barbados and his mother was white and was born in Liverpool. Eric started to develop signs of dementia around 1997. He is in the later stages of it now and is cared for at home by his wife Joan.

George Cartwright, who was an official of the National Union of Seamen, worked at the Trades Union Congress Training Centre in Hornsey for a number of years and was later Chair of the Felixstowe Ports Committee. He died in 2006. – Editor.

'Pat Gallagher' steadfastly refused to write his story for this book and did not wishto have his name appear in it. This pseudonym has therefore been used throughout. – Editor.

Alex Moumbaris and Marie-José Moumbaris

I constructed this from emails I exchanged with Alex in 2007-8 when he and his wife were living in Paris. Marie-José declined to write her own story. Alex has approved the entire text. – Editor.

I was born in Alexandria, Egypt, on the 4 December 1938. Both my parents were Greek. I am a second or third generation Greek born in Egypt. My paternal grandparents were natives of the island of Khios, while my maternal grandparents originated from Volos. My parents divorced in or around 1945.

In the forties and early fifties Alexandria, more so than the other main cities in Egypt, had a very multiethnic, multilingual and multi-religious population.

In 1952, after King Farouk was overthrown, my family felt that Egypt held no future for us. Consequently the family dispersed to Greece, France and Australia. I went with my grandmother to Australia, where, when I became 16, I acquired Australian nationality.

A few months later I left for France with my grandmother to join my mother, where I stayed for four years. There being no real openings for me, when I was 21 I returned to Australia, where I stayed for another three years and studied for my matriculation in the evenings. I worked for Reuters Sydney and then for the Bank of New South Wales and a couple of other jobs. At about 23 I left for France, where I tried to continue my education at university, but as this became impossible, in 1964 I left for the UK with the equivalent, in 2009, of about £1000.

Eventually Comtel (part of Reuters) offered me a job in the evening – American markets. I started at two or three in the afternoon and finished at 10 or 11 pm.

After a few years I said to myself, I'm not going to bury my life in that job. Thankfully computers turned up. We had a test and I was one of those selected. It was around 1966-67. This had some important political consequences for me; it was turning point.

Concerning what made me become a Communist, it was triggered by the situation in Reuters, where after six months of hard work in the computer section I got a raise of about two shillings and sixpence. It was about then that I 'declared war on the bourgeoisie'. I became interested in trade union activities, tried to join the Communist Party of Great Britain. To this was added the putsch in Greece, the Vietnam War and South Africa. All this along with a distressing background of living in bed-sitters with a salary one could just subsist on.

It is a fallacy, so far as I am concerned, that I joined Umkhonto we Sizwe, and later the SACP, for anti-racist or pro-South African reasons. This does not mean that I was not anti-racist or that I had no interest in South Africa. The object of my struggle, however, was the struggle of the workers. I happened to be involved in South Africa, where this took the form of a struggle against racism. More precisely it was an anti-racist struggle, in a specific anti-colonialist context of national liberation, which was part of the national and the international anti-imperialist struggle.

In a way all of us, the foreigners involved in the South African struggle, were a direct expression of international feeling of condemnation of, and opposition to, racism even though the motives of each individual could be different.

I was not recruited for ANC work, I was recruited by Umkhonto we Sizwe. I was never a member of the ANC. At the time of my recruitment, in November 1967, I was a member of the CPGB and I left for my first mission in December 1967.

My integration into the South African struggle evolved in stages. First I started participating in demonstrations about Vietnam and Greece. The League for Democracy in Greece was a place I used to go to sometimes and it was situated just below the office of the ANC.

If my memory is right, this is where I met David King,[23] who was a member of the YCL and the CPGB. We saw more and more of each other. At one point he said to me that he would be

23 See Appendix 1.

away for a while and that if he did not come back, 'not to make a fuss about it'. I found what he said somewhat weird but I said nothing. Some days later he asked me if I was prepared to go on a mission to South Africa. I agreed.

Some days later – I was working for Reuters at the time – he arranged an appointment with Ronnie Kasrils. It was a rainy day, and the 'A1 Café', where the three of us sat to have a chat, was miserable. Next time we met was inside St Paul's Cathedral. There Ronnie gave me £500 or so, for my fare and stay in South Africa.

The first mission – which I thought would be my only one – was just bringing letters in a double bottomed suitcase and posting them at the main post office in Durban. I do not remember the content of the letters. I just posted them to newspapers, journalists etc. Maybe there were a couple of hundred letters that I posted from Durban Central Post Office at a precise date and time.

Having done that, I had to stay a bit longer because of the air ticket being issued for a minimum number of days stay in South Africa. So I also spent two or three days in Johannesburg.

A second such mission followed in June 1968. This mission was to Durban again with letters containing a leaflet about the Wankie campaign. There were much fewer letters but I had to make a banner about ten metres long, writing on it "The ANC fights". In the banner were rolled about five hundred leaflets which, as the banner unrolled from the top of the multi-storeyed garage in the Indian market, flew everywhere. The unrolling was activated by a time device based on acid that ate through a wire. David King, joined by his then partner Deirdre Drury, carried out a similar operation in Johannesburg, involving a loudspeaker message from the ANC.

The real recruitment came later, when I was sent to the Soviet Union for a two or three month course, and that was around August 1969.

By the time I came back from the Soviet Union, I was a full time salaried – just enough to live on, that is – operative.

After a few driving lessons from Stephanie Kemp[24] and some filming from Strassy,[25] I asked for a decent camera, a second hand Pentax, which was quite expensive compared to what comrades were used to. I got an 8 mm camera and lots of cine-film transformed into photo-films. Anyway, it worked well. I got an international licence from the Automobile Association (I repeatedly failed my ordinary real driving licence test).

My mission was to reconnoitre, for future use, a number of landing points, some in remote places, others in quite crowded ones. I had maps drawn with secret ink, which I developed as I went along and destroyed when I had finished.

So I arrived in Durban, bought myself a fishing rod etc., hired a Ford Cortina and started my attempts from the North – Kosi Bay, which is just near the Mozambique border. I went to the nearest game reserve but failed to go any further as access was restricted – because of 'terrorists', according to a game warden. Going south there was St Lucia, Richards Bay. All that involved staying in game reserves or hotels. I have stayed in almost all the game reserves close to the coast.

So much for the north part. Toward the south there were various places: Port Grosvenor, Ntafufu, Agatha Beach north of St Johns and plenty of others. In fact I know the entire coast from East London to the Mozambique border.

If the place was deserted, I went alone; otherwise I took a 'gilly' with me. He did all the work and I just held the fishing rod. I played and lived like a 'master', which, I am ashamed to say, was not all that painful. If you were white you were almost part of the family – everybody was nice to me, except of course the Hertz manager whose car I wrecked. Having done all the photographing and filming, which I sent by post as I went along, I came back to Durban and flew back to London. I spent the next two months preparing a report with slides and film.

For this purpose (this was in 1970) Ronnie found me a room with the Thelma and Stephen Nel in Muswell Hill and

24 At that time Stephanie Kemp was an ANC exile living in England. – Editor.
25 Ivan Strasburg, from Durban, who became a leading TV and film cameraman in Britain – Editor.

it was there that I did all my homework – mission reports, etc. concerning the landing. I was there 'incognito', as a Greek communist, and I was surrounded by many South Africans opposed to the apartheid regime.

By that time, I had been meeting Ronnie quite often in Golders Green and been a few times to his house where I met Eleanor. In her cheerful, casual manner she gave the appearance of just being Ronnie's wife and the mother of Christopher and Andrew – at the time they were very young. But it is only now in 2009, after her painfully untimely death, that I found that she was a cadre in MK and the SACP, and that she had been active in clandestine operations logistics, communications, liaison, recruiting as well having acted as the driver for the Secretary General of the SACP, Bram Fischer, a highly delicate and responsible task. I knew about her escape from custody, but then in South Africa you did not need to do much to get arrested. Consequently, it was no wonder Ronnie did not seem to worry much when she walked unexpectedly into the room one evening while we were projecting slides of the Hluhluwe game reserve, fruit of my last mission in South Africa. From that moment on we could no longer pretend that I was just a Greek expatriate militant. Once 'she knew our secret' (which she must have probably known all along), we talked also about Brigit, her daughter from a previous marriage attending school in Durban and with whom she was out of touch. I proposed to contact her in Durban on my next mission. My suggestion was, of course, turned down. (Much later, in 1996, when Ronnie was a government minister, he and Eleanor befriended my family and organised our stay when we visited South Africa on the official invitation of the ANC.)

Just before the next mission I met Daniel Ahern who was to participate in the landing reception team. I cannot remember where we met in Moscow, but we were together in Baku for renewed training in landing. We met the same Soviet comrades, a small (very small) ship and did some training in navigation and landing.

Mission number four took place in 1971. The object was to check some of the landing points by night with Daniel. The result of the mission was nothing; that is, nothing happened in the beaches at night. They were even more deserted then. Consequently for mission number four there is nothing very much to say. Four landing points were rechecked. We went back to London.

The Landing that did not take place

The landing that did not take place involved 19 comrades, arms and ammunition that were to come in on two dinghies. The ship that was to bring them close to the coast was the unfortunate *Avventura*. I was in command of the landing and Bob Newland was with me on the main beach. There was an alternative beach where 'Vincent' [*i.e. Daniel Ahern – Editor*] and Bill McCaig were to be ready in case something unforeseen happened. The signalling had been arranged and also walkie-talkie communications, which were brought in by Bob Newland.

After this mission when 'mother died' [*i.e. the project was aborted – Editor*] we all went back to London. A while later Ronnie Kasrils approached me about helping six comrades, in two groups of three, to cross from Swaziland to South Africa. I was to guide them to the crossing points and then go and pick them up on the other side.

When I announced to my wife that I would be leaving on a mission she said something like 'No way, unless I come with you'. I said 'Oh.' By then she had realised, and I had admitted, that in fact I was not working for the Greek resistance against the colonels but for the South African resistance. So I said this to Ronnie and he said 'Oh' and that he should take it up with higher comrades. A few days later he came back and said that after all it was a very good idea. A couple would be a good cover. He also asked me to take care of the transfer of nine other comrades from Botswana into South Africa, following the same procedure. We agreed but decided not to tell him that Marie José was 2-3 months pregnant.

We went to Swaziland through Portugal and Mozambique. We called the groups 'Anthony', 'Bertrand' and 'Charlie', etc. The first group, Anthony, arrived by air from Nairobi, transiting through Johannesburg. The airport was sealed and we never found out why. Our comrades had lost their luggage in Nairobi – which meant that they had no money, no false identity cards, etc. We hoped that their luggage would arrive by a later flight, but nothing happened.

We had decided to transfer the first two groups simultaneously, from two different crossing points. The second group, Bertrand, arrived and, inevitably, the two groups recognised each other. The transfer on the Swazi side was carried out successfully, except for minor mishaps, such as wrecking the carburettor on a big piece of coal that had fallen off a truck.

The problems arose on the other side. We left the Bertrand group on the Swaziland side of the border; Marie José and I got through the border post normally and we were to pick up the Bertrand group on the South African side of the border. We were to help them get further inside South Africa. However, the Bertrand group was not at the rendezvous. Also we were stopped by the police on what was supposed to be a routine check.

But that was not all: Kombela, one of the Bertrand group, went straight away to give himself up to the South African police and he knew who the other five were. (He became a state witness).

After the police stopped us, we gave up on 'Bertrand' and went to meet 'Anthony'. We passed the rendezvous point twice and there was no sign of 'Anthony'. We spent the night in the car and next morning decided to have another look. By chance we came across Gladstone Mose. (The other two comrades, Petrus Mthembu and Justice Mpanza, told me that Gladstone was to give me the signal but had failed to do so.) We took him to the border of the Transkei. We found out later that we were closely followed even after we had picked up Gladstone Mose, and that they had lost us as they were following us by helicopter. Had we not found Gladstone Mose we would have stopped the operation and gone back. (Gladstone Mose was also later to become a state witness.)

Money was running out. We gave up our Mercedes and took another smaller car for the Botswana operation. We stayed at the President hotel in Gaborone, Botswana, and there we met 'Charlie' (one person) and another group of three (let's call it 'Denis') including Menye dressed as a priest. (Later he also was to become a state witness).

We took the four to the border, twenty-four hours before the rendezvous on the other side, to give them time to cross. I did not want a repeat of what had happened in Swaziland. I gave instructions to them that at 18.30 they were to be at a specific point on the road, a couple of kilometres inside South Africa, and if I was late they were to progress along the road away from the border, with one person on lookout and the other three behind cover.

(Now there were two other groups that were to come: the 'Freddie' group of two and the 'George group' of three. These two groups did not come through. I believe that Comrade Mtshali was one of them.)

At 18.15 we crossed the Botswana-South African border and as we filled in some form at the border post ten to fifteen policemen fell upon us.

They grabbed Marie-José by the hair and one of them put a strangle hold on me and another put handcuffs on my right arm. I yelled at them that Marie-José was pregnant. From then on we were separated. They started interrogating us separately and in the night we were transferred to Pretoria. We both started a hunger strike that lasted seven days for me and eight days for Marie-José.

We left for Pretoria. Marie-José was in a separate car with Colonel Schoon and they followed us all the way to Pretoria. I sat in the front seat between captains Gloy and Van Niekerk. They were driving at 80 mph. I seriously thought of grabbing the wheel and bringing the car crashing against something, but the thought of Marie-José being behind us made me abandon the idea. Marie-José was taken to the women's prison in Pretoria Central where she was interrogated mainly by Captain Trevor Baker.

At one point, when she was being examined by a doctor (I suspect his name was Burns, but cannot be sure) she saw him getting ready to put his weight on her belly to make her abort. She had the reflex to stop his hands.

It was evident that Marie-José was an embarrassment to them. She was French and pregnant, and whereas I could be considered an international terrorist with apparently no real national attachment, this was not the case with her. The relations between France and South Africa were very important and the political pressure that started to mount in France forced them to release her four months later. We met on two occasions: the first one, eight days after our arrest, when I asked her to stop her hunger strike; the second just before she left. I remember the enormity of her belly and the thinness of her legs. Prison experience had taken its toll.

She was courageous and irreproachable in prison.

She pursued anti-apartheid work in France and did all in her power, together with other friends and comrades, to have me released. At one point she was made president of the BIAA (Bureau d'Information sur l'Afrique Australe). Subsequently she discovered that the BIAA was used as a cover for the Okhela conspirators. She immediately closed the BIAA and went to London to inform the SACP and the ANC.

At the trial we were six at the box. We were numbered in this order: myself, Theophilus Cholo, Justice Mpanza, Petrus Mtembu, Sandi Sejaka and Sean Hosey. That is, the comrades from Swaziland plus Sean Hosey whom I first met in the van that took us to court.

Sean was caught following a letter sent by Justice Mpanza after he and Petrus Mthembu were arrested. Justice had a code to signify that he was under arrest, just as I had. It consisted of a line under his signature. Unfortunately the Security Police guessed what it was and cut off the letter just above the line. This is how Sean was captured. He was not betrayed.

I got 12 years (plus one year awaiting trial), the South African comrades 15 years each, and Sean Hosey five years (the minimum, what some comrades called a parking ticket). The reason I obtained less than the African comrades was that I was not South African and consequently I was not accused of treason. I was defended by George Bizos, the South African comrades were defended by *pro deo* appointed lawyers, and I cannot remember who defended Sean Hosey. The prosecutor's name was Rees and the Judge was Boshoff.

Alex Moumbaris finished his story at this point.

Together with two South African comrades he dramatically escaped after seven and a half years and he was re-united with his family. The amazing story of the escape is told in Inside Out – Escape from Pretoria *by Tim Jenkin (Jakana Education, South Africa, 2003), though an earlier version can be read online with the title* Escape from Pretoria *(see http://www.anc.org.za/books/ escape0.html)*

OF BOATS AND BORDERS
Daniel Ahern

In the 1960s, when I was in my late teens and early twenties, I was a member of the North Kensington Young Communist League in London. I was brought up in a Communist family in nearby Paddington.

After leaving school, indeed all my life, I had many different occupations. First, I was a printer, then a bookshop assistant, then a labourer in Holland Park. In the 1960s this was simply the prerogative of youth and not recommended or prescribed by neo-liberal 'philosophers'.

In 1967 I was working as a clerk at the Farma Cream Product Company in Chalk Farm, the last of three or four white-collar jobs I suffered at the time. In those days there were thousands of vacancies for general clerks in London, partly because the work was very, very boring. (The demeaning word 'clerk' is not used now, of course. This was a period when the working class was ascending, though not ascendant, so sitting at a desk shuffling pieces of paper was regarded with contempt by the proletariat, the radical and the rootless. Later, Thatcherism persuaded clerks to get down to the gym and look tough.)

One day George Bridges, London Secretary of the YCL, phoned me and asked me to meet him in a pub near Farringdon Road. I had met George first in the summer of 1954 when we went to a Black Sea resort for young people in Bulgaria with about twenty other Communist children. The phone call was rather unusual and I knew something mysterious was afoot – after all, I was only the treasurer of the local branch. When I arrived at the rendezvous George was accompanied by a largish character, a bruiser with a broad grin, who looked me over carefully. George introduced me to Ronnie, though it would be some time before I knew his surname, Kasrils.

Ronnie Kasrils was a serious man but was outgoing and friendly too. He sometimes used South African phraseology which he had to quickly 'translate' and used slightly out-of-date terms like 'Gosh!' when he was really surprised. When George had left, Ronnie told me he wanted someone to smuggle a suitcase full of ANC leaflets into South Africa. I asked for 24 hours to think it over.

Actually, I didn't think about it for too long. After all, if you're working as a clerk at an artificial cream company, you're not going to turn down an adventure like this. Politics did not enter into this decision directly – like most Communists and anti-imperialists I knew about Nelson Mandela, Joe Slovo, Yusuf Dadoo and Oliver Tambo; I knew Aziz Pahad, a serious man, and a serious partygoer too. The ANC's struggle was very naturally mine also.

On the other hand, like many English young people in the '60s, I disliked the gloom, wind, rain and puritanism of my own country and worshipped travel and the sun. Having now travelled quite a bit, I know that every nation looks to another as an example, not realising that its picture of the other is rather distorted. Still, the sun *is* better than the rain.

The following day I met Ronnie again and accepted the job.

The first part of the plan was this: I would take in the leaflets, tie them in bundles and attach the bundles to, say, a railing on a tall building; then a pocket parking-meter timer, set so that I had time to get away, would start ticking. When the timer started buzzing, a Schick razor attached to it would turn and cut the string holding the leaflets, scattering them on the rush-hour crowds far below.

The second part of the plan was to take a train to Beitbridge on the Rhodesia/South Africa border, find out how vehicles were checked by customs, note the clothes worn by lorry drivers and how many were black and how many white. At rather comfortable flats in Hampstead Ronnie and I experimented with the timers. The system seemed to work. I was given a big suitcase with a false bottom where the leaflets were stowed. I assumed that others might be carrying out the same tasks but I never knew anything about them.

It was still summer in England, but winter in South Africa,

when I set off. I was a little apprehensive at Johannesburg airport but in those days foreign whites were not under particular suspicion so all went well. Usually, suitcases weren't opened by customs anyway.

I booked into the Hotel Victoria which was very large and very anonymous. At dinner that night, in the colonial-brown dining room, I was served by giant black men wearing red fezzes and white gloves. It was at this moment that I realised that I was in a slave state. This was what it was like in the Roman Empire – served by slaves!

I was warned that it was dangerous to go into the streets at night. Nevertheless, I went out (if only to get away from the colour brown) and found the streets strangely empty except for an occasional night watchman and his brazier. Only one area, Hillbrow, made up of a couple of streets of spuriously cosmopolitan cafes, seemed to be alive.

There were undoubtedly outgoing and energetic whites but slavery could not produce culture in the 1960s. Because of the storm of censorship the bookshops looked more like newsagents; you had to wear a tie at your (five-course) breakfast in the hotel; and no women were allowed in bars!

It was a provincial but violent society.

Actually, the difference between a sociopath (an aggressive slave-owner) and a psychopath was minimal. I will give an example: once, in a seaside resort, I was sitting in a bar with Alex Moumbaris. Suddenly, at 9 pm, a siren wailed over the town. Nobody turned a hair. I asked the barman what it was and he explained it was curfew time for the blacks! I burst out laughing and the men in the bar turned to stare at me. Alex flashed me a warning look. Later, after I had left, he had to intervene, in a joking manner of course, to stop the black potman from being beaten up by drunken whites. The joke for these whites was that the black man was out after curfew!

Anyway, from the Hotel Victoria I went out to find suitable buildings for the operation, plus substitute places in case there were problems. I awaited the date that had been agreed in

London. (The leaflets, incidentally, were issued in relation to important dates in the South African progressive calendar and often called on the people to help the armed liberation forces when they arrived.) Unfortunately, this first time, I was told to make myself scarce after the job so that, having fixed everything up, I never knew whether the preparations were successful. (In 1969 we used a different system, involving acid that was supposed to rot the string binding the leaflets).

I returned to one of my sites in Cape Town a little later but the bundle was still hanging high up on the building. On the other site I had prepared a banner reading "ANC LIVES" which had had to be stuck together in a hotel room. Acid cut the string on the banner.

Obviously, these systems were rather fiddly, especially since the acid or blade had to be set after the package was hung up. You can imagine that I was nervous at precisely this moment. And, by the way, breaking open the false bottom of a suitcase in a hotel room is very noisy.

After the leafleting events in 1967 I set off by train to Beitbridge. The trains in Africa are amazingly slow, never above 50km an hour – and then you'd be lucky – but the carriages were comfortable and there were always cheap five-course meals to be had in the whites-only saloons. As it happened, this particular train was full of police cadets.

Then I had to stay in the small town of Messina for a few days which made me conspicuous (maybe I was waiting for money) before crossing the border. Anyway, I made the observations that I mentioned earlier, partly by writing 'letters' while sitting at a roadside cafe. I then took a bus and train through Rhodesia to Lusaka, the capital of Zambia. The first bus driver, a Rhodesian, was furious that a white man would ride in an ordinary bus - most buses were exclusively for blacks. He was adamant that I sit next to him in an uncomfortable section at the front.

In Lusaka I contacted the wrong ANC (a particularly clumsy mistake) – Harry Nkumbula's Zambian party, but Nkumbula was discreet and I eventually reported to Oliver Tambo himself.

The reader should remember that at this time the ANC was not such a big organisation and this meeting is not as extraordinary as it sounds. Many of the important people I met only briefly and for a very specific purpose (to report on the lorry drivers and customs procedures at the Beitbridge border crossing, as instructed) and that is why, alas, I cannot give the reader a vivid description of them.

The 1967 trip was for 6-7 weeks.

On a shorter visit in 1968, I took in piles of leaflets and letters that had to be posted at various remote pillar-boxes in Cape Town. I had to lick hundreds of stamps too. However, in London I had received a large black eye, a broken tooth and a broken nose (free of charge) so I was conspicuous every minute of the day in Notting Hill, never mind Cape Town. Ronnie, used to such incidents, was unconcerned.

What was my cover story in England? These first trips could be presented as holidays. Indeed, I stopped off at Naples and Marseilles so that I had something to talk about. However, later, when I worked full-time for the ANC, I explained that I had an old friend in Zambia (which was true) who could fiddle company expenses for air tickets so I could go and visit him occasionally. In London I said that I was working as a messenger so that if I was seen around in the streets during the day, this would seem natural. As a young man I had done all sorts of jobs – and was to do quite a few more – so the 'messenger' story rang true.

Nevertheless, one or two right-wing friends were suspicious. It is unlikely that they will read this text, but if they do, they now know their suspicions were justified.

Returning to the UK was like entering a foreign country. It was the advertising that stunned me the most. This oppressive hucksterism after the light, space and colour of Africa was really nasty.

The *Avventura*[26] Episode

In 1969 a new project began – the *Avventura* episode. For the next three years I was to work full-time for the ANC. My code-name[27] was 'Vincent' after Vincent Price, the film actor. Ronnie told me that he wanted me to do a survey of the beaches along the coast of South Africa so that a site could be chosen for a landing of guerrillas. First, I learned to drive and then to type and then I was taught rudimentary photography by Ivan Strasburg, an accomplished South African photographer. Finally, I was shown how to write with and develop invisible ink.

I was to receive more serious training in Moscow and Baku. To obviate Soviet bureaucracy I was given a medical inspection by none other than Yusuf Dadoo! First, I flew to West Berlin where I waited one cloudy afternoon at a suburban railway station. I half-expected to see a bearded balloon-seller in dark glasses out of the corner of my eye but a very ordinary, well-built man asked me the way to the zoo and soon we were travelling by underground to the border. After a night in a well-guarded, rather special hotel I flew to Moscow in a military plane.

In Moscow I was given a Soviet passport but lived in the foreigners' section of various central hotels, moving every ten days or so. Victor, a smart man in his forties, with the ubiquitous gold teeth of Eastern Europe, was my 'guide'. The KGB arranged for me to learn the Morse Code, the development and printing of film, handling guns and methods to avoid and recognise surveillance. This latter course proved to me that I needed glasses. I was shocked.

After three months in Moscow I was ready; and in 1970 I flew to Durban, hired a car and set off down the coast to Mossel Bay. I photographed a series of designated beaches and sent the rolls of film back to London. Using specially prepared pages in an ordinary book I was able to write invisible reports on the back of seemingly innocuous letters home, but I don't think I used the

26 A contemporary report, found on the Internet, spells it as 'Avventura'. This tallies with the Italian word for 'adventure'. However, 'Pat Gallagher' informed me that he himself painted the name on the ship's side with only one 'v'. – Editor.
27 Curiously, this was also the code-name for Pete Smith, but only after 1985. – Editor.

double-transposition code I had been taught.

The Garden Route is in fact one of the great scenic areas of South Africa, so the hotels were packed at the weekend, which slowed me down somewhat. It was a beautiful journey and a lot of good work was done.

The *Avventura* episode unrolled in three parts. Now came the second part, when I was introduced to Alexandre Moumbaris, who is essentially Greek despite a French/Egyptian/Australian background. Alex had covered the eastern coast up to Richards Bay (which didn't exist as a port then) and the Transkei area, which was then chosen as best for a landing. Both of us were to cover this coast again and decide on the best site.

When we arrived in South Africa we bought fishing rods and stuck them on top of a hired car. It has to be said that neither of us were particularly good drivers – I drove too fast and Alex too slow, though this is all relative of course. We had different temperaments and, as any old spy will tell you, this can have an adverse effect when two people are working closely together. When I drove too fast Alex put his foot down on an invisible pedal and beseeched me to be careful. In the end, I had to agree to drive only on dirt roads and never above 50 mph. As a result of this I was irritated when Alex suggested we release the pressure in the tyres for the long drive on a dirt road to Port St John's. I resisted this; within a kilometre a tyre had burst and we skidded all over the road. We sat there and Alex looked at me like Oliver looks at Stan. Anyway, we brought back our conclusions. The tension between us now evaporated and everything was sweetness and light. Ronnie, however, was concerned.

In 1971, Alex and I travelled separately to Moscow. This time I took a conventional flight, stopping off at Amsterdam overnight. At the airport an excited immigration officer noticed the peculiar arrangement of stamps in my passport – Moscow *and* Johannesburg? He made some notes, and then waved me through. Later, when I told the KGB about this, they told me they would check if there had been a leak to western agencies, but they claimed that nothing had been recorded – or if recorded, I suppose, some mole had destroyed the evidence.

Alex and I lived in a big, sombre flat in Moscow and had discussions with the Soviets about the landing sites. (Alex had been trained in Moscow at the same time as me, the year before).

Next we flew to Baku where we lived on a boat (probably a patrol boat) in the military section of the port. We were surrounded by what was quite literally a sea of human shit; I was very relieved when we left that harbour! There was a military advisor aboard (but we all wore naval uniform), constantly wiping the sweat from his round face. He was purposeful and lively while the captain was, as you'd expect, more taciturn. The crew seemed to be all young conscripts.

It was a happy ship but the food was exactly the same every day - carrots, carrots, carrots and more carrots.

We passed a small island on which there were thousands of rabbits. Some sailors from a ship moored nearby were running about bonking the rabbits on the head. Our captain addressed them through a loud-hailer, explaining that he had started the rabbit colony to help everybody – do not kill too many! The frenzy on the island abated.

The purpose of our voyage was to experience landing by night in a dinghy. I went first and then we waited for Alex. The sea was getting rougher and rougher and Alex's party had left the ship but there was no sign of the dinghy. The advisor was worried but my shallow optimism led me to believe that nothing serious could happen to us. Eventually, Alex's boat bobbed into view and was suddenly thrust onto the shore. There had been some danger but I was annoyed with Alex that he took it so lightly, though a few moments before I had been annoyed that he took so long!

We were very sick in the rough seas home, especially since we were in the bow as it rose and fell, crashing into the waves. The following day, our trainer and the captain invited us to a hilltop restaurant overlooking Baku. So we had at least one wonderful meal. Despite the oil rigs, much of the town was charming, and more relaxed than Moscow. I liked it very much.

At this time I was reading an enormous amount about Stalin and Stalinism. In the aftermath of the Soviet intervention in Czechoslovakia, a large number of memoirs and historical accounts were published. When we flew to Baku I was reading a rather unremarkable book about the Soviet-German war and on one page there was a photograph of Stalin. This caused great excitement among the passengers though I don't know why – photos of Stalin from the war period were published in Soviet books also. The British and Soviet Communist Parties had differences over Czechoslovakia (I supported the British position; the SACP supported the Soviets) but this was never relevant in my work for the ANC. Alex, Ronnie and I didn't talk much politics anyway – there was a frame which we all accepted and that was that. Besides, the internal politics of the ANC had to remain secret.

1972 would be the year of the landing. First, Ronnie, Alex and I met Joe Slovo at yet another comfortable house in Hampstead and we argued all day about what to do if this or that happened on the crucial day or what to do if such-and-such didn't happen. The meeting lasted all day long – the only meeting I've ever been to that was utterly exhausting. It was hoped that we two agents would get along together as we had done in London and Moscow.

When we arrived in South Africa we first visited the two sites that had been selected on the Wild Coast. Alex had hired a camper van which I didn't want to drive, so there were no silly arguments about driving. After our visits to the coast, quite separately, Alex met 'Whitey' (Bob Newland) and I met Bill McCaig. We based ourselves in hotels in Durban.

Bill McCaig had been living and working in South Africa for some time. He had been an electrical engineer in the merchant navy and was highly disciplined in his approach to everything we did. Our job was to look for discreet places, which could also be easily recognised, where arms could be hidden. Putting it simply, this meant digging holes. We travelled around hole-finding and hole-digging. We were to be on the substitute beach and both parties would have walkie-talkies to communicate with the mother ship.

Unfortunately, my relations with Alex deteriorated and London had to intervene. I have mentioned some quarrels over driving but this was only a minor expression of our differences which were usually over a string of petty issues. Anyway, contrary to good conspiratorial practice, all four of us were ordered to meet and put an end to the bickering. This seemed to do it.

Now we changed hotels but sat and waited in Durban. I used a pseudonym in the new hotel and once sat blithely in the lounge while my 'name' was called over and over again. So, all you would-be revolutionaries out there, remember your name! Remember who you are!

In the end, tragically, the boat never came. It was sabotaged at its base in Somalia by a bunch of scoundrels.[28] A new crew couldn't get things underway. However, both Alex and I think that, if the ship had arrived, the operation would have had a very good chance of success. How might South African history have been changed?

Alex, Whitey and I returned to England. I took up a printing job. Then one day in autumn 1972 I opened the newspaper and suddenly the name Moumbaris caught my eye. Alex had been arrested in South Africa! About three weeks later I met Ronnie, who gave me a broad explanation: Alex had been caught waiting with a car for a group of guerrillas near the border in South Africa.

The trial of Alex and his comrades ensued and he was sentenced to twelve years in jail. Seven years later, he escaped with Tim Jenkin and Stephen Lee. This was a truly amazing getaway, well told in Tim Jenkin's book *Escape from Pretoria*.

In January 1980 a meeting was held in London to celebrate the extraordinary feat of the ANC trio. I was an old-age student at the time and took the train from Stoke to London just to be at the meeting. Ronnie Kasrils was also there. Afterwards, I talked with Ronnie in the pub about this and that, but a thin, ordinary-

---

28   This 'sabotage' version of events is disputed by Roger O'Hara. – Editor.

looking man at the bar was watching us carefully (lip-reading?) so we walked outside.

My cover had been blown by the Moumbaris trial but Ronnie suggested we keep in contact. Nothing happened, however, so in December I went to Algeria to teach at a lycee in the desert for six months. After this, we met again.

Deep in Disneyland

This next job was rather more passive and was mainly arranged in London by Eleanor, Ronnie's wife, who worked at the London College of Fashion. I was to live and work in Swaziland, acting as a front for 'illegals', including Ronnie himself, who moved between ANC headquarters in Maputo, Mozambique and the Swazi 'front line'.

Swaziland is known as the Switzerland of Africa – it has marvellous forests and mountains. Politically, it's more Disneyland. There were no political prisoners at the time but, whatever the king's alleged sentimental attachment to the ANC, the Swazi police worked closely with the South Africans.

I flew to Swaziland in January 1982. There had just been a hijacking of the only Swazi plane in a failed coup against the progressive government in the Seychelles. The Swazis were in a terrific panic. Every passenger at the airport was thoroughly searched and their suitcases ransacked – even my toothpaste was partially squeezed out of the tube! Luckily, I was 'clean'.

Something went wrong at the initial rendezvous: I was supposed to meet someone at a Mongolian restaurant in the suburbs of Manzini. (A Mongolian restaurant in Swaziland! And I'll bet it's still there too!) In the end, I phoned an emergency number, met my contact and settled in for a couple of weeks at the Salesian school where at least two ANC agents worked and a CIA man taught carpentry. The CIA man invited me to a hotel bar where he suddenly switched from small talk to intensive interrogation, interrupted all the time by the resident prostitutes who solicited you by sitting at your table. The prostitutes in Swaziland were very irritating but in this one case they did do me a sort of service.

Then I started work as an English teacher at St Mark's High School in the capital, Mbabane. There were a number of other expatriates on the campus, some on very lucrative British contracts. It is common in Africa that teachers live in a residential area in the extensive grounds of the school. The houses are cheap and usually pleasant enough though they always need to be partially furnished. I moved in to one of these bungalows.

Nkosazana Zuma (later Minister of Health and then Foreign Minister), working as a nurse at the local hospital, arranged that I 'buy' her car. In fact, this car would be for Ronnie's use when he came over the border. I parked the car outside my bungalow but for about a week I didn't use it; a walk across the park took me to the centre of town. The big mistake I made – my one big mistake in Swaziland – was that I didn't tell the headmaster, a black South African, about it. You should always have an explanation for everything that you do.

One morning I was shaving when I heard a series of clanking sounds and the running of chains outside. I did not pay much attention to this but when I went out a few minutes later the car had vanished! Even before I checked I guessed what had happened – the headmaster, thinking the car had been dumped, had phoned the police.

I phoned Nkosazana at the hospital and, after teaching in the morning, I walked across the park to the police station. I explained the situation, that it was all a mistake, and was led into a small room in which sat a small number of plain-clothed officers. I signed some papers and off I went, but – were the officers deliberately assembled so that they would recognise me again? It's impossible to say.

I rented a house to the north of Mbabane for a senior ANC operative in the eastern region, Ebrahim Ismail, and furnished it. A TV was installed, of course, but Ebrahim and Ronnie couldn't understand my passion for the American evangelists on Swazi TV; their biblical demagogy and anti-communism were expressed with all the power of outdoor speakers; even if their commitment was insincere, it *was* a (vulgar) kind of commitment.

Ronnie arranged for me to meet June and Michael Stephen, who lived in Mansion. They had a very young daughter. Michael was a teacher in a local girls' school but was not very happy in Swaziland, although he enjoyed working for the ANC. (Naturally, I never knew what they did.) I liaised with the family only occasionally, for security reasons.

In order that I could experience a particularly common task, I accompanied the Stephens (with daughter) and Ronnie, one night, to a flat, lonely countryside near the Mozambican border. Ronnie took his rucksack and set off down the road to the border fence. When he had disappeared, Michael decided to walk along after him to see that he had got over. This was not a good idea.

Time passed and Michael didn't return. June and I sat in the car and considered what to do. The little girl slept. Then, far along the road, we saw lights, torches, and heard men talking. From a distance, Michael hailed us.

He was surrounded by Swazi soldiers. Michael told us that he had explained to the sergeant that we had broken down. June and I quickly showed how worried we were – what were we to do, lost in such a remote area in the middle of the night, with a tired child too?

The sergeant listened sympathetically, whether he believed us or not. He took our names, then we could go. Remarkably – and everyone showed their astonishment with cries of relief – the car started immediately and we skedaddled as fast as we could.

After I had lived in Swaziland for eighteen months I had had enough of it. I told Ronnie it was time for us to part. We had not arranged any particular contract period and there is only so long you can live in a rather sleazy resort.

Before I left, I spent a month in Maputo, a strange, beautiful, ex-colonial city full of individually-designed Portuguese houses. A few people sat outside the cafes but no food or even coffee was served. The abandoned, but not decrepit, look of the city was both futuristic and poetic.

Zimbabwe Interlude

I met Mr Kasrils once again after this, in Zimbabwe in January 1987. I had been working as a teacher in Harare and was staying for a month at Eve and Robert McNamara's house while they were on holiday. I had first met Eve and Robert in Swaziland and, although they had some differences with the ANC, they were prepared to help out when it was necessary. The house was full of cat fleas due to Eve's sentimental notion that these fleas couldn't possibly molest human beings because pussycats are so lovely. Our legs were swollen with bites.

Ronnie phoned out of the blue. He arrived later with Roger Allingham and unrolled maps of South Africa on the garden table. They were planning a reconnaissance mission for Roger, who was to record details of vulnerable police stations and other targets suitable for attack. I kept away from these discussions.

Towards the end of the month Ronnie suggested I take a trip to Swaziland to spy on a big police convention there. He wanted to know the licence plates of the cars. (There was more to it, I am sure, but he never divulged all the details until the last moment.) He gave me a roll of money that I tried to stuff into my socks. However, at the last moment the phone rang, Ronnie answered, and I was told the project was cancelled – on the other hand, maybe it wasn't cancelled but a different arrangement had been made. One never knew.

In 1990 I was back in London, in Islington, and I contacted Eleanor to tell her I was going to Botswana as a teacher for at least a year. However, at this time the South African struggle was entering a confused, transitional phase so I spent a year of straight teaching and that was that.

Some Conclusions

It should be mentioned here that British Intelligence also used teachers, both in schools and universities in Africa, to obtain information. I met a couple of these characters; and, as you would expect, the British government (and its intelligence service) supported a profitable big business presence in the slave state.

Today it is not so easy as it once was to keep up with the complexities of African politics from afar. This is unfortunate because southern Africa is always full of dynamic struggles with lessons for all of us, all over the world.

I met Alex and Ronnie again in June 2005, at a gathering held at the South African High Commission in London. After forty years neither of them seems to have changed much. If we went back to the 1950s even – fifty years – are they very different? I have certainly mellowed, but there's still something of the tearaway in Ronnie, and Alex is still, I am sure, a lousy driver.

ONE LIVERPUDLIAN'S INVOLVEMENT IN THE SOUTH AFRICAN STRUGGLES
Bill McCaig

I was a member of the Communist Party of Great Britain from 1964 and became a merchant seaman in 1966. After the 1966 seaman's strike I was working for the Union Castle line which had a regular six-weekly mail run to South Africa. I came ashore at the end of 1967 but was asked by Gerry Cohen, the Merseyside Party Secretary, whether I would go back to sea as the South African Party and the ANC were looking for comrades sailing to South Africa and he thought I would be able to help.

Initially I was involved in propaganda work. There was a need to get MK propaganda booklets into South Africa, particularly into the hands of dockworkers. I was supplied with the material, which I distributed around the cargo holds, so that when the cargo was being taken out it was there for dockworkers to pick up.

Similar material was also given to me in envelopes, which I took ashore and mailed when I docked in South Africa. Clearly it was much better for material to appear to be posted within the country, rather than being sent from abroad. Trying to smuggle bundles of letters out of the docks when you're in a very hot climate presented a bit of a problem as the clothes I was wearing consisted of shorts and loose fitting short-sleeved shirts. I'd find myself with an extra beer gut as I strapped on bundles of letters round my waist, hoping I wasn't sweating too much.

I was also asked if it was possible to smuggle people in or out of South Africa on the merchant ships I was sailing on. I explored the possibility on one of the ships and created a hidden compartment in my electrical workshop, which was situated on the afterdeck of the ship. I'm not sure why, but this arrangement was never taken up and used.

Whilst we were going up and down the coast I also looked over the ports and at possible landing sites on the coast itself for putting guerrillas ashore. Examining the ports was easy but the coast was a different matter. It wasn't a very practical proposition, because I wasn't always on deck and I couldn't really stand there with binoculars, viewing the shoreline – you didn't know who you were sailing with. For instance, I sailed with an engineer who, while drinking too much, let slip he was involved with the South African Security Police and had been involved in infiltrating anti-apartheid groups in the UK and still maintained his contacts with the police. I passed this information back to my contact in London, Ronnie Kasrils. Another of the officers was from Rhodesia, and his father was involved with the security services there. There were, however, some positive contacts on ships and I recall holding discussions with an Officer Cadet from Kenya, who struck me as very progressive. I thought he would be in a very good position, when he went ashore in South Africa, to visit areas or people I would have found difficult in this apartheid state because I was white. I passed details of this contact to Ronnie and he sent another black comrade to hold discussions with him when we docked in London. I still don't know if he was recruited or how useful this contact turned out to be.

In early 1970 Ronnie asked me if I could go out to South Africa, which I agreed to do when my next voyage finished at the end of August 1970. Initially I went down to London and had discussions with John Gollan, the general secretary of the British Communist Party,[29] Ronnie Kasrils (my contact in London) and Joe Slovo.

While I was in London I had some training which consisted of being able to check on whether I was being followed. The idea was to look in shop windows and mirrors, ask people directions so you could look back in the direction you came from, sitting in good positions in restaurants and bars when you first entered, so you could see who followed you in. I was also given a means of communication with my contacts at home – pretty primitive, but very effective. Ronnie supplied me with a book, an English/

29 I.e. the CPGB – Editor.

Afrikaans dictionary, in which certain pages had been treated with some chemical. I don't know what it was but if you knew what you're looking for, you could just about make it out, as it gave a whitish look to the page. What I had to do was to put a piece of paper behind the page, then a piece of glass underneath so I didn't get an imprint in the book, and then another page on top of the page and then I'd write my coded message on that. This would leave the underneath sheet with an invisible message on it. I would then destroy the top copy that I had written on and subject the other sheet with the hidden writing on to steam from the kettle in order to erase the indentation of the writing. I would then write some sort of letter on the other side, to my Aunt Fanny or someone. In addition to this I used another book for the code. I'd draft out anything I wanted to say and then translate it into a certain code. You had to pick out line numbers, letter numbers. You could never make any sense of it unless you had the same codebook. It was very simple, but very effective. They used to communicate with me in that way. I had a supply of capsules which I eventually used by dissolving them in boiling water. They produced a red looking liquid which stained any pan you boiled it up in, so I used empty tin cans which could then be thrown away. This brought out the invisible writing. Then I went out to South Africa on a 'holiday'.

It turned out to be a couple of years' holiday. I lived in Durban and I got a job working as a marine electrician for a firm on Durban's docks. This provided me with the opportunity, not only to meet incoming ships, and therefore any possible contacts on them as well, it also gave me the perfect excuse to constantly move around the docks to see the opportunities for bringing people in and thus bypassing the port authorities. The job proved awkward at times as there were sensitive areas in the docks that you weren't allowed in, e.g. oil depots, unless you had a pass. As I was, strictly speaking, an illegal immigrant, and officially only there for a holiday, I had never had a visa to work in South Africa. This presented me with the problem of how to get a valid pass, or explain to my employer why I could not

apply for one. Fortunately, even in the strategically vital area for
apartheid of oil, you didn't have to apply for a pass – you simply
borrowed somebody else's and used it to wend your way around
any place on the docks, sensitive or not.

I received word that I was to meet another contact in Durban,
which I did. I now believe his name to be Daniel Ahern, though
I knew him as a Mr Johnson. We hired a vehicle and together
went down the coast to the Transkei. Our job on the coast was to
go round looking for suitable cache sites where the arms were to
be buried for future distribution. Having found a suitable site,
we spent our time digging big holes in the rock-hard ground,
putting a piece of plywood near the surface to cover the hole
up and then covering the board with soil so the hole couldn't
be seen. Photographs of the scene were taken so they could be
found again. You then had the problem of explaining what you
were doing if someone saw you digging or just parked in the
middle of nowhere; the explanation we used involved carrying
a toilet roll round with us. So we always came back to the car
with this toilet roll, and if anyone was there waiting, it was fairly
obvious where we'd been. On top of the car we had fishing rods,
so it gave the impression we were going along the coast fishing.

I've since found out what the operation was. The ANC
had got their hands on a ship called the *Avventura* which was
apparently loaded with guerrillas, guns and ammunition in
Somalia. I found out later that another Liverpool comrade, Eric
Caddick, another seaman and a friend of mine, joined the ship
in Somalia. Ronnie Kasrils, in his book *Armed and Dangerous*,
said 'the engine seized up off Mombasa, and the plan was
aborted'. Eric informed me that there were obviously some non-
comrades in the crew and by the sound of it they had sabotaged
the ship. I believe they poured sand in the oil and the bearings
of the engine had seized up. When they got back to Somalia the
authorities there were prepared to have the saboteurs executed.
They couldn't repair the ship so the whole thing fell through. Of
course we were unaware of these events at that time.

It was decided that I should clarify my legal position in

South Africa, so I got the correct documents and applied to stay on a permanent basis. I was rejected and consequently I had to pack up the job that I was doing in the docks, move house and disappear. I found a new job in an oil refinery by Durban Airport. While I was there I received some money from the UK and a communication that they were sending some materials to me for delivery to another comrade: documents, IDs, etc. While waiting for this parcel to arrive I received a message in the refinery that somebody wanted to see me at the main gate. As I cycled towards him I saw a guy standing waiting by the main gate. I thought 'this is a cop'. He explained he was with the police force and asked me 'if I had anything to tell him' to which I replied 'such as what?' He said he had received a communication from someone in the refinery that I had something to tell him; did I think it might have been one of my workmates? I said that was highly likely as I worked with a lot of jokers. He then started to 'pass the time of day' and, while doing so, to quiz me. He started to talk about London and asked if I knew it well, namedropping areas of London that I knew from my training there. I replied I knew areas of London, as I had family there but didn't know it really well. I thought that this would give me room to squeeze out of any difficult questions. He clearly wasn't there to arrest me at that moment and left. From inside the refinery I was able to ascertain that for the rest of the day the police were still outside the oil refinery in the car park just outside the main gate, obviously still keeping an eye on me. This gave me time to collect my thoughts. It was obvious the police knew something, but I couldn't quite figure out exactly what they did know. When I got home there was another unmarked police vehicle overlooking my flat. So I presumed my position was fairly well blown. I knew of course a parcel was coming and I presumed they'd got their hands on it and were waiting for me to lead them to other people. It was clearly time to go.

Late that same night I headed for Johannesburg by train. When I got to the airport the flight that was usually so regular had been delayed, which was the last thing I wanted. But it actually worked better than I thought. The woman at the check-in desk said: 'Were you on a flight this morning?' There was a flight from Durban to Johannesburg, which I hadn't taken in case they were monitoring the airport, so I said, 'Yes.' And she said 'We're putting you all up in a hotel.' I said: 'Good!' and went off and stayed in the hotel, courtesy of British Airways – and there was no record of me at all, because I hadn't been on the flight! When I arrived at the airport to check in, the immigration officer said to me: 'You haven't got a valid pass, you're an illegal immigrant. You came for a holiday and you've been here for two years!' I replied the reason for this was that I had applied to stay, but this is how long it had taken them to refuse me; with letters going backwards and forwards to Pretoria, they had only just turned me down. 'That's why I'm leaving now'. Much to my relief, he said 'Okay then'. So off I went.

Back home I rang up Ronnie Kasrils, my contact in London, and spoke to him. It came as a total surprise to him that I was back and that the police in South Africa were involved, but I am not sure if I was believed. I had the distinct feeling that he felt that I had 'overreacted'.

As I understand it, the sequence of events was that Alexander Moumbaris had been arrested, and the South African police were using his cover to request funds from his London contacts to establish the links in the chain. This is how they had found where the funding was coming from. I presume they looked for other transfers going to people in South Africa from similar sources in London and came across my name that way. When they contacted me they were only presuming there might be some sort of connection between us. I understand that, as a consequence of not believing me, and the comrade in South Africa still needing his documentation, Sean Hosey was sent out to complete the job and as Ronnie says in his book 'Sean walked straight into a trap. The man he exchanged passwords with outside a store in a small Natal town turned out to be a black security policeman.'

The training I was given I believe stood me in good stead.

Without it I would not have recognised that my cover had been blown and I may well have joined my other comrades in a South African prison. For this, I am extremely thankful.

Another consequence of that training is that even to this day, whenever I am in a restaurant or a pub, I always sit in a place where I have full view of the doors and can see whoever enters the room. It is a habit that my family found intriguing and upon examining this behaviour came to realise its origin.

I worked for the Communist Party for about four years in the 1970s and worked as an electrician until the 1980s. In 1983, after having a mid-life crisis, I went to university to study Economic History. I now teach history at a grammar school in Merseyside, where I still live.

I'm proud to have played a role, however minor, in the liberation of the South African people and the establishment of democracy there. I have named my house 'Mandela' in honour of both the man himself and his compatriots.

Bob Newland

I first became involved in politics while I was at school in Bognor Regis. When I was fourteen a very good friend, Michael Harrison, introduced me to the Campaign for Nuclear Disarmament (CND). He was an active member although he was also chair of the local Young Conservatives. Unfortunately Michael died aged only eighteen as a result of a leaking gas fire while visiting a friend in Paris.

Our CND group was very broad, involving Young Liberals, Conservatives, Labour and Communist Party members, church people and many other non-aligned individuals.

It was the Young Liberals who rapidly persuaded me that the solution to the moral outrage which I felt about nuclear weapons could only be found by political means. One in particular: John Kingsbury, who went on to become a local Liberal councillor, one of very few in a town dominated by the Conservatives, became a very special friend.

By the time I was seventeen I had been convinced by Kevin Kewell, a local poet and Chair of the Communist Party branch in Chichester, that it was the Communist Party which offered the political solutions I so much sought.

This was the beginning of a lifelong commitment to socialism and internationalism which was to lead me in a very few years to active involvement in the struggle to liberate South Africa as one of the 'London Recruits' engaged in covert support for the efforts of the African National Congress.

Since I was fifteen I had been regularly spending weekends in London and was involved with the then Movement for Colonial Freedom (MCF), now known as Liberation. It was the MCF which had launched the Anti-Apartheid Movement of which I also became an active member.

The struggle for the liberation of southern Africa was rising to new heights. Massive public meetings were held in London with such speakers as Joshua Nkomo, leader of ZAPU from Zimbabwe, Samora Machel from Mozambique and many other leaders of the liberation movements. These were attacked by the National Front and other racist groups and a stewarding organisation was set up by MCF to protect the meetings. This was organised by Don O'Hanrahan, an ex-para[30] and Communist Party activist.

I had previously met Don at Unity Theatre[31] and became his lieutenant in the stewarding organisation. Later Don was to provide me with accommodation and a lot of support during rocky times. He was one of the most generous comrades I have ever known, happily sharing his home, food, wine and experiences with anyone who needed them. Don was to become a surrogate father to me in later years before tragically dying of a heart attack.

I eventually moved to London and, aged eighteen and unemployed, became involved in the campaign at the London School of Economics (LSE) for disinvestment from the then Rhodesia. Little did I know at the time that another interloper at the LSE was Ronnie Kasrils who was subsequently responsible for my South African adventures.

The LSE campaign culminated in an occupation which was eventually ended by force. I joined with many hundreds of others in going to Bow Street to demonstrate late at night against the arrest of several students who were held responsible for the occupation and were charged with criminal damage for physically removing the 'gates' which had been erected to restrict the movement of students from one section of the college to others.

We sat down, blocking the road, outside the Royal Opera House and dozens of us were arrested and charged with various public order offences as a result. I had the extraordinary experience of sharing a cell with a very posh drunk in bow tie and dinner jacket who had wandered into our 'sit in' on his way home from the opera and had been arrested along with us.

Very shortly after this I re-established contact with the

30 i.e. a former member of Britain's elite Parachute Regiment.– Editor.
31 A left-wing theatre in north London, later destroyed by fire. – Editor.

Communist Party and became an active member of the Young Communist League (YCL) in Islington where I lived and worked in a sweat shop button factory. Among my closest comrades was Pete Smith who eventually recruited me to work for the ANC.

At this time the international communist movement was deeply divided; particularly over the invasion of Czechoslovakia in August 1968. The YCL was split 50/50 and I and a majority of my branch were supporters of the Soviet intervention.

This also coincided with a decision by our South African comrades to involve young white Britons in their struggle. There was a pressing need to carry forward a publicity campaign showing that the ANC and their armed wing Umkhonto we Sizwe (MK) were alive and well and fighting to end apartheid.

The repression in South Africa, exercised particularly through the restriction on movement of the black population using the hated Pass Laws, meant that outside help was needed to publicise the underground struggle being carried out by the ANC and MK.

An obvious source of such 'recruits' was the British Young Communist League. Because of our divisions some were recruited through official channels and others like myself through personal contact.

I have a strong memory of Pete Smith calling me aside one evening in 1971, taking me for a walk and solemnly cautioning me that he was to share with me a very important secret. He went on to tell me that other members of the YCL had been fulfilling their internationalist duty by assisting the ANC in South Africa.

Pete then went on to surprise me further with his announcement that I had been selected for the same honour, that it would be dangerous but that it would represent a crucial contribution to the struggle for the liberation of South Africa. It seems strange to me now that I never thought for a moment about who had 'selected' me for this honour (for a great honour it was). I was just 21 years old.

My response was an immediate 'yes' and within weeks I

was to be flying off to Johannesburg with Pete on a mission to distribute leaflets using a unique 'leaflet bomb' developed by our ANC comrades.

Pete's lecture on the gravity of our mission and the importance of security remains with me today. Over the 35 years since I was recruited I have only discussed my involvement with a handful of people. With the publication of this book I have been persuaded to share my experiences with a wide audience in order to help new generations understand that internationalism and solidarity are positive ideas that can help to change the world.

Before our departure I met Ronnie Kasrils at his 'local' and the 'theatre', both code words for a pub in Golders Green and for the Dominion Theatre in London's West End. Training in the use of the leaflet bombs was also provided along with some advice as to how to behave if captured.

Before flying out to Johannesburg I had to buy tickets for myself and Pete. A rendezvous was arranged for me to meet a comrade who, after the pre-arranged coded greetings, correctly exchanged, handed over to me £700 in one pound notes.

The same day I had to buy the tickets at South African Airlines. How young and foolish we were. I rushed from my clandestine meeting down to Regent Street clutching my bundle of one pound notes and bought our tickets. It seems that the dirty hands of BOSS (the Bureau of State Security) didn't stretch as far as that stressed young counter clerk who had to count her way through my enormous bundle of used oncers.

Pete and I were flying out via Rome and Nairobi. Our journey was relatively uneventful except for a very bumpy landing at Nairobi airport. When we took off again to resume our journey to Johannesburg the reason for this was shared with us. We had just survived the first landing at Nairobi Airport by automatic pilot.

We stayed at the Victoria Hotel in central Johannesburg. Our leaflets were packed into false compartments in the bottom of our suitcases. I remember to this day the distinct check pattern on the lining as we cut our way in. The explosive tubes for launching the leaflets were hidden in tins of Fortnum and Masons biscuits, a present for an old friend!

We also had hundreds of addresses to which we were to post copies of the leaflets. The leaflets had been printed on very thin paper and were celebrating South Africa Freedom Day,[32] which was June 26th, to commemorate the adoption of the Freedom Charter at the Congress of the People in Kliptown in 1955.

Many of the names were unknown to me but some are world renowned; Winnie Mandela, Albertina Sisulu and many others. The addresses were strange but most were in Soweto (South West Township), Alexandra or others of the horrendous shanty towns in which millions of the African population were forced to live.

South Africa was then a country of twenty million blacks and four million whites whom they were forced to serve. Nothing demonstrated this more powerfully than the train stations and main streets of Johannesburg at 7am every weekday. At night the city was white and largely deserted. Suddenly, as the trains arrived from the townships with the thousands of domestic and other workers, the street literally turned black. No wonder the ruling white elite lived their lives in fear.

We spent our first few days checking out the area where our leaflet bombs were to be set off. Our targets included a main railway station where we could leaflet a large number of African workers. Our preparation included working out a detailed escape route through the one way systems so we didn't end up going full circle into the inevitable police presence after the bombs went off.

Our evenings were occupied by stuffing leaflets into the hundreds of envelopes and licking them to seal them. After a few nights Peter announced he wanted to go out for a drink to the north of the city. I must have been suffering from the effects of all the glue because I was feeling very nauseous and decided to stay back in the hotel.

Some hours later I was awoken by Pete with a confused

---

32 Bob Newland has confirmed that the actual date of the action was in August – Editor.

story about a shooting. Pete was suitably terrified but I could barely take it in. I'm sure the drama of it all was added to by the hallucinogenic effects of the glue on our envelopes. From then on we acquired some sponges, damped them and sealed the rest of our envelopes with them.

After a few days we were ready to post the letters so that they arrived in time for the big day. Pete and I set out on the long trek to post them. We had decided, after some discussion, to deposit them in as many boxes as we reasonably could in the hope that even if some were identified the rest would get through. Subsequent reports suggest we were very successful and most of the intended recipients duly received their surprise package.

There were a couple of days to kill before the due day, so we set about passing some time sightseeing and attempting to relax. Things started well. We went to the main park and spent a couple of pleasant hours rowing a boat on the lake. This had to be followed by a very special curried mince in the restaurant and a couple of local beers to quench our thirst.

We then decided that we would like to have a look at Soweto (from the outside). As we drove past we got involved in a massive funeral procession. Police directed us out of the queue but inadvertently we took the wrong turning and found ourselves driving through Soweto. What a shock. The rows and rows of tin shacks went on for miles and miles. We didn't want to turn back because of the large numbers of police with the funeral procession. We didn't want to hang about for fear of being attacked or stopped by the Soweto police.

Eventually we found a right turn, which we took, and drove out of Soweto with a great sigh of relief. So much for relaxation. The next day we did very little except prepare our bombs, test the mechanisms and timers and check and re-check our routes.

The big day began with a big breakfast. We had been given a specific time to detonate the bombs. I think it was 3 pm. Off we set. The bombs were hidden inside paper carrier bags. I was driving and Pete had them sitting between his legs. We were sitting at a set of traffic lights when I happened to look at the car next to us. It was a police car. The driver was leaning over looking inside our car. Pete was completely unaware of what was going on. I feigned a bout of coughing to distract the policeman and fortunately at that moment the lights changed and off we drove.

We had two targets, one of which was the railway station. Previous reconnaissance had identified a convenient litter bin where we could place our carrier bag with bomb. There was only a three minute delay planned, in order to avoid the bomb being discovered while giving us just enough time to escape. Our second target was not far away and we reached it without any problems, deposited the bomb and proceeded along our escape route.

Then all hell broke loose. The area was flooded with police from all directions. It was only on our return that we discovered that another group was operating in the same city and we had unwittingly planned our escape through their target area.

We were to get hint of this the next day when we were at the airport waiting for our flight. Pete had gone to purchase some snacks and I saw two people across the concourse I thought I recognised. I quickly found Pete and we moved to a quiet corner where we could see and not easily be seen. Within a few minutes Pete identified three people we knew well from the YCL. These were Graeme Whyte, and Sean Hosey whom we knew from London, and Denis Walshe, who Pete knew from his home town of Southampton.

Fortunately we all managed to get back to London without difficulty. Unfortunately Sean was to be arrested the next year while participating in another operation.

The second stage of my ANC work was much more serious. In the following year, 1972, I was introduced in London to an amazing comrade, Alex Moumbaris. Alex was a Greek Australian married to a French woman living in Paris. He had been involved for some time in MK operations and had spent many months carrying out surveys in South Africa to find suitable places to land MK fighters from the sea.

Our task was to meet these groups with essential supplies and communication equipment and transport them to locations where they could collect weapons and move to operational bases.

During the planning stage of our operation I visited Alex at his flat in South London. He showed an active interest in Stalin and I lent him a copy of one of my books. Before I left my home in Bognor Regis I stamped my name and address with a rubber stamp and red ink inside the cover of all my books.

After Alex was arrested his home was broken into by the South African security services and a number of items removed including my book. This was subsequently to be produced as an exhibit during his trial in Pretoria as part of the evidence to prove he was a dangerous Communist.

Our operation was code named 'Mother' and communications for it were based on observations relating to the health of 'mother'. My code name was Whitey. Alex and I were to work directly together and there were two other comrades, Dan Ahern and Bill McCaig working through Alex but of whom I was unaware in the first instance.

My initial role was to transport the communication equipment to South Africa. Radio equipment of this kind was still illegal in Britain so had to be collected from France. It was being transported in the false bottom of a tea chest which was full with camping equipment. To avoid two trips through UK customs I was to deposit the tea chest in transit in Southampton and then transfer to a Union Castle Line ship going to Cape Town.

As arranged I met Alex in Paris to collect the tea chest. Previously I had been supplied with cash to cover the initial stages of my journey and to be sufficient to satisfy immigration at Cape Town. Unfortunately there had been some problem with other funds and Alex had to take the bulk of my cash from me.

All went well with the journey back to England and I departed on the Windsor Castle bound via the Canaries to Cape Town. I had recently injured my finger in an industrial accident so my cover story was that my father owned the button factory (the sweat shop where I had been working) and he had sent me to South Africa to recuperate. Friends were to join me there for a sight-seeing and camping trip.

It's only in circumstances like these that you come to realise how important it is to have an effective cover story about which you can discuss. Fortunately I knew a fair amount about button manufacture and some of the rich clients who my 'father' serviced.

I shared a cabin with the son of a South African wine producing family. At my table, much to my distress, was a young Rhodesian secret policeman who was returning after several years working in London.

At every meal the policeman kept saying he thought he knew me. His favourite haunt was Camden Passage market at the Angel in Islington. What he never worked out was that every Saturday morning I was at the Angel selling the Morning Star. He certainly did know me. Throughout the journey I made sure I never picked up a newspaper in case the association jogged his memory.

The journey was not without its drama. As we set off through the Bay of Biscay a storm brewed up. Some hours later our ship was hit by an enormous wave which succeeded in smashing in the foot thick steel doors at the front of our deck. Passengers were thrown all over the place. At least two sustained broken limbs.

Apparently the Captain should have held back in view of the weather forecast but was too busy drinking on the First Class deck above us. The Commodore of the Fleet happened to be on board and relieved the hapless Captain of his duties. For us passengers the rest of the journey went very well as they opened the bars round the clock and stopped taking payment for drinks.

On arrival at Cape Town the immigration officers come on board. This was another tense moment as I had virtually no money left. When asked where I was going I replied

Johannesburg. The nice man suggested that I might consider staying at the Victoria hotel as it was very friendly to Europeans. Of course I knew it well from the previous year but was going nowhere near it.

He then proceeded to ask me how much money I had. Worried that he might ask me to produce it I quickly responded by saying my father had been concerned that I might lose it in transit so I had enough for my journey and he was to transfer additional funds once I arrived in Johannesburg. This seemed to satisfy immigration and off I went on the next stage of my adventure.

Alex was in Port Elizabeth and I was to travel by train to meet him. The small amount of money I had left didn't cover a first class fare so I had to travel second class. My compartment had three other occupants: warders from Robben Island. Fortunately they were not prepared to speak English so left me completely alone.

At our pre-arranged meeting point I found Alex and we departed for an overnight journey through the Transkei to Durban. I was driving and it poured with rain. To help keep me awake I had taken copious numbers of caffeine tablets. The road disintegrated as we drove along it.

Our van skidded from one side of the road to the other. Below us was a drop of thousands of feet. As the van slid to the edge I would jerk the wheel and hope that it turned. It did and we eventually arrived in Durban at our holiday cottage, exhausted but safe. It did however take me two days to recover from the effects of the caffeine and to get some sleep.

Now started a long waiting game. Unknown to us, the ship bringing our three groups of MK combatants had suffered technical problems. For us every day seemed to last forever with little to do.

We spent some time checking out our routes and making sure we knew them blindfold. On one such trip my van got stuck on a beach in the middle of the night. Luckily, Alex was very strong and threw a rope over his shoulder and dragged us up the beach as I revved the engine very loudly. This woke up the dogs in the nearby African village and we eventually fled the area with the sound of barking dogs ringing in our ears.

It became necessary for us to move several times. Firstly because of the delay exceeding our reservations but also because it was very suspicious for us to spend so much time inside when we were supposed to be tourists. The problem was that Alex was waiting for messages.

On some occasions he had to book into hotels overnight in order to use the telephone. Such was the limitation of technology, combined with the repressive system, that you could only make international phone calls from private phones, hotels and main post offices. We spent some of our time on the beach and a great deal of it playing Backgammon, a game which Alex taught me. He was a good teacher and much to his distress I took to it very quickly. We played for points and such was my success that by the time we returned home Alex 'owed' me 1,600 points. At a maximum 64 per game that was quite a victory.

In the middle of our stay we were stood down for a few days when it was known that the boat had not set off on schedule. In order to allay suspicion Alex and I split up. I went off to Johannesburg to visit a family who had befriended me on the outward journey on the Windsor Castle.

They were recent British emigrants who were joining other family members who had lived in South Africa for some years. The brother was employed by the South African company responsible for developing the South African version of the French Mirage jet fighter in defiance of the United Nations arms embargo.

In his cups he bemoaned the disasters that this development was confronted with. He also talked at length about the army plans to deal with insurrection within the townships. I was able to scribble extensive notes on these exchanges and prepare a detailed report on my return.

Reunited with Alex in Durban, we set about the final preparations for the landings. Our purchases included vast quantities of medical supplies, anti-snake bite serum and glucose tablets.

Messages started to come through which caused us great concern; 'mother is unwell', 'mother is very ill' all of which suggested there was a serious problem. We had no idea what it was. Had we been betrayed? Had we been discovered? Where was the boat?

Our operation was planned to last between three and four weeks. It was now week eight. Suddenly we got the abort message 'mother has died'. All we had to do was get out as quickly as possible.

Alex managed to get the first flight. I stayed behind another day to get rid of all the supplies we had amassed. It was a tense 24 hours. Were we blown? Were the police waiting for me at the airport?

Our immediate fears were unjustified. We both returned home safely and met Ronnie for a debrief. Only years later was I to discover that the boat had been sabotaged.[33]

My family were not aware of my involvement, nor would they have understood or been sympathetic to my participation. While I was away I had my twenty-second birthday. Various relatives were ringing my mother asking where I was and what presents I wanted.

All my carefully planned explanations for my absence had fallen apart after the first month. Two months later when Alex approached me to return to South Africa to complete our aborted operation overland we had a long discussion about the security implications of my blown cover.

Amongst my comrades I had planted a story that suggested I had been victim of a breakdown through exhaustion and had gone to Bristol driving mini buses. Unfortunately political protagonists had also challenged this cover and exposed me.

It was decided that it would be too risky for me to return. That was a serious blow to me. My commitment to the cause was very deep and my sense of an unfinished task even greater.

33 See Roger O'Hara's story, where this is disputed. - Editor.

This distress was made worse when I discovered shortly afterwards that as there was little time to find another comrade to go with Alex he had decided to take his wife Marie-José with him.

One of the fighters taken across the border with them surrendered himself to the police. As a result Alex and Marie-José were arrested and consequently Alex was sentenced to 12 years imprisonment. He served seven years before escaping from Pretoria Central prison. But that is his story.

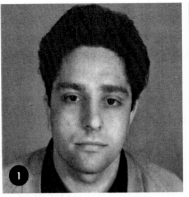

1 Eddie Adams c1970
2 Daniel Ahern 2005
3 Bob Allen
4 Roger Allingham in his South African Navy
  uniform
5 [left to right] Ron and Tom Bell outside the
  Helmsley Hotel, Cape Town, 1970
6 George Bridges, Trafalgar Square, 1967
7 Eric Caddick holding banner on left

8 Mary Chamberlain
9 Bob Condon with his wife Mavis
10 Seán Edwards
11 Sean Hosey
12 Gordon Hutchins
13 Ronnie Kasrils 2003
14 Ken Keable 2011
15 Jo Lewis and Mike Harris in action, 1990
16 Norman Lucas
17 Steve Marsling
18 Bill McCaig 2001
19 'Alice McCarthy', Signal Hill, Cape Town,
   14 February 1970
20 Mike Milotte 1970
21 Alex Moumbaris
22 Marie-José Moumbaris

23 Bob Newland 2012
24 Pat Newman
25 George Paizis 2010
26 Ted Parker
27 Dr Ron Press
28 Lucia Raadschelders, Swaziland, 1987
29 John Rose 2004
30 Stuart Round in the Africa Hinterland truck
31 Danny Schechter, Occupy Wall Street, 2011
32 John Simpkins
33 Pete Smith with Ronnie Kasrils at launch of
   Armed and Dangerous, 1993
34 Denis Walshe
35 Gerry Wan
36 Graeme Whyte

37 Stuart Round and the Africa Hinterland truck in Malawi, needing repair

38 In Port Elizabeth c1989 fully loaded. Stuart Round is on far left, the others are all tourists

39 The truck at Liliesleaf Farm Museum at Rivonia

George Bridges

During the late 1960s and early 1970s, at the request of the African National Congress, a number of British Communists and Young Communists went to South Africa to carry out illegal surveillance and propaganda actions. They were risking heavy prison sentences and one, Sean Hosey, served five years in prison. In writing this I would like to pay tribute to the courage and strength of commitment of those who went.

I joined the Young Communist League at the age of 15 in October 1956, at a time when hundreds were leaving. From a longstanding Communist family tradition, I was well aware of the revelations about the Stalin era at the 20th Congress of the Communist Party of the Soviet Union, so I never fell into the worship of the USSR and Stalin that characterised Communists up until then. Although I generally supported the action of Soviet troops in Hungary I always hoped and believed that the Krushchev era would usher in the kind of reforms that would democratise socialist countries. Up until the invasion of Czechoslovakia this was a plausible position which I shared with most of my YCL comrades.

We had always seen ourselves as fierce opponents of racism in general and apartheid in particular. In 1967 as London Secretary of the YCL I was sent to a World Federation of Democratic Youth (WFDY) conference in Sofia. On the way out I was briefly detained by the police at Heathrow. They said I resembled one of the Great Train Robbers currently on the run but I was too short (at 5 foot 6 inches) so they let me go on my way. I have often since wondered if this was a pretext to keep tabs on me.

On the coach to the plane I met Ronnie Kasrils. You can generally tell immediately a kindred spirit. Ronnie had an infectious smile, great sense of humour and an iconoclastic view of authority which we shared. WFDY was a cumbersome body of largely ageing (in youth organisation terms) bureaucrats from existing socialist countries which tried to create an international front of youth organisations including young communists and other democratic and anti-colonial organisations. It organised regular World Youth Festivals of varying success over the post-war years and probably its main function was channelling funds and other support from the USSR to allied groups. (Although I can honestly say the British YCL never received any to my knowledge). The YCL were an irreverent bunch at the time and our nickname for WFDY was the 'World Federation of Bureaucratic Youth'. The WFDY anthem was 'One great vision unites us though remote be the lands of our birth'. We parodied this to 'One great schism divides us though remote be the date of our birth'. This was the time of the Sino-Soviet split and it dominated this conference and led to hours of pointless discussion. Despite this, Ronnie and I had a good time socially together at this event and it served a valid purpose – to bring young people involved in political activity together from different parts of the world.

Afterwards we met socially on a couple of occasions. Then Ronnie approached me in more serious vein. He explained that the situation in South Africa was getting really tough for the ANC and anti-apartheid movement. BOSS, the South African secret police, had cracked down on activists and long prison sentences were being handed out. Mandela had had a 25 year sentence confirmed. A certain defeatism was creeping in. On the other hand there was an opportunity for non-South Africans to enter the country fairly easily due to the boom in tourism. Would I be prepared to recruit YCL'ers to undertake illegal work in South Africa? He made clear the risks, and said it had been cleared with the Communist Party of Great Britain.

Although my first response was to agree enthusiastically, it did pose some moral dilemmas. The CPGB and YCL had nearly always operated in conditions of strict legality. There was sometimes some pushing and shoving on political demonstrations, but in general we respected legality (even bourgeois legality). In fact we tended to have a moralistic view of sexual behaviour and drug-taking, even in the Swinging Sixties, partly to avoid giving the police a justification for intervening openly in our organisation. Illegal political action in face of a fascist state was another issue altogether, and completely justifiable as the only expression of opposition. A few years before, the General Secretary of the YCL, Barney Davis, had travelled to Greece to distribute leaflets opposing the military dictatorship. So my conscience was clear on this score.

The other issue was danger to innocent bystanders – what became known as 'collateral damage' in Pentagon-speak. There is always a moral issue where political action involves a threat to the lives of others. While we were never pacifists, as YCL'ers we had never been called upon to inflict physical harm on others in pursuit of our political aims. This was a luxury afforded us because of the times we lived in and the political system which allowed a democratic process to unfold. It was this issue which Ronnie refers to in his autobiography *Armed and Dangerous* where he discusses the disagreements we had over whether it was easier to be a communist in Britain or in South Africa. I still aver I was right – to be called on to stand on the high road selling newspapers, trudge round knocking on doors, marching in the road carrying banners is as nothing compared to putting your life and liberty on the line faced with the armed wrath of a racist state. But it was not always so for British Communists. Towards the end of the Second World War, the Communist Party was urging its members to volunteer for the D-Day landings to set an example to others. The father of my best friend Mike Power volunteered and was subsequently killed in Normandy. No pacifism there then.

'Terrorism' is a slippery term which has acquired many different connotations. The classic opposition to terrorism enounced by Lenin, and Communists since, generally refers to the anarchist tactic of assassinating political leaders and other symbols of bourgeois society. This tactic was deemed ineffective and counter-productive and I would not have supported any move in this direction. It was never suggested, despite the many assassinations of anti-apartheid figures by BOSS. Terrorism as a designation to abuse the armed struggle of national liberation movements we also rejected. What we did was often called terrorism – but it is a long stretch from leaflet bombing, loudspeaker vans, transporting false documents, and surveillance of border crossings to the suicide bombings of today. So this issue did not arise in this case.

Nonetheless I wanted to get an assurance from Ronnie that the tasks our YCL'ers would be given would not involve violence to anyone or the danger of injury to bystanders. He agreed, and that resolved this issue.

The other dilemma was personal. I did not want to ask anyone to perform a dangerous task that I wasn't ready to do myself. I'm no hero and would have been terrified to have been asked to go myself, I readily admit. At the time I had a young wife and two young children as well as having a relatively high profile as a leading Young Communist. We agreed that we would only be asking those with little or no family commitments and who were unlikely to be publicly well known. That left me off the hook and I can't say I wasn't a little relieved. This feeling only increased my admiration for those who went.

I looked through the membership for YCL'ers who would fit these criteria. Ken Keable[34] happened to be the first one who came to mind and I was gratified when he readily accepted, and relieved when he returned safe and sound. When asked by Ronnie to find someone who could discreetly visit the border between South Africa and the then Southern Rhodesia, Dan Ahern seemed to fit the bill ideally and he did a great job.

After I was involved, these restrictions were not entirely adhered to and I wasn't entirely happy about this at the time.

The stories of the individuals who went will speak for themselves. They say that living in constant fear heightens your experience and I think this emerges in their accounts.

In his autobiography, Ronnie refers to his views on Dubcek and the Prague Spring. During our clandestine meetings in Central London pubs we had many hours of discussion on this. As he states, we greeted joyfully the changes which 'socialism

34 Other evidence shows that, in fact, Daniel Ahern was recruited before me. – Editor.

with a human face' heralded. It looked at last as though the renaissance of democracy in the context of a socialist system would vindicate all the reservations we had had about the Soviet Union and the heritage of Stalinism. I remember getting a phone call from the National Organiser of the YCL, Pete Carter, on August 21st 1968 about 8.00.a.m. saying 'they've done it.... They've invaded'. I think I knew in my heart of hearts then that the game was up, that the project that for me began in October 1956 was basically doomed. Although my soul mates and I in the YCL and CP soldiered on throughout the '70s and '80s, pinning our hopes on the Euro-communist surge, I think we knew it was over.

I think Gorbachev did his best but he arrived 20 years too late to save the socialist project.

I can partially understand why Ronnie was convinced by his seniors in the South African CP to believe in the necessity of 'defeating counter-revolution'. Apart from the ideological issues, there was a lot at stake for the South African CP if they broke with the Soviet CP. We know now, although I don't believe any of us in the YCL knew then, that the CPSU was channelling relatively large sums of money to the CPGB and presumably much more to the South African CP. It is not so much the fact of the solidarity, which could be justified, but the secrecy, which cannot. This was kept secret not only from the Soviet people, who could hardly be said to be so affluent as to afford it, let alone give their consent, but also the recipients (apart from the privileged few). The resentment I now feel, as someone who worked full-time for the YCL, in the time spent organising jumble sales, raffles etc. being entirely unaware of pots of money in an attic, unaccountable and arbitrarily distributed, is immense. What is worse, while during the sixties we were low-paid, no pension, etc., in the seventies, as the YCL and CP declined, some full-timers were hardly paid at all.

So after 1968 my relationship with Ronnie cooled somewhat as the bitter debates over the Soviet invasion of Czechoslovakia broke out in the CP and YCL. I moved on from the London

YCL and handed over to the new secretary, Bob Allen, who undertook the responsibility of liaising with Ronnie.

For obvious reasons I kept no records of my work with Ronnie, so I am hoping that with our collective recall the events are recorded accurately. One puzzle which I have never resolved in my mind is why, from our end, the security was never breached as far as we know. I guess there is a file on me and other YCL'ers somewhere in the security services, and being a small organisation there was plenty of gossip and rumour about what we were doing. MI5 have since boasted that they had a mole in the YCL leadership in the 60s, although I cannot guess who it could have been. Perhaps they did know but did not pass the information on to BOSS, although there is other evidence of collaboration.

Tragically one of our comrades, Sean Hosey, was caught in a trap resulting from a breach at the South African end.

Googling Sean's name, there are two sources which bizarrely accuse him, and a Greek, Alex Moumbaris, of unlikely, impossible acts. One was to suggest that non-South African whites were planning to take over the liberation struggle from indigenous blacks. The other was that Sean was involved in smuggling arms into South Africa as part of the armed struggle. Neither is remotely true. As far as Sean was concerned, all he was doing was carrying false documents which were intended for someone to be able to escape from South Africa – for which crime he received, and served to the day, five years in prison.

I think Sean was the last of the British YCL'ers to go on such a mission.[35] The situation in South Africa had changed and the opportunities for indigenous action improved.

Though clearly our contribution was a minor one, I like to think it was something we can be proud of. We spent much of the '60s marching against apartheid, picketing the South African Embassy and boycotting South African goods. YCL Executive Committee member Jim Brookshaw climbed onto

---

35 This assumption, which is not quite correct, reflects the long self-imposed silence by those involved until this book came to be written – Editor.

the roof of the Rhodesian Embassy and tore down their flag. Those brave YCL'ers, and others who went into dangerous situations, brought some cheer to the anti-apartheid forces in South Africa at a time when things looked bleak. We showed the apartheid regime that they were not invulnerable. The defeat of the apartheid regime was one of the few clear victories that the progressive movement can claim in the 20th century. Generally speaking what we set out to do as a YCL we did not achieve, although I am not ashamed of the efforts we made. We did the best we could.

THIS WAS NOT IN MY JOB DESCRIPTION!
Bob Allen, London YCL Secretary,
1969 to 1974

I became immersed in 'revolutionary politics' from an early age, thanks largely to my Dad, a passionate, life-long Communist. In 1960, I joined the Young Communist League, at the age of 15, adopting a whole new 'life-style' of political debate and action, believing, like other comrades, that we would change the world. There was a seemingly endless round of intense debates, meetings, campaigns and demonstrations, conferences, as well as periodic internal and external conflicts. All this was wrapped up in large doses of the '60s youth 'counter-culture', albeit in a particular 'right-on' form – or so we thought!

We seemed to inhabit a parallel universe, with a determined 'can-do' mentality. The 'struggle' and collective action was what mattered. This was fed by a simplistic world-view, the certainty of victory for socialism and communism. Peace and banning the bomb, stopping the USA's war on Vietnam, opposing racism and defending civil rights, ending apartheid in South Africa, defending trade unions, trying to create 'socialism with a human face', resisting the fascist coup in Chile and defending Cuba's revolution, above all, building a better world for ourselves and our children. It seemed like we were involved in it all! Were we naive? Yes. Were we idealistic? Yes, but why not? Was our 'political project' flawed? Undoubtedly so. Were we better people for participating in the struggle? Definitely! Did we change things? I believe so, although not quite as we envisaged in our original 'cunning plan'. Any regrets? One or two, but overall, I wouldn't have missed being involved for the world and the struggle against apartheid illustrates why, in my view, it was worthwhile.

In 1968, I met and married my soul mate Ros, a fellow teacher, and together we continued in the 'struggle'. Over the years, her contribution has been huge and, thankfully for me,

Ros has remained my wife and best friend for 38 years.

In 1969, I was made an 'offer' I couldn't refuse, the chance to leave a secure job in teaching, which I loved, to become a fulltime official for the YCL. I was largely financed by Ros, as my 'wages' were somewhat inadequate and irregular! No, I'm not complaining, as my five years working for the YCL and the same again for the Communist Party were an incredible experience – warts and all!

Thus in the summer of 1969, we moved to London and I took over from George Bridges, as London YCL Secretary – quite an impressive act to follow, especially for two supposed innocents from 'the North'. Shortly after, George and Jack Woddis, the Communist Party's brilliant International Secretary, made another offer I couldn't refuse. This interesting and unofficial addition to my job description entailed liaising with a certain Ronnie Kasrils. This apparent South African student was actually a leader of the then illegal South African Communist Party and the ANC's underground army, Umkhonto we Sizwe. My task? To identify and convince particular individual YCLers to go on covert missions to South Africa, to support their bitter struggle against apartheid.

To put it simply, I was asking others to put their lives at risk, in a country thousands of miles away from their homes. This was the reason we tried (not always successfully) to restrict the missions to those who were unmarried and without children. The risk for me was minimal, because fortunately, as a fulltime official, my supposed 'high profile' excluded me from consideration for such missions. The worst I could have expected from the British state was arrest and questioning by the police Special Branch. The other comrades faced possible arrest, torture and death. Each and every one was a person I respected and trusted, having already made major contributions to the YCL and yet, potentially, the ultimate sacrifice was now being asked of them. My admiration for them remains immense! For what it's worth, my heartfelt thanks to all of you – you know who you are.

To some people, this could sound like the stuff of 'Roy of the Rovers' or 'James Bond', but it wasn't at all like that! A very real difficulty, for me, was the considerable sense of responsibility for the volunteers' safety and the fact that I could not discuss this with anyone else, least of all Ros and close comrades. I have to admit I was racked with guilt and worry each time I helped send someone to South Africa, and then wallowed in relief on their safe return. Similarly I was deeply worried for Ronnie and the permanent terminal threat he faced from BOSS, the fascistic secret police of South Africa. However, he always appeared quietly unconcerned and just got on with the job, and history shows he did it superbly, just like the many other brave women and men involved.

Periodically, I would select a 'victim' and discreetly approach them about volunteering for covert activity, without saying what or where. If the conversation was going well, I would then be more and more explicit, until I finally popped the key question. Remarkably, the response was always the same – 'OK, I'm up for that!' Then I would arrange another 'public' and yet 'secret' meeting with Ronnie, usually in a particular pub near to Tottenham Court Road tube station. I would take a roundabout route to the station, to avoid being followed, than wander into the pub and stand next to Ronnie, without any indication we knew each other. During a brief conversation out of the sides of our mouths, I would give him a name and contact number for the next volunteer and he'd update me on any other relevant matter. Then one of us would leave, whilst the other would quietly depart later on.

After each of our 'assignations', I returned to my official job. Throughout this time, I would run the full gamut of emotions – excitement, fear, apprehension, worry, guilt, relief, but always with the conviction that we were part of a necessary and just cause. My recollection of some of the details is somewhat mixed, but the experience remains very vivid to this day!

I felt both humbled and proud to have been involved, if only in a small way.

Pete Smith

Pete wrote a much longer piece which he intends will be the beginning of his autobiography. I have cut it down drastically and edited it considerably for this book. This has been difficult, partly because Pete's account is not sequential, but mainly because his writing skills, (even with the benefit, I hope, of my editing) fall far short of the greatness of his deeds. The final text has Pete's approval. – Editor.

African National Congress and Young Communist League

I was born in 1949, the eldest of four children, into a working-class family in Southampton, then the third largest passenger port in the world. My father was the equivalent of a medical sister during the Second World War, based mainly in Italy, after which he worked in the meat trade, then the fruit trade, became a postman, working finally in the sorting office. He was the first communist postman in Southampton to be acknowledged for his role in the union on his retirement. When I was ten years old my mother took up work as a cleaner in hospitals, having completed her nursery task in the upbringing of the children.

I grew up on a purpose-built working-class estate, called Millbrook, next to the shipyards of Southampton dry dock. It was built just after the end of the Second World War. The countryside was a short walk away where you could participate in apple scrumping with your friends (we only got caught by the police once) and take a family walk during the autumn for the purposes of blackberry picking.

I failed my eleven-plus exam at primary school only to be sent to the 'lowest of the low' secondary modern technical schools. I surprised everyone, including myself, by coming out with six GCE '0'levels. I was diagnosed as a late developer but it was through my developing political consciousness that I recognised that unless I took school seriously I would not benefit in later years from studying at university. I would probably have never met Ronnie Kasrils either.

One of the books I studied at school was "Cry the Beloved Country" by Alan Paton.

I went on to a local grammar school where I obtained two GCE A' levels (Chemistry and Pure-and-Applied Mathematics) enabling me to go to the Polytechnic of North London to study for a degree in Chemistry, starting in 1968.

Having joined the Southampton Young Communist League branch I transferred to the branch in Islington, London, where I met Ken Keable. This led to my involvement with the African National Congress, working with Ronnie Kasrils for some 20 years, including from 1985 to 1990 permanently underground in Southern Africa.

In Ronnie's book *Armed and Dangerous. My Undercover Struggle Against Apartheid* he writes:

Chapter 14 'Disneyland', page 235.

Of additional concern was the knowledge the driver had of one of my longest-serving assistants, 'Vincent', a schoolteacher from London, whom I had recently brought to Swaziland. I had brought him out to give special assistance to Ebrahim, but felt that he should be withdrawn. When the Swazi police visited him a short time later to check on his passport and work permit, it put our decision beyond dispute.

Chapter 16 'Turning Point', Pages 278 to 281
Vincent, who had changed identity after his transfer from Swaziland, had prepared a safe house in Gaborone. Within a week of leaving Malanje we had Damien's unit assembled under its roof.

The plan was to fly the unit to Lesotho from where they would descend the Drakensberg Mountains as a climbing party and slip into one of the Natal nature parks. A contact would meet them at a hotel, and they would later link up with Susan. Heavy snows had fallen over Lesotho and their departure was delayed. Then the Motswana couple from whom Vincent had rented the house unexpectedly returned from abroad. They gave him a month's notice while they stayed with relatives, but were constantly dropping by. They were obviously disconcerted to find their home filled with bearded white males who might be mercenaries bent on destabilising Botswana. Vincent explained that we were a group of friends from Britain who were touring southern Africa. I was introduced as a publisher and the couple brought over a knowledgeable friend who grilled me on every facet of the profession. 'Vince', I said, 'tell your landlord you're taking your pals off on safari. We'd better be on our way.'

We had a second-hand Landrover, and for months Vince and I had been reconnoitring routes westward through the Kalahari desert and then south to the remote northern Cape border with Namibia. We loaded up with supplies and weapons and dodged the road blocks, permanently mounted by the Botswana Defence Force along the solitary national highway that runs like a spine along the country's eastern border with Zimbabwe and the Transvaal. This was the main MK infiltration route, and comrades often started by slipping across the Zambesi River by boat near Livingstone. Joe Modise had instructed me to investigate the Kalahari as an alternative.

I was at my happiest in the field away from headquarters and the interminable meetings. After being holed up in the Gaborone house, everyone in the vehicle was in high spirits and I was soon hooting at gaggles of ostriches showing us their heels along the dusty roadway. Botswana is a sprawling, dry country with scattered villages. The haunting Kalahari Desert stretches endlessly westwards from the handful of towns along the north-south highway.

We struck camp on the edge of the desert, near the diamond-mining town of Jwaneng. As dusk descended and we were enveloped in a star-studded sky, relaxing with mugs of coffee around a camp fire, the banter was carefree and confident. Some days later, back in Gaborone, I read in the local newspaper that Pik Botha, South Africa's Foreign Minister, had visited the Botswana Prime Minister's brother in Jwaneng on the same night as we were camping nearby.

Late the following afternoon, after a full day's precarious navigation along interminable sand tracks churned up by huge cattle trucks, and stopping at times to admire the ghostly salt pans shimmering in the desert heat, we arrived at a remote point on the border previously ear-marked for a crossing. The dried-out bed of the Molopo River forms the southern frontier with South Africa, a well-constructed border fence running alongside it. The scrubland of the area is supplemented by a fringe of bush along the river-course which provides additional cover and we parked the vehicle a kilometre from the crossing point. We were a couple of hundred kilometres north-west of the Army Battle School at Lohatla and I wondered how the Seventh Division was getting on with their exercise. If they were going to reinforce the units on the Namibian-Angola border, they would be overflying our position within weeks, as well as using the Upington-Windhoek highway south of us.

Meanwhile, I led my own invasion force through the scrub and thorn trees to the crossing-point. We lay on our bellies in the fading light and watched through field binoculars as a police vehicle drove along a gravel road on the South African side...

As soon as it was dark we moved off and began slipping over the fence. I left Vincent on the border with an AK-47 to cover us and, keeping low, escorted the unit half a kilometre up to the gravel road. We were armed with AKs and grenades and were ready for any eventuality. I placed two empty cans of Coca-Cola at the side of the road some 40 metres apart, by way of a signal for a vehicle that was due within ten minutes. I had contacted an operative in Johannesburg with whom I had worked out such a pick-up in an emergency. There was no way a unit could safely hike the 600 kilometres to Johannesburg in this terrain. We had no contact with the local people. Although after the 1990 lifting of the ban on the ANC, I discovered how militant the people of the Northern Cape, and other rural areas could be. We deployed in two groups and waited.

Long before it arrived, we heard the whine of an engine. Everyone crouched low as headlights appeared and in a cloud of dust a farmer's van sped by. I was pleased since we could do with a little traffic as a screen for our own vehicle. It arrived within

minutes, coming to a halt by the second can. I had a word with the
driver while the four scrambled inside. As the vehicle disappeared
I wished that I too was travelling to Johannesburg. For days I had
been considering accompanying the group to their destination – at
least for the weekend – figuring Modise would not get to know. In
the end, discipline prevailed over a desire to face the odds with the
unit.

So how does someone from simple working-class life as a youth,
leaving Southampton at the age of nineteen, find himself, at the
age of thirty-nine, on the other side of the Equator, lying on their
belly on the cool sand of the Botswana desert at night, staring at
small white pairs of shining eyes on the other side of the border
fence separating Botswana from South Africa, pointing a fully
loaded AK-47, ready to fire, waiting for the return of Ronnie
Kasrils on the South African side of that fence?

Well, I developed a political consciousness; unwittingly
I hasten to add, as a youth in Southampton. This began by
listening to my father's opinions in my early teens, as he
commented on the news, and guided by my mother's humanity.
How the Steel Was Tempered, a book by Nicolai Ostrovsky, was
to influence my revolutionary enthusiasm through which I
was to agree, without any reluctance, to assist Ronnie Kasrils.
The South African experience that followed was to temper that
enthusiasm into a deeper pragmatic understanding of Marxism
in later years.

On joining the YCL I had immediately recognised, on the
membership card, the extract from *How the Steel Was Tempered:*

Man's dearest possession is life, and since it is given to him to live
but once, he must so live as to feel no torturing regrets for years
without purpose; so live as not to be scarred with the shame of a
trivial and cowardly past; so live that, dying, he can say: 'All my
life and all my strength were given to the finest cause in the world
- The liberation of Mankind'.

I quoted this extract at my father's funeral. He died just
before the dawn of the year 2000 having celebrated his fiftieth

wedding anniversary in February 1999 and his eightieth birthday in August. There would be no further illuminating political discussions down the local pub with my father, a staunch supporter of Palme Dutt, that I would look forward to when I visited my parents during the holidays.

My father, as I have indicated, would always comment on the news on television, although I had no knowledge at the time that he was previously a member of the YCL in his youth and a member of the Communist Party of Great Britain in the army medical corps. I was only to learn that after I joined the Southampton YCL at about the age of sixteen. Further I was to find out that my father's father, my grandfather Harold Smith, was a member of the CPGB and a holder of the TUC medal for organising a strike on board ship during the Second World War and being marched off that ship at gun point.

At the secondary technical school, to prepare for an English lesson the teacher asked her pupils to bring into the school the daily newspaper their parents read. Well, I walked into the lesson, innocently not anticipating the impact, with a copy of the Daily Worker (now the Morning Star) and was immediately branded in a negative way as a communist. This was the trigger that directed my natural curiosity to find out what was so bad about being a communist.

During the last two years of my secondary school I developed a thirst for reading, which included: all the James Bond novels by Ian Fleming; a banned copy of *Peekskill* by Howard Fast (I shall never forget 'if you can change a cop's nature, you can change human nature'); *The Ragged Trousered Philanthropists* by Robert Tressell; David Guest (a lecturer at Southampton University who went to fight in Spain where he was killed) on Dialectical Materialism which I found in the house of my father's father; and several communist classics including *The Communist Manifesto*, Engels' *The Origin of the Family, Private Property and the State* and Lenin's *Left Wing Communism, an Infantile Disorder*.

Later on in London, whilst studying at the Polytechnic

of North London, I was to read all of Howard Fast's novels, followed by those of Emile Zola, and I came across a book, whose name escapes me, by Jack Woddis on Southern Africa. I also found a book entitled *The British State* by James Harvey and Catherine Harwood.

I was soon persuaded to join the Southampton branch of the YCL. This doubled its active membership to two. When Dave, the elder of my two brothers, joined soon afterwards this increased its active membership to three.

I soon became Branch Secretary and branch delegate to the 1967 bi-annual national congress of the YCL at the NUM holiday camp in Skegness. It was the only time in my life where I became a representative without any competition. In the space of two years we built the branch membership to forty strong. We also built the Hants and Dorset District Committee of the YCL, and I became its Treasurer, building active branches in Portsmouth, Basingstoke, Eastleigh and Bournemouth.

In the YCL we were preparing for the 1968 Ninth World Youth Festival, to take place in Sofia. The heroic liberation armed struggle of the Vietnamese people was to be highlighted at that festival and the YCL had embarked on a campaign to collect money to purchase bicycles to be sent to Sophia and handed over to the Vietnamese delegation. We had arranged for a comrade at Southampton University to provide a message written in the Vietnamese language. That message of solidarity from the Southampton YCL branch was transferred to a metal tag and fitted to each bicycle purchased.

At grammar school I found I had a natural talent for badminton. (This was to prove useful in Lesotho in 1978, passing the time whilst, unsuccessfully, trying to find work, and later on in Botswana in 1987, where I played against the national badminton champion, to help deal with the boredom of staying alone in a safe house for some three months. In the late 80s I also found myself playing tennis against Ronnie Kasrils at the Soviet Ambassador's residence in Lusaka, when we were both in town at the same time of course. The completion of the match, which Ronnie inevitably won, was followed by a social chat with the Ambassador over a bottle of Soviet vodka.)

In September 1968 I enrolled in the Polytechnic of North London, living in bed-sit land, above a pub. Unbeknown to me at the time that pub was a five minute walk from the London ANC Office. It didn't take me long to get involved in the National Union of Students at the height of its activities following the 1968 student riots in Paris. During my second year at the Polytechnic I had been elected as Vice-President for External Affairs and was involved in a series of sit-ins which led to one-third student union representation on the Academic Board of the Polytechnic. We also formed the first joint student/lecturer Polytechnic CPGB branch and by then I was an active member of the Islington YCL branch as well.

Also during the second year a Terrence Miller from South Africa arrived as the new Principal of the Polytechnic, which led to a further series of sit-ins and strikes to express solidarity with the Anti-Apartheid Movement.

During my first two years, September 1968 to July 1970, for Part One of my degree I opted to study Russian and Economics. I ended up getting a University of Exeter diploma in Russian. Obtaining a second class honours degree in July 1973 I began work at the Ozalid Company in Debden, Essex. By then I had done two missions in South Africa, the first with Ken Keable and the second with Bob Newland, and a couple of missions in Paris with Ronnie Kasrils. I was in regular contact with Ronnie, who persuaded me to move into teaching so that I would have more flexibility with longer holidays. Another factor was that the Ozalid company was about to send me to the Soviet Union for six months to set up an analytical laboratory, which Ronnie thought would jeopardise any further assistance I could give him.

In 1975, having already moved to live in the London Borough of Newham, I took up a teaching post at a local all-boys' school in that borough in September of that year. This was to completely change the future I had planned, from that of a trouble shooting analytical chemist travelling the world, and probably settling down to raise a family, to that of a fully seconded Divisional Secretary in Newham for the National Union of Teachers. (I now represent some 2,000 teachers and recently settled down with an understanding partner, but too old to raise a family.)

Just before I became a teacher I carried out a solo mission for Ronnie to Lesotho and another in 1978 when I met and got to know Chris Hani, who was sadly assassinated in Johannesburg not long after the ANC entered government.

Then in 1985 I was to join Ronnie to work directly under his command in Southern Africa until the end of 1999 when it became clear that the ANC's armed struggle was to contribute to the changing internal social-economic climate in South Africa resulting in the ANC taking state power. At the end of discussing this matter with Ronnie I indicated it was time for me to return and participate once again in the political struggle of the country of my birth.

I hope this brief account gives you a background to understanding my involvement with the ANC. It will certainly help and encourage me to complete my autobiography, to be titled 'Living under Sod's Law'. What happened to my political party membership? Well, in 1991 the CPGB dissolved itself and I joined the Labour Party. At the time I recalled my father's remark on my return, that the working class could not afford the luxury of two working-class parties.

Well, to the purpose of the book: an account of those involved in missions during the early 1970s, to help spread the word amongst the people of South Africa that the ANC was well and alive and, at the same time, allow the ANC space to rebuild its underground. Thinking about the period this book covers, the rebuilding of the underground was done with great speed and this is a tribute to the maturity of its leaders, of whom Ronnie Kasrils was one. I was to become a comrade and friend of Ronnie and over the years get to know his wife Eleanor and their two sons Andrew and Chris.

In giving this account I state that I have the greatest respect and trust for Ken Keable, with whom I undertook the first mission in 1970, and Bob Newland, with whom I undertook the second mission in 1971. We all had limited training and that should not be taken as a criticism of the ANC. It was a reality under which the ANC lived and was fully understood by all three of us. Ken and Bob, in discussions with me about missions, took seriously the nature of the mission and paid strict attention to the question of security. We were to make mistakes, but importantly report back our experiences and, in discussions with Ronnie, learn from those mistakes.

My apologies to Bob Newland that I might recall more about the mission I did with Ken Keable than with him.

I cannot recall how Ken asked me to join him on a mission to South Africa, other than that he told me he had done a solo mission about a year before. I do know we met through the YCL, becoming firm friends as well as comrades.

Our mission was to go to Durban to let off three leaflet bombs and a tape recording. I was introduced by Ken to Ronnie Kasrils. My first memory of the impact of a leaflet bomb was in our hotel room in Durban.

The story begins at Heathrow airport. We were booked on a BOAC VC10 plane to fly to Johannesburg via Rome and Nairobi, then changing at Johannesburg to fly to Durban. This was to be the first aeroplane flight of my life. I was still a student at the Polytechnic of North London and had not confided with anyone, except Ken and Ronnie, where I was going. There was no need to, even though my brother Dave was then living in Hampstead. The next thing that happened was to change my attitude to this.

I think the arrangement was to meet Ken at Heathrow Airport. When we went to book onto our flights Ken did not have his tickets. He had told me his cover story with his father that he was spending a couple of weeks with the Woodcraft Folk. Ken decided to go home and see if the tickets had been left there by mistake. In those days if you were late you could catch the next flight.

Whilst he was gone his name was announced over the public announcement system. I went to the appropriate place to be informed that his tickets had been found. I explained what Ken had done and asked if I could phone his home to tell him. They agreed but must have listened (unbeknown to me, and it didn't occur to me to check) to the telephone conversation I had with his father. I indicated to his father what Ken was doing and to inform him that the tickets had been found. On his return Ken told me the airport had rung (they must have thought my message somewhat strange) and that his father now understood his son was flying to Johannesburg. Ken's father then arranged to purchase a ticket to go to Johannesburg should things go wrong and we had ended up in prison. That we found out on our return.

With every subsequent mission I did I informed Dave, with strict instructions that, should I get caught, everything should be done to prevent my father attempting to fly out.

As far as I can remember, the flight went smoothly. On arrival in Durban we booked into our hotel. The name escapes me and I was only to visit Durban once again in 1986 for a few days.

We needed to hire a car. Ken was the driver as I was not to obtain a driving license until 1975, when I became a teacher and could afford the driving lessons. We hired a Renault. The first time we used it, having parked it in the hotel, it wouldn't start and it was only by accident that we found out the choke was incorporated with the movement of the accelerator. I was later to learn that these seemingly small things can be most important in determining the success of a mission.

We bought the appropriate materials, such as the buckets, which could not be hidden in the suitcase. We discussed the tape recorder and had come across a sort of cave, the archway of which was secured by an iron gate. Inside were what we assumed to be miners, all black of course. We decided the best thing to do was to purchase a bicycle, fit the tape recorder to it and chain it to a lamp post in such a way that the broadcast it emitted would be directed to those black miners.

That meant purchasing a box to hide the tape recorder to be placed on the bicycle. The cassette had to be spliced and a piece of string exiting the box to be pulled to start the recorder once the bicycle was secured to a lamp-post. For good measure the box had some white candles attached to look like dynamite with a message attached that disturbing this would result in its imminent explosion. The whole thing was wrapped in brown paper.

I do not recall the reconnaissance to place the leaflet bombs. However, they had to be tested to make sure the clockwork egg timer would work. First each bucket would be prepared. Of the two metal contacts that came together to send an electrical charge to ignite the gunpowder, only one had a plastic covering, the theory being that if the plastic covering was left in place it would prevent the circuit connecting when the two metal arms met at the end of the time delay associated with the egg timer. Of course, when it comes to doing the drop, the leaflet bomb is placed and only then is the plastic covering removed and the egg timer activated. Well, it was the evening before the drop. Sod's Law came into play and then went into reverse.

I am not certain if it was the first test or the third test. Anyhow, the bucket was set up and the timer released. The timer came to an end. The next thing we heard was a fizzing sound, even though fireworks were exploding outside the room. This shouldn't happen. Instinct took over and it was 'dive for cover!' The sound of one big firework echoed in the room. There were leaflets all over the room. Then came a knock on the door. Ken was quick to the door which he held just ajar for him to be seen but not the inside of the room. The conversation went to the effect that Ken had also heard the explosion and it must have something to do with the firework display outside. The person, whom I never saw, must have been satisfied, as the conversation came to an end and Ken closed the door.

Well, we cleared up the room and rescued the leaflets, placing them into the other two leaflet bombs. At least the leaflets wouldn't be wasted. The following morning, the day to carry out what we had prepared for, I woke up and the first thing I saw as my eyes opened was the pelmets associated with the windows looking out of the hotel room. On top of them were some more leaflets from the bomb that went off in our room the previous night. We had missed them in the clear-up. They were quickly rescued and added to the other two leaflet bombs. The first task that day was to purchase the bicycle. That was my job, as Ken was driving the car. I had the broadcast with me and went into a shop on the outskirts of Durban we had previously identified. I purchased the bicycle with cash, took it out of the shop and attached the recorder to the appropriate place at the back. A chain and padlock had previously been purchased to secure the bicycle to the lamp-post. Carefully, taking account of the surprising weight problem at the back, I cycled to the pre-arranged spot. In securing the cycle to the lamp-post I was interrupted by a policeman asking me what I was up to. I didn't tell him the truth and he was satisfied with the lie. As he moved away I pulled the string to set off the broadcast and proceeded to join Ken at a pre-arranged place to finish our mission and place the leaflet bombs for detonation.[36]

I was wearing a jacket which could be turned inside out and hadn't shaved for two days. This was deliberate as I was more exposed than Ken when purchasing the bicycle and securing it to the lamp-post. When we had placed the second leaflet bomb we parked near a store and I went into the toilets and came out with my jacket turned inside out. I got back into the car and, as we drove along, used a battery shaver to remove the stubble from my face.

I recall agreeing with Ken about wishing to go back and being able to bring back evidence of the impact of what we had done. On our return Ronnie informed us that our mission had been successful, though he asked why we had not chosen the railway station to place the broadcast. Yes, we did report the leaflet bomb going off in our hotel room, and the lessons learnt materialised in the next mission with Bob Newland; can you work out or

36 Pete's memory of some details differs from mine. It was a long time ago. – Editor.

guess the change that took place regarding the plastic covering? Even though Ken was an experienced electrical engineer he was never blamed for it. It wasn't until I spoke to him in May 2005, when he suggested the production of this book, having not seen or spoken to him since 1973 when I left Islington to move to Newham,[37] did I find out that he felt responsible. My first response was that he was not to blame and I explained the subsequent modification which would never have taken place if the leaflet bomb had not gone off in our hotel room.

So, a year later Ronnie approached me about a second mission, with Ken not being available. By then I had been working with Bob Newland who had recently joined the Islington YCL. I think by then we were sharing the same accommodation and had been involved in promoting the National Union of School Students.

Again I do not recall how I approached Bob to assist me, though you will see from his account how that was done.

Our task was to set off six leaflet bombs and post God knows how many letters, again hidden in false bottoms of similar suitcases. We set off from Heathrow on the same flight path as the mission with Ken. It was not until 1976 (I think that was the year) that I no longer had to transit in Rome.

Thinking about it, I must have spent more time in Johannesburg airport than any other airport in the world. I even think I have spent more time in Lusaka airport than Heathrow airport. Not bad for someone who is still just an ordinary working-class person? I digress.

We booked into the hotel in Johannesburg. It was the Victoria Hotel in Eloff Street.

We visited, and relaxed in a boat, in one of the parks, Zoo Park I think was its name (which I revisited in 1994 by myself and videoed the experience). We also went out for a drive to relax and ended up in Soweto, one massive black township on the outskirts of Johannesburg. That massiveness meant it was

---

37 I remember briefly meeting Pete twice during that period, at political events in London. – Editor.

a long time before we could find a route back. I think we also visited a few cinemas, which I was to do later on in my stays in Johannesburg to allow time to go by and check if I was being followed.

Well, as to the mission, we set about the reconnaissance to place the leaflet bombs. To practice, I remember taking a plastic bag behind a wall, stooping to pretend to do up my shoe laces, leaving the plastic bag behind as I stood up to continue my journey. There was just rubbish in the plastic bag and no one seemed to take any notice of me.

We bought the stamps and envelopes (spreading out the purchases over several shops), along with plain nail varnish. The latter was required for handling the papers to prepare the envelopes for despatch by the local post. It would last for about an hour, preventing finger prints appearing on the paper and envelopes, only to be replaced and allowed to dry before continuing stuffing the envelopes. A discussion took place about the posting of the envelopes – whether to put them in one central posting box or spread them out. It was resolved that distribution had a better chance of success, should they be intercepted, if we used several post boxes.

One evening when we were sticking stamps on the envelopes, using our own saliva, Bob was not feeling too well. I went out that night by myself to visit the Hillbrow television tower. I had not had the opportunity to visit the one in England. I was walking along, approaching Jouebert Park, singing quietly to myself. One could argue this was due to the current success of our mission, or the illusion created by licking so many stamps. The next thing that happened was that I witnessed an attempted drive-by shooting, dangerously close to me. Sod's Law, I thought.[38]

The next time I was to see a bullet exit a gun was in the Botswana Desert in 1988. As I opened the passenger-side door of an old Toyota Land Cruiser, the commander of the team I was with had just about finished the process of disarming

38 This incident is mentioned in Bob Newland's story. – Editor.

his weapon. He pulled the trigger which resulted in a yellow flame, like an active Bunsen burner, appearing in my eyes. He immediately apologised as he had forgotten to check if there was a bullet left in the barrel. I never saw that bullet and have no idea how close I came to feeling its impact.

Before placing the six leaflet bombs, we had to test each egg timer, but this time both metal pins that made contact when the timer had finished its cycle had plastic coverings. Did we get it right? Not one of them went off in our hotel room. Mind you, one had to remember to remove both plastic coverings otherwise the old theory might still work and the leaflet bomb would not go off where it was meant to.

On the day of completing the mission, yes, Sod's Law was to raise its head. I think we had placed two of the buckets as planned, only to come across police activity. Somebody else had been doing the same thing. Internal operatives, I thought. The plans were dropped and Bob now had the task of driving the car around and stopping to allow me to jump out, place a leaflet bomb, and jump back in.

The next morning we went for breakfast and I was reading the Rand Daily Mail. The report indicated that more than six leaflet bombs had gone off, one much to the annoyance of a female reporter. If she had taken one further step the leaflets would have been captured within her skirt which brought a smile to my face as I read it. I hasten to add that smile was simply a response to a leaflet bomb going off where I had placed it.

I think it was the next day we made our way to Jan Smuts Airport to return to England. Before checking in, Bob pointed out to me two members of the YCL. We decided to ensure we would not meet them and retreated upstairs where we could observe them. We then spotted another team, one of whom had been the Branch Secretary of the Southampton YCL when I joined in 1965.[39]

We observed them check in and proceed through the

---

39 This was Denis Walshe. Bob Newland also mentions Sean Hosey and Graeme Whyte. - Editor

departure lounge, leaving our departure to the last minute so that we would not make contact with them.

I returned to work at the Ozalid Company (having taken two weeks holiday), with a copy of the Morning Star reporting on those leaflet bombs going off in South Africa. That was the only mission I did with Bob. It was not long before he was involved in another operation (code name 'Operation Mother', as you will see from his account). My only role in that was to regularly check a house in Hampstead for correspondence which I would pass on to Ronnie. One day, when I was checking the mail while the owner was abroad, some other people entered the house and I had to hide under the kitchen table until they left.

I am now left with the two missions (I think it was two) that I did with Ronnie during the period this book covers. If my memory is correct this was during my second full time session at the Polytechnic of North London; September 1971 to July 1973.

This involved flying to Paris with Ronnie, spending a few days there and then returning carrying bags which had false bottoms hiding certain materials. I have to say it was a pleasant feeling being able to fool British Customs. The second time I had to return by myself, deliver the bags to Eleanor, Ronnie's wife, and then fly back out again, and return with him, again carrying the bags with false bottoms. We got to know each other very well. I was just a courier and was not always told what I was carrying. Some of it was explosive materials for the leaflet bombs to be made in London, sometimes it was sterling currency in large amounts. I am fairly sure that a man I met briefly in Paris with Ronnie at that time was Joe Slovo, though I was not told his name. I was to meet him properly much later.

As I have already indicated, I was to continue my close association with Ronnie. I will mention one amusing story, about my passport. They are valid for 10 years and when it came to my second mission with Bob Newland I had to change my passport, because it had a German Democratic Republic visa stamp on it. I couldn't renew it as it was still valid.

Discussions took place about what should be done, which included giving it to a dog to tear apart. I decided using black ink to spoil it. I took it, so blackened, down to Petty France[40] and they agreed to replace it. In 1975 I had to change it again, when it was still valid. This time I left it in my clothes as they were cleaned in an automatic washing machine where I was sharing a house with a married couple. The outcome was barely recognisable, but the wife of the married couple was not very happy with the impact it had on her new washing machine. I again proceeded to Petty France with what was left of my passport and they kindly responded by providing me with a new one. In 1978 I had to change it again and placed it in a dish of glue. I transferred the passport soaked in glue into a clear plastic bag and yet again took it along to Petty France. And yet again they provided me with a new passport.

I have often wondered if anyone at Petty France looked at the record of my passport or the South African Authorities questioned a Peter Smith from England visiting them in 1970, 1971, 1974 and 1978; each time with a new passport and each new passport having a ten year life span.

I was to repeat this trick one more time in 1986 at the British High Commission in Lusaka, when I had to leave Swaziland and move to Zambia. Subsequently there was no need for me to do this, as within a year I was travelling in and out on three different passports, one giving me an age 10 years younger. I know that many people at the age of 40 onwards would wish to prove they were ten years younger.

I believe the YCL trips had finished by then but I still kept in touch with Ronnie and did two further solo missions for him. The first was in 1976, to deliver a Fortnam & Mason's box with plastic explosives to Lesotho. I had to remember the face of someone on a London tube train, getting on and off after two stations on the Central Line, with Ronnie indicating the individual involved without the individual or I acknowledging

---

40 Where the Passport Office is situated, in London. – Editor.

one another. He was a white ANC member who was nicknamed 'the Professor'[41] I think, and I was later to stay with him in Bristol for a few days and learn how to make leaflet bombs and hide materials in cans and aerosols. I then flew to Nairobi and met this man outside the main post office, again not making contact. He had the Fortnam & Mason's box with him. He then walked away without taking it and I took it with me to Johannesburg airport, where just the first layer was checked by customs. I hired a mini, taking the box in the boot of the car and drive to Lesotho. I unloaded the box at the hotel and delivered the appropriate material to a deputy head teacher, Chris Hani's wife I believe, at a local school.

The 1978 mission was started by Ronnie, but he left for Southern Africa permanently before it was completed, and I began to work with Aziz Pahad. I had to smuggle a lot of English currency (there was a limit on exporting sterling at the time) in a briefcase, flying from London to Maseru, staying at the same hotel and met by Chris's heavily pregnant wife. I was given details of where to meet Chris and clandestinely give him the cash.

On both occasions I tried to find employment (each time having resigned my teaching post) but was unsuccessful.

There were two other missions arranged by Aziz, though I do not recall when as they never materialised. For the first, I recruited a white female member of the YCL. If the mission had gone ahead we would have driven a caravan, with weapons hidden in it, through Botswana into South Africa, posing as a honeymoon couple. The second was to interview (after being briefed by Joe Slovo and 'the Doc',[42] in a pub in Tottenham Court Road) a high ranking ANC comrade, whose name escapes me after all this time, who had just been released from Pretoria Prison. The purpose of the interview was to bring back a report about the situation of other comrades inside. I remember meeting Aziz to pick up the money to buy the air tickets only to

41 Dr Ron Press has confirmed that this was he. – Editor.
42 Dr Yusuf Dadoo. – Editor.

be informed that the mission had to be cancelled because three comrades had just escaped. One was left to wonder what would have happened if it had taken them a few more days to escape. I was to meet Tim Jenkin, the one who prepared the wooden keys, in Swaziland in 1986 and retell the story to him.[43]

Nothing further happened until 1985, when I received a message from Ronnie to go out permanently, as arranged by Eleanor, Ronnie's wife.

I left London at the end of August 1985 and within two weeks I was in Swaziland. I became a teacher at a secondary school there and undertook numerous missions into South Africa, which consisted of military reconnaissance and delivering illegal materials to dead letter boxes. For a while I stayed at the house of June and Michael Stephen, who were in Swaziland working for the ANC.[44] In early 1986 I shared a house with Ebrahim.[45] (June and Michael had smuggled him out of South Africa by hiding him in their vehicle). Ebrahim and I had many enjoyable evening hours of political discussion (he was studying the works of Kim Il Sung at the time) for some three months. He was supposed to leave with me but decided, against orders as I understood it, to stay on, and he got arrested. The next time I met him was in 1994 in the House of Parliament in Cape Town as his guest; he was then a Member of Parliament. I had received a tax rebate which paid for a six week trip to South Africa in the summer holidays of 1994. His political brain was still sharp as we relaxed, taking our time drinking tea in the parliament's restaurant.

By June 1986, the police visited the school where I taught, having stopped a car that I used to own, with weapons being smuggled into South Africa. I then left for Zambia.

Most of my time in Zambia was spent on the ANC Farm and in October I was sent to Cuba for three months training

43 See *Inside Out – Escape from Pretoria Prison* in Appendix 4. – Editor.
44 See Appendix 1- Editor.
45 Ebrahim is the man mentioned by Ronnie in the quotation on the first page of this chapter. He is Ebrahim Ismael Ebrahim, who entered parliament in the ANC victory in 1994. – Editor.

as a counter-intelligence officer in a police training camp. That also had its funny side, including being hospitalised after Karate training; I was too old to do that. In fact when I came out of the hospital they put me back on Karate training only for me to end up in there again, much to the annoyance of the sister. An interesting fact was that it did not take long to disregard the colour of skin – you forgot there were black and white Cubans and just saw them all as Cubans.

1987 and 1988 saw me in Botswana, with the same four-wheel drive Toyota Land Cruiser, setting up two safe houses. I was to enjoy the peace and tranquillity, sometimes two weeks long, in the Kalahari Desert.

Towards the end of 1988 I was in the Soviet Union being trained by the Red Army as an intelligence officer and being observed by the KGB. The political education classes were interesting as one lecturer was supportive of the changes taking place and another was not.

1989 saw me back in Zambia, which became my base for carrying out missions into South Africa, some of which had to be cancelled at the last minute. By the end of 1989 I was staying in a safe house in Zimbabwe awaiting a mission to Cape Town, a place I had never been to, and wondering if I would get to visit Table Mountain. Whilst waiting in the safe house I studied Lenin; there was a bookshelf with his collected works. In particular I had the time to study his 'new economic policy' and things began to fall into place.

It became clear that changes were to take place in South Africa and I went back to Zambia where I met Ronnie and informed him that I felt there was no longer a role for me and it was time to pick up in England where I had left off. I was given the choice of staying on in South Africa but that was not for me. Roger Allingham, a white English colleague, underground in South Africa, whom I had met in Botswana in 1987 and worked with for two years, decided to stay on and joined the South African Navy.

In 1985, when I left London, I was the Divisional Secretary

for the Newham Teachers' Association (part of the National Union of Teachers) about to be seconded full time. I returned in 1990 and by 1992, and ever since, I was elected again as the NTA Divisional Secretary, but this time full-time seconded.

I am honoured to have been asked by Ronnie to assist him in his work for the ANC. I still try to make sure, when I go into a restaurant, to sit with my back to the wall and when I am driving I still automatically check whether I am being followed.

'Alice McCarthy'

Editor's note: Alice McCarthy is not her real name. Her former partner, with whom she went to South Africa, wants anonymity for professional reasons, and she is using a false name to protect his identity.

Where to begin? I joined the Communist Party in 1967. My partner had been approached to go to South Africa soon after we had got together. He worked for a bookshop, and I worked as a telephonist. My partner, whom I shall call James, I seem to recall, was first approached by a party member called Dave,[46] but James can't remember his name. (Time has somewhat placed a mist over events in our minds, James and I have laughed at the fact there are parts which are very clear and others not so). James had agreed to go out to South Africa before we had started to live together, so he suggested to Ronnie we should both go. Ronnie was not very convinced – after all, I was an unknown and a new party member - but he agreed to meet me. I don't think I struck Ronnie as a woman with a revolutionary commitment. He looked at an Eastender who at the time wore false eyelashes and the shortest of mini skirts – not the image of a communist intellectual. Ronnie did however agree I would go with James (I believe after talking it through with James). Our training sessions began when we met Ronnie at offices off Oxford Street. Our first assignment was to be in a town called Port Elizabeth. We were to place buckets of leaflets at the bus station. The buckets held a small explosive device with a timer, which would scatter the leaflets, giving a dramatic effect at the crowded bus station at the end of the working day. Ronnie showed us how to set the timers and how to use the right amount of explosive, also talking through with us the right times to place these at the bus station. James and I both phoned in sick because to apply for leave may have in time been traced! Ronnie had said we were not to tell anyone about our movement, but

'James' later confirmed that this was David King. – Editor.

we were homeless at the time and had been kindly given a room in a house of a comrade. He had three teenage children living at home at the time and one other at university and we felt his wife was quite surprised when we turned up one night with him. (We felt indebted to our comrade, and the family got used to this odd couple sleeping in his small study.) We did tell him we were going into South Africa. We trusted him fully. He had been in the Communist Party since a youth after fleeing from Nazi Germany and we thought it only right he should know. (He never mentioned it on our return or ever – not one question in all the years we knew him).

Speaking to his wife recently about this book she was so surprised to hear about the events, and smiling said 'well that was another secret he took to his grave'.

On a cold winter's day we set off for Heathrow Airport to fly to South Africa. I had never been on a plane before. Ronnie had supplied us with two hold-alls with false bottoms in which was stowed the timers and explosives. In a hidden compartment in a suitcase lay the leaflets. We arrived in Johannesburg, then flew to Port Elizabeth and hired a car.

Pulling into a garage for petrol, we witnessed a car being driven at full speed trying to hit a black South African. It was terrifying, in such a confined space. James had to hold my arm, reminding me not to react but to think about what we had in the boot of the car. We got out of the garage pretty quickly, only to drive down the wrong way of a one way street. James turned the car around calmly and we moved off sedately but terrified. I was not psychologically prepared for such things. Witnessing someone trying to injure or kill another person was not within our experience (not that growing up in East London did not hold for me its own level of violence at times). I realize, thinking back, that I must have been a bit of a liability in the first few days.

In Port Elizabeth we stayed in a small hotel for two nights and then rented a beach apartment, which was on the edge of town and secluded. We could assemble our buckets without interruption.

James felt it would be better if he went to place the buckets on his own. It would not attract attention, a single white person in a bus station full of black workers returning from a day's work. We had not thought this through – I did stay behind to wait but began to realize I did not have a proper escape plan. James and I had discussed that in the event of him not returning by nightfall I was to leave and make my way back to Johannesburg and home to England. But I did not have the car; James had taken it (he could not have walked through the streets of Port Elizabeth with our 'buckets'.) He had not taken any identification with him. Sitting and thinking, I decided if he did not return in the given time I would have to burn his passport, return ticket and clothes and then walk to town and get a taxi to the airport. But I did not have much money even though I had a return ticket. How to get out?

James did return. We both felt very good with what he had achieved but spent a restless night and left early in the morning to return to Johannesburg and on to London. We had carried our clothes and few belongings in the hold-alls with the false bottoms. We did not have enough money to dump these, so we returned with our clothes in them. Where we had removed the false bottoms there was a distinct line of glue around the inside a couple of inches from the bottom. We just had to take the chance that they would not be searched. They were emptied and searched at Heathrow but no comment was made; the inspection was for contents – we only had grubby clothes. (We used these hold-alls for many years as our weekend bags.)

Our next trip was by ship into Cape Town and flying back from Johannesburg. The assignment was a massive posting and to contact someone in Lesotho. Once again a false bottom held the materials to be posted but it was a very large sea chest this time. I remember taking it in turns to buy hundreds of stamps at different places/ post offices. It was a relief to arrive in Cape Town. I had been very sea sick for most of the trip. Cape Town was such a beautiful city. I did not feel the same edginess I had felt in Port Elizabeth. We stayed in an apartment in an area which was considered to be a 'good area'. The woman who managed the apartment insisted (barking in Afrikaans) that the 'maid' (a worn-out middle-aged black woman) carry our entire luggage up to our apartment, which was on the first floor. Of course the sea chest was far too heavy for two people, let alone one worn woman. James and I made a joke about having brought all our household things from England, as we did not intend to return but were going to settle in the Cape. When the owner went back into her house, we three (the 'maid', James and I) struggled up the stairs with our heavy secret. Ronnie had practised with us how to write the addresses. I can remember his dismay with me, 'Alice - no curves please, remember!' he said again and again. It's not easy to change one's given way of writing, at least for me. The posting was such a good way to extend the idea that there was a massive movement 'out there' ready and willing to bring down the apartheid system. There was a mass movement, but many had been locked away, murdered or forced to flee, living in exile. Therefore any support for the committed and determined South Africans (both black and white), who were not going to allow their beautiful country to continue to be a place without morals or compassion, was a positive contribution. We stayed in the flat writing addresses, putting the literature into the envelopes and sticking on hundreds of stamps. But we had a problem: we had to hide our work because each morning the 'maid' came, wanting to clean and cook. We said she would not be needed for a few days but she said (with eyes downcast) 'Mrs would not like that'. We did not want to jeopardise her so we hid our work in the bedroom and kept it locked and said we were eating out every day, enabling her to go early so we could get on with the work at hand. The posting went well but was not so easy. James and I drove to as many mailing places as we could find. It rained very heavily, which was good for us – riding around in a car loaded with so many packets of post might have drawn attention. There were packets on the back seat, covered over, and the boot was packed as well. It was a great relief to get it all finished.

The other part of our work was to go into Lesotho to contact someone. We had a letter to give and a message. I think we flew into Bloemfontein and hired a large Mercedes car to take us into Lesotho. Bloemfontein was like stepping back in time. There seemed to be very few women about and it was so very quiet and watchful (or was this me again?) We drove to Lesotho, pleased to leave Bloemfontein behind. The first checkpoint was with the South African border guards who asked us to step inside the hut to check our passports and wanted to know why we were going into Lesotho. They checked the boot of the car as well – I think we had to open our bags. Then we crossed the bridge into Lesotho. On the other side there was the Lesotho guard on his own – he seemed to jump out of his hut, the gun coming first (a rifle). He was very tall with a huge smile; he took our passports but did not check the car. He also asked us why we had come to Lesotho. Again we repeated we heard Lesotho was a 'must' visit if doing a tour of South Africa. (I am not sure if he kept the passports). He said we had three days to stay – if we wanted to stay longer we must go out back across the bridge and re-enter! We did not question this.

We realised we were the strangers in town – people were staring at us. We checked into the only place to stay, an inn/hotel. Ronnie had advised us to go to the post office to find the address of the person we were to contact, not to ask about him – this would draw too much attention. I think he was a solicitor. The post person showed us the place to go, which was not difficult for it was such a small place. It was an office with a few people waiting. A woman came out of a back room looking very surprised to see these two white strangers. We said we wanted to speak with Galakie Sello - we needed advice. She said he was not in. We sat down saying we would wait, we did not intend to leave the office without seeing Galakie. Going out and then returning would only have drawn unwanted attention. She left the room and, coming back, asked us to wait in another room at the back of the office.

When Galakie came he looked at us very uncertainly. We also were on edge and by now very tired. We handed him the letter and I think we gave him a code name. He relaxed and with a big smile shook our hands warmly. He told us to follow him to his house – he did not want to talk in the office. The message we had for him was to leave Lesotho and meet up with others. At his house he showed us his large car, a Mercedes (one could not be up to conspiracy driving around in a Mercedes, could one?) He said that each week his wife drove out of Lesotho, getting the guards used to her coming and going. His plan was to leave in the boot of the car one day. We agreed not to talk at any personal level, as the less we knew of each other the better. But he knew we were English and thanked us for coming 'all that way' but advised us to leave as soon as possible as strangers drew too much attention to themselves. We planned to leave the next day. That night in the Lesotho inn was one of the most frightening experiences for me, we were so exhausted but all through the night there were gun shots very close, as if there was a gun fight going on outside the window. We left the next morning, not using up our three-day pass.

Returning to London, we met with Ronnie and talked through with him all our experiences (we now had a place to live, a flat.)

Shortly after our return Ronnie asked if we would think about going back to open an import /export business. We said we would think about this. We decided not to take this up. Going in and out was one thing but to live 'by choice' would be another. Also it was to be the end of our trips into South Africa because I answered the phone one day to hear a heavy South African accent asking to speak with James and Ronnie using their full names. He said he would ring back. We contacted Ronnie. He came over with his partner, Eleanor. Ronnie spoke to them. It was the South African secret police, Ronnie said, up to their usual intimidating tricks. He advised us to change our number and go ex-directory. We never found out how they got hold of our number or that we knew Ronnie. I only read

Ronnie's book two years ago. I was very moved by the events and his commitment to the struggle and only now realize what a lucky escape Eleanor made.

I feel this time and experience was a turning point for me in so many ways. There we were in England able to campaign openly, for a way of life without fear of imprisonment. We were members of the Marx Memorial Library, James was in the Young Communist League but we decided to join our local Communist Party branch as well and became more active in our local community. I joined a group of women to open the only women's aid centre. James and I took part in so many issues at that time, both national and international, and of course selling the Morning Star (very interesting selling outside tube Stations late on a Friday night!). I made life-long friends in this close committed political group. I had left school in the East End of London at the age of 15 years and worked as a machinist in Brick Lane and Middlesex Street for 9 years before becoming a telephonist. I had my first child, a son, in 1970 at the age of 28. Stopping work to be with my son gave me the opportunity to 'move on', in my way of looking at life and just 'being'. (I had another child, a daughter, in 1973). I began to take GCSEs at night classes, but the comrades said this would take forever – 'Sit the London University entrance exam'. I was not confident about this, but they insisted, so I applied and sat the exam. To my surprise (not theirs) I passed and used this to do teacher training. I was only there a week (having said to the comrades I cannot be active, I really must get my head around this course) when the student union occupied the college because of cuts taking place in education. I joined the communist student branch. How I ever got through my teacher training I don't know. After many years of working as a teacher, and more studying through the Open University (with much encouragement and support from my present partner) I became a Head Teacher of a large primary school (as the song goes 'it's a long way from here to there'). I took early retirement in 1998. I am fortunate to have taken part in a small way in the struggle of the South African people.

I still live close to where Ronnie Kasrils used to come with his big smile, patience and encouraging words, always optimistic and absolutely convinced that the people of South Africa would overcome those terrible times to construct a 'state of South Africa' based on Liberty and social commitment.

Eddie Adams

My direct involvement with the South African struggle started in 1969. Previously I had been London District Organiser of the YCL. Then I had been one of those taking the YCL Medical Aid for Vietnam coach around different parts of Britain. I was also involved in trying to stop our local authority, Kensington & Chelsea, investing in the apartheid state as the chair of West London Anti-Apartheid Group.

George Bridges approached me and this led to a meeting with Ronnie Kasrils, a South African comrade. I readily agreed to go – perhaps too quickly. The first part of my introduction to what was needed was a training session with Ronnie in an empty office in Charlotte Street W1. We crouched behind some desks while he explained and showed me how to operate a street broadcast. The second session related to what we called 'leaflet bombs'. These consisted of a domestic plastic bucket with a platform over a tube with explosive powder in it. On the platform was a pile of propaganda leaflets. This was set off by a timer of the type used by motorists which you set when they parked their cars. They buzzed when your parking time was up. This device would send leaflets a hundred feet into the air.

On reflection, this type of leaflet bomb must have been new because Ronnie arranged for us to go to Richmond Park for a try out. We tramped to what we thought was quite a remote part of the park, but every time we were ready to have a go, up popped a courting couple. This continued and it was much later when we found an empty area. Things didn't go to plan. Instead of going up, it went horizontally like a rocket, and made what seemed to us a very loud bang. We then realized it was getting dark, and the gates to the park were being closed.

We made our way back to the parking area, which was some distance away. Luckily there was a park warden there who was only interested in clearing the park, not what we were up to, and directed us to the one open gate.

On my next briefing with Ronnie I was given a suitcase which had a false bottom and some money and I was warned about picking up any women, particularly if I wasn't sure of their ethnicity. To be seen with anybody other than a white woman could compromise the mission. My task was to post, internally, letters that I had in the false bottom of my suitcase, let off a couple of leaflet bombs and organise an illegal broadcast.

I had to have certain inoculations for my trip and I approached Steve Fisher, a local Communist Party doctor. I couldn't tell him what I was doing but I made it clear it was for the movement and he obliged. I booked my ticket and made my way to Heathrow. I passed through customs and was waiting in the departure lounge when all of a sudden I was approached by this plain clothed man. I immediately realized who he was and he asked to see my passport. It was then that it came home to me that it listed me as a youth worker (YCL fulltime) and it showed me wearing a YCL badge! Not too clearly, luckily.

Before he could ask me any questions, I said 'I've given all that up now'. I didn't explain what I had given up but I felt we both knew what I was talking about, and I added, 'I am taking a short trip to South Africa to see if there is any chance of getting a job and starting a new life there'. He smiled, nodded, gave me my passport back and left.

I tried to imagine what would follow this encounter. My immediate thoughts were: should I abandon the trip or take a chance and continue? I was very nervous but I decided to continue. Our first stop was in Italy – Florence I believe. We stopped for a couple of hours, and I sent a cryptic message back to Ronnie saying I thought I had been rumbled.

We stopped again at Nairobi and I remember us passing Kilimanjaro with its snow covered top. At Cape Town I sailed through customs with no problems.

I booked into a hotel not far from the centre. It was run by an Indian family but the clientele was white. As agreed, I attempted to send a telegram to Ronnie to tell him I had arrived safely. Entering a post office, I saw an empty counter and went up to it. The person behind the counter, instead of serving me, started shouting at me. The more I tried to explain what I wanted the more he shouted. In the end my nerve gave out and I walked out, puzzled by what had happened.

Finding another post office, I studied it closely before trying to get served and realized that I had tried to get served at the blacks-only counter. This time I was able to send my message.

The next day I started to reconnoitre Cape Town. I walked into the biggest building in the city and asked if I could go up on the roof and have a look around. They said 'yes' and gave me a guide. I took photographs, and got a good idea of the town's layout.

I also went up Table Mountain and visited the old colonial fort. Then I got down to making the broadcast. I purchased a speaker and visited a do-it-yourself shop. I bought wood to make a box and very strong mesh to protect the speaker, and chains and padlocks to secure it so that no one could halt the broadcast before it had finished.

I had to make up the material in my hotel room. This wasn't easy; a lot of sawing and banging might raise suspicions about what I was doing. So I spread it out over a period of time. Each morning the rooms were cleaned, and I had to make sure I hid the materials from sight.

I had noticed that in the evening the road alongside the main Cape Town Railway Station was filled with thousands of mainly black workers going home. Above the station there was a car park overlooking this road. I made my way to this car park, climbed over the railing on to the ledge above the road and secured the loudspeaker to the railings. To start the broadcast there was a small hole with a wire protruding. I pulled this and beat a hasty retreat.

My first bucket bomb I placed in a small alcove next to a phone box not far from the Parliament Building. As I walked away I had only got about 400 yards when it went off.

I turned, and saw the leaflets make a perfect column about 60 ft high in the air, then taken by the wind, and scattered. Within minutes they were being picked up.

The following day I found a small market area, though I cannot remember exactly where it was. This time I placed the leaflet bomb, which I was carrying in a shopping bag, into a wastepaper bin. This seemed to me a perfect cover. I didn't wait around for it to go off! My mission was now complete. I had posted the letters shortly after my arrival in Cape Town, so I spent a couple of days sightseeing while I waited for my flight home. On arriving home I had acquired a slight tan which didn't quite fit in with my story that I had been visiting relations in Leeds.

Eddie has checked his passport and found that he arrived in South Africa on 7 Nov 1969 – Editor.

Eddie Adams and John Simpkins

The following year, 1970, I was approached again by Ronnie Kasrils about another trip to South Africa. This time he asked me if I could recruit somebody to go with me. I approached John Simpkins, a friend and member of the YCL. He readily agreed. Ronnie again gave us some training in an office near Tottenham Court Road. He was a little concerned that both of us had been on TV in relation to a local protest. We had to have yellow fever injections. This time we cut our hair short and wore suits; the idea being that we were supposed to look like businessmen.

From the previous trip we realized we had made a few mistakes. Flying directly to South Africa could raise suspicions with the wrong people so John and I visited Air France in Piccadilly. We booked our destination via Paris and this gave us a night in Paris and meant we left from the European departure building. Armed with our false-bottomed suitcases, which contained leaflets, timers, glass tubes, explosive powder and radio cassettes, we left for Paris. In Paris we had a good night out, but had difficulty finding our way back to the hotel!

This time the plane stopped at Nice. The runway was next to the sea and it looked very beautiful. Our next stop was Brazzaville in the Congo. It was a tropical night with lots of insects, drums in the distance and heavily armed guards looking bored with life.

At Johannesburg airport we were checked by two very big immigration officers, but it was okay. Our taxi driver was white, and a local Boer. We told him we wanted a cheapish hotel. He took us to the Johannesburg market area. The hotel looked more like a warehouse than a hotel. It was cheap and we thought, at the time, ideal. We were amazed at the number of lamb cutlets offered us at breakfast and the big steaks with pineapple and salad for lunch.

Buying the materials we needed for making the speaker boxes was fairly easy. The one difficulty we encountered was that we needed a Philips tape recorder and this proved difficult to locate. John remembers we found one in a small shop which looked as if it was about to close down. It seems they had been pushed off the market by cheaper Japanese products.

Our next step was to hire a car. I had got myself an International Driving Licence before we left London and we hired a Mini which I was used to driving. We drove out of Johannesburg and the countryside (veldt) had a wispy sort of beauty.

Back at the hotel we started to make our speaker box and bucket bombs. I believe we made four bucket bombs and one speaker box. The next day we set off to a pedestrian underpass near an elevated roadway.

We parked on an empty building lot and were messing about getting our stuff organized in the boot of the car. John closed the boot and I for some unknown reason dropped the keys of the car in, just a second before he closed it. My mind must have been somewhere else. We had to leave the car and go back to the hotel and ring the car hire firm. Luckily they explained that if you took the back seat of the car out there was only a curtain between that and the boot. We were delayed but relieved.

A lot of people passed through the pedestrian underpass at home time. There were road works and lots of material lying around which proved to be a good cover for our bucket bomb. I seem to remember we had got some distance away when it went off, making a very loud bang. This was mainly because the sound waves hit the underneath of the motorway above and echoed all over the place.

It was reported in the *Rand Daily Mail* on the 14 August 1970, in relation to the leaflet bomb near Faraday Station, that a Mr. Samuel Nkosi, a council night watchman guarding building equipment near the scene, said: 'I was about seven paces from the explosion. Lots of paper shot into the sky and some were hurled as high as the overhead motorway.'

On returning to the hotel later that day another problem loomed up. John and I noticed that the hotel lighting was dimmed, and that a number of oldish looking business men were coming into the hotel around about dusk, accompanied by African women. It was obvious that the apartheid laws were being flouted. We realized that this was a dangerous situation for us. The police might raid the hotel at any time, and we decided that we would have to find another hotel.

We moved to a modern hotel more in the centre of Johannesburg and we felt a lot safer. We found a market area known as Diagonal Street for our next bucket bomb, which we placed near a telephone box. The next day one of the daily newspapers (*The Rand Daily Mail*) complained that it had gone off near their rival's office so the following day we placed our forth bucket bomb near their office. This time a security person saw it and took it into the office foyer. Whilst he examined it, it went off, singeing him a bit. We were pleased with our efforts. Two of our bucket bombs had reached the people, and we had got maximum publicity in the press.

The same day as the Diagonal Street leaflet bomb (which, by the way, was near the offices of the Star newspaper) we drove out to the Witwatersrand University campus. There was a special student day with club stalls etc outside the buildings. We placed our third bucket bomb near a column beside one of the stalls. There were lots of students milling around. We drove away and stopped about half a mile down the road and waited. We clearly heard it go off.

The following day we located one of the stations bringing people from the townships. The layout was very suitable for our purposes. The entrance was in a dell, with high ground surrounding it, with a fence that looked down on the station. John and I padlocked the speaker box to the fence. While we were doing this there were black policemen down below but their attention was on the people leaving the station. They didn't look up once, I am pleased to say.

We set the broadcast off and left. We had now completed our mission and the following day we found a local park which was quiet and deserted and got rid of any tools and materials we hadn't used behind some bushes.

John and I felt very relieved once we had passed through customs and were on the plane home.

Eddie Adams & John Simpkins 1 July 2005

THE LONDON RECRUITS – MY PART
Tom Bell

INTRODUCTION
the route from Southwark to South Africa

I think I became a socialist in the womb. I think the passion for socialism that flowed through my Mum's veins crossed the placenta and entered the foetal Bell's blood. And there it remains to this day, buzzing around, occasionally getting me into trouble.

So it wasn't a terribly difficult journey, from Southwark to South Africa. After making my life debut at Guy's Hospital, it went via a crappy education, Greenwich Young Communists, an electrical apprenticeship and that moment of realisation that, actually, the world makes sense from your viewpoint, not theirs. Armed with that youthful certainty I found myself, with my big brother, on a flight to Cape Town, to play our part.

My education, the highlight of which was acting a communist in the school play, and the lowlight acting a fairy in another school play, was pretty forgettable; except Mr Graham Clarke, my class teacher. He taught pottery and English and he was an inspiration. The headmaster wasn't too keen on me – he must have worn out a whole bamboo bush caning good behaviour into me. But if Charlton Secondary School for Boys was like the inside of an old teapot, the kids tumbled from its crooked spout into a world of bright dawns and hopeful sunsets. It was the sixties.

The fifties was a seminal decade, but it was in the sixties that seeds sown ten years earlier sprang into a glorious profusion of life. From new visions of democratic socialism that Khrushchev's speech unlocked,[47] through the triumph of youth culture that had its Genesis with Elvis et al, to the mass peace movements that started with the first Aldermaston march – all had their origin in the fifties. But all came of age in the sixties, and the

---

47 To the Twentieth Congress of the Soviet Communist Party – Tom Bell.

same applied right across human society. Of course, much of that exuberant growth has withered and died (or been killed) but the sixties have nonetheless left an indelible mark on the world in which we live today. The dominance of the Right has yet to bury the sixties completely.

I say all this because it is the context in which I cut my political teeth – a time of unbridled optimism, of passion for justice and desire for a better world in which human beings would at last really become *human*. It led me to do many things in my life that would otherwise have been beyond me – like writing this chapter in this book.

My brother Ron and I (and of course our lovely little sister, Jackie) were born into a working-class family. My father (who died when I was eight years old) was an electrician who joined the Communist Party in 1935, my mother a typist who joined the CP a year later. They were both active in the CP and labour movement – my father in his union, my mother in the tenants' movement. Indeed, my mum founded the first modern tenants' association in Britain – in Southwark, during the Second World War.

Due to my birthday falling in August, I was still only fourteen when I walked out of my old school for the last time, turning as I left to stick two fingers up at the hated building and vowing never to enter that door again (I eventually broke the vow – I did a GCSE there many years later, after it had become an FE college). At 15 I became an apprentice electrician – reluctantly following the family trade, in which I had no great interest. Just after my fourteenth birthday I joined the Young Communist League, Greenwich branch. I had met them in 1962, when I was twelve, while on my first Aldermaston march. In theory that was also my first political activity alongside my brother who, being almost seven years older than me, was supposed to look after me. However, virtually on arrival at Aldermaston, he set off with his mates in search of a good time, no doubt involving the opposite sex, and I just got on with enjoying the whole exhilarating atmosphere of the march. I recall that I had obtained a large trilby hat from somewhere – far too big for me – that amused my fellow marchers and enabled Ron to pick me out at a distance.

So began that wonderful, inspiring, educational and formative period of my early political life. It started at Aldermaston, accelerated when I joined the YCL, and ended with my election as its National Secretary in October 1970, a little after my twenty-first birthday.[48] On the way I revelled in the dynamism of an exuberant South East London YCL, enjoyed my first foray into trade unionism, was elected to the League's London District Committee, and given the hapless task of District 'Challenge' Organiser;[49] then elected to the YCL National Committee,[50] and given the even more hapless task of National Treasurer. And I took part in the ANC loudspeaker and leaflet bomb campaign of August 1970.

What happened thereafter is another story; except to say that, unlike my first years in youth politics, it was distorted by the fault line which, by then, characterised communist politics. The Eurocommunist movement was seeking a vision of a democratic socialism that distanced us from the decaying Soviet model, and I identified myself with it. I wanted to continue the new kind of cultural, hegemonic politics that characterised the League in the sixties, but the faults that had opened then became a schism in the seventies and our venture didn't stand a chance. Before I retired from the YCL in 1979, I proposed a new constitution that deleted references to Leninism. It was accepted, but was by then of no consequence. What happened in the eighties and thereafter is now a history that bears bitter testament to how right we were.

The battles fought between two historically doomed tendencies within British Marxism were indeed grim. Yet the Recruits narrative is a story of how we all, in this critical struggle at least, were fighting on the same side – albeit unknowingly at the time!

48 Subsequently this became General Secretary. – TB.
49 *Challenge* being our monthly – if we were lucky – paper. – TB.
50 Subsequently this became Executive Committee. – TB.

When we gathered for the first time, at the South African Embassy in June 2005, I recognised faces from both sides of the CP schism (plus some from the non-CP left) and, despite all the width and depth of the schism and all the contending views, I felt an immediate bond with them – my fellow London Recruits. Like me, they had this precious secret, something we hold in common, and I cherish it and respect them all deeply. Perhaps only the party of Mandela could work such magic! So, my fellow Recruits – I salute each and every one of you.

JOURNEYS' START

It was at a party at George Bridges' flat – one of many held there in Forest Hill. My brother Ron approached me and said, 'I've been asked to do a job.' I looked at him, sensing something odd. 'Eh? What job?'

'Well, Bob Allen has asked me to do something – for the ANC.'

'Oh, yeah….what?' I recalled the time the then YCL International Secretary Jim Brookshaw had got onto the roof of Rhodesia House and thrown the flag of the illegal Smith regime to the pavement below. Perhaps it was something like that.

'Well, it involves going to South Africa and doing something – something illegal – out there, that is – it'll be dangerous.'

'Hmmm!' – I couldn't think what to say, my thoughts were racing.

'And I need someone to go with me – who I can work with;' I knew what he meant, and my heart beat faster. He looked at me again 'So – you comin'?'

'Well, yeah!'

Ron then told me as much as he knew about what we would do – a job that required whites, doing very risky stuff, helping the ANC. I was the obvious choice of partner for him in such a venture, because we got on so well. Everything we did was with a laugh. Among our South East London YCL mates we had dubbed ourselves 'The Fabulous Bell Bros'. We had a 'Fan Club', which had two members (including the FBB themselves) and one female secretary who, looking back, was probably not entirely serious about it – it was just part of the daft fun we had back then. So, this was a real job for the FBB! The conversation was held in taut, whispered tones in the hallway, while the revelry in the living room continued, happily unaware of what the FBB were discussing.

Soon we had arranged to meet a bloke called Ronnie Kasrils, who would show us what to do. We met, as I recall, in a café and he took us to the office of a book publishers – I think it was in Soho. There were piles of books on desks, with very little spare space. In that office, over the next few weeks, Ronnie Kasrils taught us what to do.

UNDER INSTRUCTION

We were to go to Cape Town and carry out two tasks. One involved purchasing and adapting two tape cassette players (they were the size of a large book, with a row of tab buttons – common in the pre-Walkman seventies). After modification, which entailed fitting a large speaker and associated electronic parts to the player, they would blast out a message to the people, from the places where we had hidden them. We were to buy a soldering iron and a few small tools to carry out the modification, as instructed by Ronnie. The other task required us to buy five plastic buckets, into which we would vertically fix a tube filled with explosive and an ignition element. Into the tube was fitted an eight inch length of broomstick. Then a plywood disk was fixed at its centre to the end of the broomstick protruding from the tube. This created a platform in the bucket onto which maybe a couple of thousand fliers (literally in this case) were to be placed. Crumpled newspaper could then be left on top of the fliers to conceal them, and the whole lot put in a harmless-looking carrier bag. All the devices would be controlled by a timer that we must pre-set for a time as instructed by Ronnie. At the set time, the loudspeakers would broadcast their message and the fliers would be blown up into the air for people to grab. Ingenious! Apart from the tape players, buckets and tools the whole lot had to be taken by us from London in secret compartments in the bottom of very large suitcases. We then had to simply assemble it all in our hotel room. Eat your heart out IKEA – the ANC were there long before you!

At some point early in the process I insouciantly announced to our Mum that, in effect, both her sons were about to stick their heads into the mouth of the beast. She looked at me without batting an eyelid and said something like 'Right, well, OK'. It was only later that I realised just how she must have been churning inside.

Ronnie advised us about placing the buckets and the homemade PA systems. Obviously we were to find places where large numbers of black people were gathered, or in transit. I remember how, one evening after an instruction session, we were walking down the street. Ronnie was carrying a bag and stopped to tie his shoelace. We waited until he stood up and we proceeded on our way. Then Ronnie stopped. 'Well?' he asked, 'Notice the difference?' We looked. 'Uh, not really…hmm… what d'ya mean?'

'The bag! Where's the bag?!' he exclaimed. Yes, it was left where he had stopped to tie his shoelace. 'So, that's how you can drop the bucket, without anybody noticing – but be careful!' he said. Next, he took us through the plan – the 'hit' had to happen at a certain time and date, we had to book into a particular hotel (The Helsmley) and keep our heads down. Once the job was done we could stay for a while and then leave South Africa when the coast was clear.

Despite the serious nature of our relationship with Ronnie Kasrils, all of this was done with a laugh. Sometimes when we were teasing him, or seemed to be making light of it all, Ronnie would just shake his head and say, in his South African accent, 'I don't know….you Bell boys!'

One final instruction was very hard to take. 'You can't go looking like that,' said Ronnie 'They'll immediately arrest you as hippie homosexual commies!' We looked at each other. I had a beard and Ron sported a droopy moustache, our hair was almost shoulder length. We sighed. Oh well, all for the cause! A quick visit to the barber transformed us into respectable, clean-cut young Englishmen who would win the trust of any white fascist Boer.

Shortly before we were due to leave, Ronnie brought us our suitcases – big blocks that looked heavy even when empty. I opened my case and my eyes went into shock. It was lined with a criss-cross patterned paper and it swam before the eyes. It was impossible to see that the inside was about four inches shallower than the outside. Thus, the false bottom safely concealed the compartment below it, which contained our self-assembly kit and fliers.

A couple of days later we met Ronnie for the last time before we left and were given, as I recall, something like a thousand pounds in cash. Thus financially armed we went to the British Overseas Airways Corporation and purchased two air tickets to Cape Town, via Johannesburg. We were set to go and on 6 August 1970 I found myself next to my brother on a flight that, in my wildest dreams, I had never expected to take.

CAPERS IN CAPE TOWN

Disembarking at Cape Town Airport was a little nervy. The clone-type customs officer looked at our suitcases... then looked at us...then waved us through.... then called us back..... to look at Ron's fishing rods! Phew!

We arrived in Cape Town, ready to embark upon the first step of our plan – and it went wrong. The Helmsley Hotel – a pleasant little building on the outskirts of the city – only had a room for one night, which we accepted. We then repaired to the Grand Hotel in town, and sent a 'Happy birthday' telegram to Ronnie: 'We are booked into The GRAND hotel, Will stay in The GRAND'. We thought it might be important that Ronnie should know of this change in case of...well, just in case. If a room become available at The Helmsley, we asked them to phone us at The Grand. The next day they called us – a room was free! So we decamped to The Helmsley, sending another telegram to a probably confused Ronnie saying that we were now settled in The HELMSLEY. And there we stayed.

On our first night in the city, we went for a walk. We were soon approached by a black man who must have realised that we were not your normal Afrikaners. He was highly agitated and was pointing to some kind of indelible stamp on the back of his hand. We couldn't understand a word he was saying, so we just moved on, leaving him behind us in the night. 'Oh well', we said to each other, 'Welcome to South Africa'.

The next few days were spent purchasing the tools and equipment needed for our task, and reconnoitring Cape Town for sites suited to it. We also hired a car.

Buckets and tools were purchased from…well…bucket and tool shops. Then, to conceal the loudspeakers, we bought two wicker picnic baskets. We also bought padlocks and chains to secure the baskets to suitable places, hoping to make their removal more difficult. We made notices to place on the baskets, warning DO NOT TOUCH – HIGH EXPLOSIVES. The cassette players were, it seemed, possibly more difficult. Maybe the police would identify the shop from which they were obtained and discover a trail leading to the FBB. So, in their wisdom the FBB decided to use an ingenious method to throw the apartheid Bureau of State Security (BOSS) into confusion – we sensibly purchased the players from two different shops, Ron buying one and me the other. BUT – and here was confirmation of seasoned espionage agents at work – we decided to speak in some other accent than our native cockney voices when making our purchases. Otherwise we may be instantly identified as… er…Cockneys. The problem was that neither of us could do accents to save our lives – which may have literally been the case here! Anyway, we both decided to have a go at Irish, that being the easiest for the sadly non-thespian FBB to do.

So I sidled into the cassette player shop and pointed to the window, in which the perfect player for Illegal Political Broadcasts was on display. I cleared my throat and mumbled "Oid loik ta buy dat player, if ya don't moind". Fortunately, the shopkeeper was more interested in my money than my voice, and I soon emerged with the player under my arm. Ron then bought his player, and we were in business.

The recce was going well, and we soon identified a number of excellent places that could benefit from our visit. Oddly, it is here my memory really fades. But I do recall a two or three storey car park. The top level was its roof, and there was a low barrier wall around the edge to stop the most stupid drivers from simply driving over it. We went up to the wall and looked down. A few feet below, running all around the building, was a ledge, protruding some two feet out. The car park overlooked a busy square or bus station area (memory failure again) that was thronged with black and so-called Cape Coloured people. Excellent! The bustling railway station was identified as another perfect location. We had now established all the locations for our task.

Meanwhile, back at The Helmsley, we were not exactly observing Ronnie's advice to keep our heads down. Indeed, at times it was like The Helmsley meets Fawlty Towers. The place was managed by a Cape Coloured woman named Millicent. Her assistant was a white woman (there was no logic in apartheid) named Sandra. The receptionist was a beautiful Cape Coloured young woman in her early twenties and she was also called Millie. I don't think they had met many London lads with that mad cockney humour before. We had a good laugh with them, urging them to form a Cape Town branch of the FBB Fan Club, and generally poking fun at the place.

The Reception area had a number of tables and chairs in it, and various patrons would sit there waiting for whatever, eating snacks or drinking coffee. One of them was in permanent residence at The Helmsley – an old posh woman with an English upper-class accent who, every time we saw her, told us that she had once been a highly popular singer. We couldn't resist goading her. 'And you had crowds of adoring fans then? Like the Beatles, eh?' The daft old bat was so full of herself it never occurred to her that we might be less than serious. Often she would burst into the only song that was apparently left in her repertoire '*I could have danced all night, I could have danced all night, and still have asked for more*'. Then she would look at us and beam. We would wince but, undaunted she would continue, '*I'll never know what made it so **exciting***' (there was a whispered accent on the last word) and we would burst into wild applause – anything to shut her up.

Then there was the old porter-cum-waiter, George. He was incredibly slow, shuffling his way across the reception with no apparent objective in mind. Ron would shout 'Whoosh! Tom, what was that blur'.

'Dunno Ron, must have been George flashing past!' Then Ron would cry out 'George for God's sake man, slow down! You'll collapse!' And George would stop and laugh helplessly, making him even slower, while bemused guests stared. We renamed George 'Flash'. I think he liked it.

One character who warmed our hearts was a chambermaid called Cut Throat – or that's what we called her. She translated Afrikaans newspapers for us, and would then issue a dire warning – one day the hated whites would all get their throats cut, and she would do it. To Cut Throat we made no secret of our distaste for apartheid, but we feigned surprise at her venom. We asked if she would kill the whites at the hotel, with whom she seemed on friendly terms.

'Yes, all of them.'

'But what about us?' Ron asked. 'Would you cut our throats? I mean, we're not racists!'

'No,' came the reply. 'I will get someone else to do it.'

After a couple of days, we wanted to sample the Cape Town nightlife and found ourselves in a big cabaret, in one of the large hotels. Apart from the waiters it was all lily white. We must have gone there three or four times, but it seemed there were just two acts – I've long forgotten their names. One was a female stand-up comedian who was about as blue as South Africa could tolerate. Back home she would have been regarded as par for the course at the Royal Variety Show. Then there was an anodyne male pop group singing anodyne covers of the anodyne end of the British hit parade. Neither act varied from one night to the next, and we soon got bored. Then we met John.

I cannot recall John's surname, but we got talking to him at the cabaret where he was as bored as us. John was a bit different. He was a Rhodesian businessman (something to do with paint) who was living in a Cape Town hotel for some reason. His main object in life appeared to be getting laid as often as possible with as many women as possible. I don't think he achieved said object over much, but his resolve never appeared to wilt, if you can forgive the Freudian innuendo. John hated apartheid, but only because it forbade him from pursuing any woman he wanted, regardless of race. 'Outrageous!' he would say. 'Why can't I fuck who I want? The government shouldn't tell you who you can fuck and who you can't!' But he was wise to the politics of his environment. 'See that black waiter who just served us?' he said to us in a café one day. 'He may be all smiles with you but, if he had the chance, he would slit your throat while you lie in bed at night. And one day they will, and I'm getting out of here before they do.' It seemed that throat cutting would be the preferred form of retribution when apartheid met its nemesis. John had the right idea.

We had told people that we were businessmen back home – we were in the tropical fish business. That was partly true – Ron was thinking about setting up a tropical fish shop. To be really convincing we explained that we were fed up with being overrun by the blacks in London. 'You know how to handle 'em here in South Africa,' we sneered, and we explained that we were over there to make contacts, with a view to emigrating there. We sold this line so well to John that he saw in us his financial salvation. He became desperately keen to set up a business with us.

John took us to a (white) party where we got into conversation with a group of them. They seemed mightily impressed with these two London businessmen from whom, John had advised them, they had much to learn. In 1970, the London docks were a cauldron of union militancy, led by the fiery communist leader Jack Dash. His notoriety had spread to Cape Town and, on hearing we were Londoners, Jack's name was thrown with bile into the conversation. 'Jack Dash,' said Ron, 'is doing a good job!' The ensuing cold silence was broken by someone exclaiming, 'You'll get nowhere here with those views.'

Then, with a swerve I could only watch and admire, Ron exclaimed, 'Well yes – he is the enemy. But to defeat any enemy you must know them, and Dash is very good at what he does. If we don't understand that, we are doomed!' The silence was transformed into warm respect for such wisdom. 'Well, yes, that's right. Of course.' Phew! How dim they were! They would have believed any bullshit delivered by this pair of shrewd London businessmen.

The last time I remember meeting John was when we went to his hotel. We found his room and knocked on the door. From inside there issued the sound of suppressed female giggling and John hissing 'Quiet'. We called out and, on realising it was us, he opened the door, ushering out two black chambermaids as he did so. 'See that,' he said. 'The law says we can't fuck. Outrageous!'

John was getting very enthusiastic about our future business relationship, so we backed off – we were due to leave shortly after the hotel encounter anyway. I sometimes wonder if he got out before his throat made reluctant contact with a sharp blade.

John directed us to a *real* nightclub, a black/racially mixed dive in the shadowy docks area. There a heavy rhythm and blues band blasted out rock music from a ludicrously high stage. We were among the very few whites there – we were not sure if we should have been there, but John assured us we would be OK. No alcohol was sold – we had to bring our own. The going fare was brandy, so we took a couple of bottles in with us. The place was a heaving mass of humanity, inhaling the smoke that hung thick in the air like a latent curse.

Before too long I was in an advanced state of merriment, and found myself at a table with a group of Cape Coloured women who were, to put it kindly, well past their prime. One of them was speaking to me, saying something like 'Do you want to take me back to your hotel?' It dawned on me, to my horror, that I was being propositioned! I hadn't travelled half way round the world for that – I was only interested in a pretty girl back in the UK who I was, in two years time, to marry. 'You're old enough to be my mum!' I slurred. Then I heard Ron's voice, 'Come on, don't you know they're on the game?!' Having never encountered a lady of the night before, I had no idea of their profession. I just wanted away from them. Eventually we slouched into the cool night air and I went to hail a taxi, but Ron pulled me back – the 'taxi' was a police car! Anyway, we found a real cab and got back to the Helmsley unscathed. We did return to that club, but thereafter I stuck to soft drinks. What a contrast it was to the sanitised atmosphere of the whites-only cabaret! Life in all its visceral form was there, heaving to the rhythm of its black music, uninhibited in its defiance of the mores of apartheid's pseudo culture.

I recount the above stories in an effort to convey what life was like in Cape Town. Apartheid was as real there as anywhere else in South Africa but, perhaps due to being a port, it somehow tried to obscure its racist essence. Hence, for example, the mixed-race jazz bands that we witnessed playing surreptitiously in the University. Apartheid is fundamentally unnatural and, even as it economically benefited the whites, it denied them the right to openly explore all human life.

OF LEAFLETS AND LOUDSPEAKERS

For all that, our real focus was, of course, on our task. We were busy planning the job. Having decided locations, we had to work out the route between them, and then we did a dummy run, which went well. We had carefully removed the false bottoms from our cases and assembled all the parts correctly. Now the day arrived for our training to be put into practice. Somehow we got everything out of the hotel and into the car unnoticed. We drove around, placing the picnic baskets and buckets as planned. We got a scare while chaining one basket to a railing.

As we crouched down over it, we looked up.... and there was a policeman, looking like some overgrown, old fashioned Boy Scout, walking directly towards us, holding a long baton. We carried on, hearts in mouths...while he just passed us by!

Then there was the car park bit. We lowered the basket containing the loudspeaker device inside onto the ledge, making it difficult to disable or retrieve. Down in the square we placed a leaflet bomb by a lamp post. Then we retreated, waiting in the car, anxiously glancing at our watches as the set time approached.

We didn't have long to wait – we had placed our little messages to apartheid as late as possible, to minimise the possibility of their being discovered before going off. My stomach was writhing as my watch hit the set time (five o'clock) and – nothing. We couldn't just sit in the car waiting for something to happen; we wanted to check the locations. But it was rush hour, and we were stuck in heavy traffic. Eventually we decided that I should check one location, while Ron slowly drove around the traffic–jammed block. Even as I write this, it occurs to me that we were probably the cause of the massive traffic problems!

I tentatively approached the first location on foot and – my heart soared! Thousands of leaflets were scattered everywhere, with black people grabbing them and stuffing them into pockets and bags. The police were rushing about like headless chickens, attempting the impossible task of preventing this. And all the while, a speech was bellowing from a chained-up picnic basket. Police were circling it like nervous dogs, wary of the 'explosives' warning. Eventually one of them gingerly prodded it with his foot, which did not explode. I left them trying to open the basket, looking more like the Keystone Cops than the strong arm of apartheid law. I can't describe the feelings racing through my very soul at that moment. We didn't check the other locations but, even if those efforts hadn't worked, this made it all worthwhile. But they had worked, as we found out the next day in the press.

I almost didn't care what happened at that point. Of course, we had considered the possibility of getting caught. We knew what that meant in the very worst-case scenario. I didn't believe that an apartheid court would pass a death sentence on us – they weren't *that* stupid. But I did countenance the possibility of being shot if caught in the act, or defenestration while under interrogation on the twentieth floor of some Interior Ministry building. But, right then, they could do their worst, and I couldn't give a damn.

MISSION COMPLETED...

All that now remained was to relax for a while before leaving. We had one more moment of elation when, the morning after the big day, we saw the newspapers. Leaflet bombs and loudspeakers had gone off in other major cities in South Africa: Johannesburg, Durban and others had also received visits from the ANC .We were not alone! One newspaper showed a leaflet, which could be clearly read, and they nearly got into trouble for helping terrorists!

Ron had taken to devising silly little poems about the Helmsley, its staff, the FBB, etc. Sandra and Millie took us out and showed us the safari park and Millie junior took us to the cinema. The latter trip was a bit worrying, as we whites were with a coloured girl, but it was OK. Millie junior had told us all about her boyfriend, and promised to bring him to London one day to meet us.

We visited the Cape of Good Hope and, on the way, found ourselves high up at the head of a valley below. The vast beauty of the scene was a wonder – until our gaze drifted down to the valley floor. There below us was a blot that was surely a township. Even at a distance one could sense the squalor, and the anger that accompanied it, rising from it like a fetid mist.

Then we had a trip up Table Mountain, the beautiful backdrop to Cape Town. From the cable car, the city shimmered below us, flowing away like a carpet that ran out to the sea. From the top of Table Mountain, we looked out to the horizon. There, in the distance but clear, was Robben Island, where Nelson Mandela was incarcerated. It felt as though I could almost reach out and take the island gently in the palm of my hand, lifting it Gulliver-like from the sea and releasing its precious captives from their wretched shackles. The image faded as I looked back inland, but I was full of hope that one day Nelson Mandela and his comrades would cross that strip of water to lead a new South Africa.

UP, UP AND AWAY

Our day of departure came and, with cheery goodbye waves and smiles from the Helmsley staff, we took a cab to the airport. In our suitcases, under the now completely visible false bottoms, were all the Cape Town newspapers. We thought Ronnie would be interested to see them. Yes, it would have been a give-away if we were searched at Cape Town Airport, but as we were leaving the country, we didn't expect that to happen and it didn't. We changed at Johannesburg and sat on the London flight as it taxied up the runway. I had the window seat and was looking at the ground below, waiting for it to fall away as we departed from South Africa. Then, with a bump, we were flying, free from apartheid! I felt a nudge in my side and looked around. Ron was silent, but his hand was extended to me. My thoughts were in such a jumble that, for a split second, I wondered what this meant. 'That's it Tom,' he said. 'Job done – they can't catch us now.' I found my voice. 'No, they can't catch us now.' We shook hands warmly.

We must have got back about mid-morning, the cab dropping me at our council house first, then taking Ron home. Nobody was home and I was jet lagged, so I went to bed for some fitful sleep. A while later I heard a key in the front door and knew it was my mum. I went to the upstairs hall and looked down at the door as my mum closed it. I leaned over the handrail and sleepily called out 'Hello mum'. She looked up, surprise all over her face. 'Son! Son! You're back! You're back!' Mum was only five feet tall, but she took those stairs like an Olympian. She rushed up to me and threw her arms around me crying and repeating 'Son, you're back! You're back!' Then, 'Is Ron back?'

As a young bloke of not quite twenty-one, I didn't know what the fuss was about. 'Yeah, mum, we're back – it went well!'

Soon after that, we had a debriefing meeting with Ronnie Kasrils. He was delighted to see the newspapers, and happy with our report. 'You Bell boys – you've done well!' he said, smiling that big, open smile of his. 'You've done well!' We had done our best but, compared to the huge and sometimes heroic struggle against apartheid, our contribution was just one grain of sand on the beach. You need to look no further than the other chapters of this book for confirmation of that point.

Ours was in fact a modest contribution, but nonetheless I am proud of it. And what I gained was priceless, because I learned something about myself from that ANC mission. I had gained new insights into myself, and a new self-confidence. I had tested my nerve, and my nerve had passed. I feel this must be true of my fellow London Recruits, and of all those who find themselves facing danger for what they believe in. There are in fact legions of such people down the centuries whose endeavours speak in eloquent reply to those who have now surrendered to the Mammon of the Market.

A few months after we got back I became National Secretary of the YCL, which ruled out any return to South Africa. I am also proud of that but, although it isn't even a lifetime away, it's now of a bygone era. As Karl Marx said, 'The only thing that is constant is change'.

FINAL REFLECTIONS...

Years later, after I had become a parent myself, I fully comprehended my mum's emotions on seeing her sons' safe arrival home. I understood the anguish that my mother must have felt every day that her sons were away and it's the one thing about this whole story that makes me feel bad. I imagine how I would feel if my daughter Emily went off to, say, Israel to do undercover work for the Palestine Liberation Organisation. I would be sick with fear until she got back. And for me, that illustrates the basic, raw reason why the search for new forms of a democratic socialism must go on – for the children, the youth, the future.

We don't have children to see them slaughtered on some battlefield, or wither from hunger, or be crushed in the rubble of their bombed home, or crumble in agony at the torturer's sick behest, or decay among the drug-laden shit of the sink estate, or suffocate on a polluted planet. We want so much for them to thrive and blossom – and that is what apartheid totally denied to millions of black children, whose families were torn apart or who barely existed in those emblems of the Afrikaner nightmare – the rotting townships. They were denied their inherent birthright because they were black in their own land.

Today, like so much of the developing world under capitalist globalisation that's in deep crisis, South Africa faces immense problems which will take decades to overcome. But the defeat of apartheid was a precondition for any progress towards equality and democracy in that beautiful country. I am proud of the little bit I did in the struggle to rid the world of apartheid back in 1970, and I am forever in debt to the ANC and Ronnie Kasrils for trusting my brother and me to do that little bit on the streets of Cape Town.

Ron Bell

Born into a CP family, I was well immersed in the ethos of freedom and anti-discriminatory practice. My father was a Trades Union official in the ETU[51] and mum, apart from standing as a CP candidate in elections (with me in her arms on the poster) had the honour of starting the first ever Tenants' Association during the Second World War.

I joined the YCL at 14 or 15 years of age but not as an activist. My activity came when joining the ETU at 16. I became active in the League in my 20s under the influence of George and Jackie Bridges, Mike Power and my kid brother Tom. So, when I was approached by Bob Allen, the London District Secretary of the League, with the prospect of being recruited to do "some work for the ANC", I readily agreed. After all, hadn't I spent many hours on picket lines outside SA House demanding freedom for Nelson Mandela?

My acceptance led to a secret meeting in Soho with Ronnie Kasrils. Over the meeting it became clear that another person would have to be recruited, as working in pairs was the preferred strategy. When it was explained to me that we would be making leaflet bombs and laying down amplified speeches, I immediately thought of Tom. Both 'sparks'[52] (well, one and a half) but Tom was always good at chemistry. I thought this would be the perfect mix, plus I knew we could trust one another with our lives. So I recruited Tom.

Several nights followed in Ronnie's company in a dingy office in Soho, where we were trained to carry out the tasks of producing and setting up leaflet bombs, mixing stuff, connecting detonators and timers. Then came the task of amplifying a simple cassette player to boost the output by many watts with the aid of a pre-amp and 12 inch speakers. I cannot honestly remember being concerned or fearful for our own safety. Looking back I guess we were rather reckless, but I suppose this helped. However,

51 Electrical Trades Union- Editor.
52 Slang for 'electrician' – Editor.

we were both very concerned for the wellbeing of others. It had by now become apparent that although we were not producing mighty explosives designed to harm people, nonetheless they might not be healthy for someone standing too close. So we'd have to situate them in high density areas to have any effect but where no one could get near them! Ronnie assured us that these devices could not maim anyone!!

We were given our cases, one each, with false bottoms filled with leaflets, timers, powder, igniters, pre-amps and audio cassettes, plus some money to purchase plane tickets and cover our hotel costs and items we would need in Cape Town SA. These included a soldering iron and solder, speakers, cassette players. I realized that, in order to purchase these objects in Cape Town, to carry out adequate reconnaissance work in a short time to enable five bombs and speeches to go off simultaneously, and to plant the devices in carefully chosen, significant areas, we would need a car. So my last task before setting off was to acquire an international driving licence.

The day of departure arrived and I remember feeling excitement. Tom and I had prepared our stories. We were businessmen visiting South Africa to explore the pros and cons of emigrating and we took on the personas of brothers with a leaning towards the racist doctrine of the country. I had my long hair cut short, shaved off my moustache, donned a suit, and was ready to go. When we made a fuel stop in Cape Verde Islands, almost on the equator, I realized that the suit, collar and tie were not the ideal apparel for keeping cool.

It was when we landed at Jo'burg *en route* to our destination that I came face to face with apartheid in action – real time. Toilets with 'Net Blankes' (whites only) on the doors. Yes, white and black toilets in the airport. I never saw the 'Blacks only' loos but the 'Whites' were pretty luxurious. On we flew again to Cape Town where we disembarked and passed through to customs and immigration. No one asked to see inside our cases. This caused us some relief as on a nearby table a black guy had his opened case tipped upside down, its contents strewn all over the place. There were only clothes, so he was told to clear it up and move on, in such a manner as if *he* had made the mess. As we walked away a voice called 'wait a minute'. I confess to feeling a tad uneasy as I turned to face the voice, with my fishing rod holdall hanging from my shoulder. For some reason I'd thought this would look good! 'What's in the holdall mate?' 'My fishing rods,' I replied. 'Mind if I look?' 'Course not,' said I, moving the bag towards my inquisitor. With just the rod tips showing he said 'No problem', looking no further, 'Have to check on gun movement'. 'Okay, thanks, bye.' And that was that.

Ronnie Kasrils had asked us to stay at the Helmsley Hotel. We thought there must have been some importance in this request so we called a cab and off we sped. On arrival, we paid the fare and hauled the large cases up the stairs to reception. Ronnie had said there'd be no problems booking in, so imagine our surprise when we were told, 'Sorry, we're full'. We must have looked very sad because the two young receptionists said, '…but we can fit you up in a twin room for one night'. Feeling tired and needing time to work out what to do next, we readily agreed. After a wash and brush up we returned to reception to chat up the girls. They told us that the Grand Hotel in the town centre would have a twin room and that after a few days they may have space here at the Helmsley. Next day we called a cab to take us to the Grand; a huge 5 star job where shoes were put outside the room at night and returned spotless in the morning, in contrast to the informal Helmsley. Nonetheless, we were very concerned because we didn't understand the significance of Ronnie's instruction to stay at the Helmsley. We had to inform him of our change of plan, so I had this idea to send him a birthday telegram. It read, 'HAPPY BIRTHDAY RONNIE. HAVING A GREAT TIME HERE AT THE GRAND HOTEL. BEST WISHES. BELL BROS.' With this sent, I went to hire a car. This done, we started planning.

Two days later we received a phone call from the girls at the Helmsley, saying they'd got a room and did we want to go back. We said we did, loaded our car, moved back and sent another telegram to Ronnie. This time it read, 'WE'RE HAVING A WONDERFUL HOLIDAY HERE AT THE HELMSLEY'. And wonderful it was too. We worked very hard at establishing our target points and how to deposit our 'plants'.

We purchased our goods. The 'speeches', we decided, would be concealed in large hampers chained to fences and padlocked with a sign saying, 'DO NOT TOUCH – HIGH EXPLOSIVES'. The leaflet bombs were made inside plastic buckets, placed in large carrier bags and situated nearby. Easy!

The girls, when off duty, took us out in the afternoons. This sorted the sightseeing and we worked on the project at night when we knew we would be undisturbed.

Come the Big Day. The car was inconspicuously loaded up the previous night. Each item had the timer set to ensure that they all went off simultaneously at 5.00pm – rush hour – in predominantly black, congested routes throughout the city, such as bus and rail termini.

I would like to point out that Cape Town concealed its harsh, racist, apartheid practices quite well and one needed to go out and explore to discover its extent. I'll never forget the contrast in the white and black railway stations. The white was like no other station I have ever seen; carpeted – yes, carpeted – with leather chesterfields dotted everywhere for seating, and pedestal ash trays around which the male black attendants negotiated their vacuum cleaners. Spotless. The contrast in the black section was staggering. Although we were not allowed to enter we could see enough, and when the trains arrived to take the workforce back to the townships it was like watching a movie, with hundreds of people packing in. Of course, a speech and leaflet distribution had to go off here!

After the bomb / speech devices had been primed and laid we chose to observe what happened at the city bus station centre, but when I got back the rush hour traffic was so bad I couldn't park. So Tom jumped out and I drove around the block. I could hear the speech when I picked Tom up half an hour later. In retrospect the traffic jam was probably caused by us because the bomb had gone up. Tom said it was 'fantastic'. The police wouldn't touch the speaker hampers because of the 'High Explosives' warning and were rushing around trying to snatch leaflets from the hands of workers returning to the townships. Eventually one khaki-shorted policeman got the nerve to kick the basket. When nothing blew up they all started to give the hamper a good kicking, but still the speech screamed its message to Vorster.[53] I must confess I felt chuffed to bits.

Of the five put down, one bomb failed and was handed in to the police, so the newspapers stated. The others went off simultaneously with five other cities. Next day, back at the hotel, we asked staff to translate the newspapers. The black members of staff with whom we were friendly read the reports with enthusiasm and actually one lady who we had nicknamed 'Cutthroat' said joyously that the day was coming and that white throats would be cut. It was difficult not to blurt out that we whites were responsible for these acts. I hope she realised in the end.

After the event we stayed on to make a holiday of it (visit safari park, Cape Point, etc) and were invited to parties, and it was here that I found myself among people espousing the worst elements of racist doctrine. What really appalled me there was that the most vehement racists were the ex-pats. To me they seemed shallow and very stupid. Here they were espousing their vicious racism with venom against the British black, immigrant population and they were here, hoping to achieve a better lifestyle by becoming migrants themselves. Anyway, after a few drinks and hearing Jack Dash's name[54] being torn apart, I expressed the view that Jack was 'doing a good job'. The room went silent and all heads turned, and an attractive woman from Essex said, 'You won't get anywhere here if that's your views'. I must admit I felt rather concerned that my guard had dropped and I was centre of attention for the wrong reasons. So I said, 'Listen, you have to know the enemy to defeat them. Jack Dash is paid to do

53 B J Vorster – South African Prime Minister. – Editor.
54 Jack Dash (1906-1989) was a Communist and a prominent trade unionist in the London docks, and was a hate figure in the British media at the time – Editor.

a job, so he does it to the best of his ability and for his union he does it well. So we should respect that or we're doomed. I'm not saying that I agree with it, but for his side, he's doing a good job.' Silence.....then another man said, 'Absolutely right: never thought of it like that. Good point, Ron.' This brought murmurs of agreement. The subject changed and we were off the hook. Sweating but rather pleased with myself I thought, 'Yes, you were right, I wouldn't get anywhere with you lot in this political climate, with my views'.

Leaving Cape Town was sad, actually. We had made some friends and, despite our 'We'll be back soon' talk, we knew that this was 'goodbye'. We brought back, along with our memories, copies of the newspaper reports for Ronnie and photographs of locations where we'd laid leaflet bombs and speeches.

Once home and 'job completed', I had time to reflect on how my preconceived views on Apartheid had altered. I realised that whites in the Cape knew of division according to race, but the terrible plight of the other races was so well hidden as to make racism seem natural to all but the most radical whites. The real evils were carefully concealed from eyes that were content not to peer too deep.

Today, especially following the High Commissioner's and Ronnie's speeches at South Africa House in June 2005, I feel very proud of the role London YCL played in the ANC campaign. I cannot lose the thought that many black South African comrades gave their lives to the struggle for freedom. This puts what I did into perspective.

The left in Britain at the time, including our own organisation, was pretty divided on many issues. But here was a situation that demonstrated some very basic moral, ethical and political issues in which we were united.

One year after returning from South Africa I had a bit of a shock. Brother Tom was still living at the family home with our Mum. I lived a mile up the road, so it was no surprise when I received a call asking me to pop down.

On entering the lounge, I was stunned to see 'Miss M', a

young woman who worked in the Helmsley Hotel was sitting alongside a young man. She looked pretty shocked because gone was the short haired, clean cut bloke from Cape Town. Here was a long haired, droopy moustached bloke. Tom also had now grown his beard and had longish hair. This is what had happened: Tom had given his home number to her, never thinking it would be used. Then one day Mum answered the phone to a woman asking for Tom. By then Tom was General Secretary of the League, working in King Street.[55] So Mum just gave the number to her. I would have loved to have seen his face when he picked up the phone. She said she was at Victoria. Tom dropped his pen, changed his pants and rushed off.

He had to take a calculated risk and put his cards on the table, feeling sure he would get a shocked but positive-ish response. He sat and explained all.

Although rather shocked at his revelation, she also had other problems she needed help with. She had managed to save enough for a return flight, sorted out their documentation and arrived with nowhere to stay. So he took them home.

That's when I walked in. Once all our blood pressures had returned to near normal we started the job of sorting out their accommodation. We fixed them up with digs at Bob and Ros Allen's in Streatham, where they stayed for a while before moving on around Europe, as was their arranged plan. We both often wonder how she is, and what she's up to now.

Of course, this was not the end of the story; many other comrades were, unbeknown to us at the time, engaged on similar activities. Many years were spent later campaigning for the release of our dear friend Sean Hosey from prison in South Africa.

I feel proud to have belonged to the same small organisation that produced such commitment in young people to change the evil face of the world. The YCL'ers.

---

55 The head offices of the CPGB and YCL were in King Street, Covent Garden. – Editor.

A JOURNEY
Gordon Hutchins
(on mission with Bob Condon)

On graduating from an Approved School (BTS Formidable, Portishead, Somerset) I joined the Merchant Navy. After several trips I "paid off" in New Zealand, where I lived (mainly in Auckland) for ten years.

I soon began to meet people engaged in a campaign to boycott South African goods. Later I joined the Communist Party of New Zealand, for whom apartheid was a major issue.

Along with others I daubed the fence of the Governor General (Lord Cobham) with the slogan "Boycott South African goods". It made the centre pages of *New Age* and a touch of the globals. We also daubed the proverbial gasometer – nothing like a good slogan to greet a new dawn. A great deal of emphasis was put on not buying South African goods. Example: asking the greengrocer for 'four oranges, but not South African, please' – often greeted with a grunt of disapproval, or more. Nonetheless, a good consciousness raiser and, for many people, an introduction to politics.

On my return to England in the early sixties I joined the Communist Party of Great Britain and, among other issues, resumed activities in relation to apartheid. Hence, daubing of a less notable sort took place. Many trade unions sent annual greetings cards to political prisoners in South Africa. London North District of the AUEW[56] adopted Dave Kitson, a well known political prisoner. Did he get them? I remember giving out coloured postcards of Nelson Mandela at the time when he and his colleagues were standing in the infamous Rivonia trial and eventually sent to Robben Island prison.

Then, out of the blue, one evening in the summer of 1971 the

56 Amalgamated Union of Engineering Workers – Editor.

phone rang. Would I like two weeks holiday in South Africa? I would have to go with a friend, Bob, as a travelling companion. We had an uneventful journey by air to Port Elizabeth via Johannesburg.

Port Elizabeth, even under apartheid, was a thriving, bustling town. There was open fraternising on the streets between Cape Coloureds and white South Africans. The restaurants were buzzing, noisy and a good night out.

Of course we had to combine our holiday with the distribution of leaflets by means of bucket (leaflet) bombs. Our mission came together when we visited the Ford Motor Works, and felt that we just had to set up a bucket bomb near the main workers' entrance. In all we "set up" six bucket bombs in various places. We heard one go off at a memorial in the centre of Port Elizabeth. It gave us a certain amount of satisfaction, but not as much as a front page photograph in the following day's paper. It depicted a plain-clothes policeman chasing a floating leaflet.

The leaflets were written in Xhosa and addressed to black South Africans.

Were there moments of trepidation? Yes, especially when I inadvertently walked into a 'blacks only' toilet. The depredation and neglect of this facility was appalling. Into the bargain I met a black South African as I left. He may well have thought 'whitey' went in for a relief other than passing water.

On our strolls around town we noticed cars parked with plain clothes police observing all and sundry. It became a game between me and Bob, to see who could spot three before lunch. Not too difficult. Whilst we enjoyed our stay in South Africa we did have several conversations with white South Africans: a fruit farmer from Cape Town, and a tug boat captain who showed us around an old lookout fort. They were both eager to talk to us. No doubt the pariah status of South Africa was taking its toll. However we were both relieved when our plane was actually airborne and leaving Port Elizabeth Airport.

Editor's notes:
Gordon Hutchins has been a seaman, factory worker, active trade unionist and shop steward. Now active in the pensioners' movement, he was born in 1933.

Bob Condon was born in Ireland. He was an Irish Army officer who resigned from the Irish Army in order to volunteer for the British Army during the Second World War, in which he served as a weapons instructor. He was also a film editor and window cleaner. He worked in the UK, Canada, and the US (New York). He spoke fluent French. He was in turn a member of the US, British, and French Communist Parties. Bob was knocked off his bicycle and killed in France in the year 2000, aged 78.

Eddie Adams has reported that he put forward the name of Bob Condon, who in turn selected Gordon Hutchins.

RECOLLECTIONS OF AN ANC COURIER ON THE UNION CASTLE SHIPPING LINE
Norman Lucas

Introduction

It was only my return to South Africa in 2007 (for a conference in Stellenbosch) that rekindled my memory of the events in 1970 and 1971 as an ANC courier. Until then I had more-or-less buried the thoughts of what had occurred. I guess that this was because I could not talk of what I had done at the time, or as long as apartheid still existed. Perhaps other people were doing similar work, even possibly through the Union Castle shipping line? As it happened, a couple of years later at an anti-apartheid rally I bumped into an engineer from the ship I was on and neither of us had any idea we had similar views despite sitting at the same dining table for months. Perhaps he too was a courier? I do not know and at that time apartheid still existed so I was unable to ask. Anyway, as time went by, and we celebrated the release of Nelson Mandela and the collapse of apartheid, it seemed inappropriate to mention anything. Following my visit to South Africa and consequent discussions with old friends and former comrades in the UK I started putting together the events that took place in late 1970 and early 1971. It was my friend Ron Bell, who also has a chapter in this book, who encouraged me to write my account and put me in touch with the editor.

From young communist to ANC courier

In 1969 I joined the Young Communist League (YCL) and became an active member for a few years in London. During that time I participated in various campaigns, one of which was the struggle against apartheid. The events leading up to becoming a courier for the ANC were in effect a series of chance events. As a young person I wanted to travel. In those days disposable income was far less, so I had to find a way of working my way round the world as best I could. Having been a sort of apprentice photographer in London and Dusseldorf I joined an agency that put photographers on passenger liners. On board my job was to take colour photographs of passengers. These were developed, printed and sold on board the ship. This made money for the shipping line and the agency. I got free board and a small percentage of the takings, which just about covered my bar bill.

I worked on a number of ships in various parts of the world but was eventually put on the Union Castle Line, which in those days cruised from Southampton to Cape Town, then with mostly new passengers to East London and Port Elizabeth, then back again to Cape Town and with another set of passengers back to Southampton. The ship I was on when I did my ANC courier work was the SA Vaal, although I previously worked on the Pendennis Castle and Windsor Castle. These were all beautiful large ships and this was expensive luxury cruising, so most of the passengers were pretty well off, to say the least.

I was on leave in 1970 and joined some campaigning that was going on at the time. In a pub afterwards I happened to mention my travel itinerary to the London District Secretary of the YCL, Bob Allen. He immediately asked if I would consider doing some work for the ANC (I found out much later that he recruited a number of YCLers to work for the ANC). This I readily agreed to do. A few days later I met a black South African, who I guess was in his late 20s, in a London pub just off Trafalgar Square. To this day I don't know his name and obviously I never asked. He explained that he wanted me to take packages across to South Africa. He asked me if I knew the risks and told me that if anything happened I would be on my own. He said I would be told where to leave the package but would not meet up with anyone in Cape Town. Simple as that. I don't know the extent to which they trusted me (I could have been a plant). Perhaps I had been checked out within the YCL. I don't know. In any case I was used three times.

A while later I was given a smallish heavy package (a little bigger that a shoe box) and told to leave it at one of the quays in the harbour in Cape Town. I don't recall the exact details but at that time when a ship moored up in Cape Town there were a number of quays and there was a post or concrete block with the number of the quay on it. I was to leave the package behind one of these numbered blocks late in the evening and walk away. Someone clearly would collect it – I assume after making sure that it was all clear and no one had followed me.

I suppose it would be interesting for the reader to have more details: names, places, etc., but the long and the short of it is – I was given the packages by someone I did not know. I never asked what was in them (I think they were leaflets but I'm not sure), I dropped them off in Cape Town at an agreed place and time and they were collected by someone who I also did not know. I'm afraid that's it. What I can give is a few more details of what happened and some of my feelings, difficulties and concerns around that time.

Some personal reflection and incidents

Once on board with the package there were two really important things for me to be careful of. Firstly, I had to hide the package somewhere on board where it would be unlikely to be found and where, if it was found, the contents could not be traced back to me. This was easy as there were many wooden panels in the cabins and officers' quarters that could be prised off and put back. Secondly, and by far the most difficult for me, was keeping my mouth shut while being on a ship with a very high proportion of white South African officers and well-off white passengers on a cruise. I assumed most of the South Africans (and quite a few British officers as well) were supporters of apartheid. The evidence for this was their non-stop defence of apartheid and attacks on its critics and opponents.

As a photographer on board the SA Vaal I was considered a civilian officer along with pursers and entertainers. This meant I was sitting each day with passengers and other officers in the dining room and mixing with them at events and in the bar. In the course of conversations apartheid would be justified by a whole number of assumptions and arguments, some of which were about the inferiority of black Africans and the phrase that kept coming was 'people should not criticise apartheid until they have come to the country to see for themselves'. Why they said this was a mystery, because what I saw horrified me. (A few of the younger South Africans did not like apartheid but said they went along with it because if black majority rule took over they would be thrown out of 'their' country.) I had to keep my views to myself – which, as friends and relatives will testify, has always been rather difficult for me. What I thought best was to adopt the charade of saying that I was really not interested in politics of any sort and I was travelling and working my way round the world for a good time along the lines of 'wine, women and song'. (There was some truth in the charade).

On one occasion we were searched by police after we had docked in Cape Town. I was later told that they were looking for pornography, which they believed was being smuggled in by the crew and sold on the black market. The officers' quarters were not searched (much to my relief). I suppose they thought that as officers (and gentlemen) we would not do such a thing. In that respect the South African authorities clearly had social class prejudices to add to their racial ones.

On one of my runs as a courier I had a particularly hard time keeping a lid on my views. We were cruising over Christmas time and every one was in Christmas mood, with carols and parties. The singing of 'peace on earth and good will to all men' was very hard to bear from people who supported apartheid. The hypocrisy of the Christmas message and the reality of what was going on were terrible and I made excuses of not feeling well to retire from the festivities before I blew a fuse. (I must confess that my attitude to Christmas, or Christianity for that matter, which was always sceptical to say the least, never really recovered from that event.)

On another occasion, after having made the drop of the package at the agreed spot the evening before, I went to the post office to post a letter to a friend or relative. Before I knew what was happening I was pounced on by two policemen who pushed me up against the wall, punched me and pushed their sticks against my throat. With an infuriated tone they asked me what I was trying to prove and why I was a 'troublemaker'. To my horror what I had done, without thinking, was to join the queue for blacks and coloured people. I think at the time it was probably the nearest or the shortest queue and coming from London the colour of the queue did not register at all. Once they loosened the stick from my throat I explained I was a foreigner, that I did not think and that I would certainly not do it again. In short I grovelled, and the policemen let me go with a warning and a lot of swearing. I remember kicking myself for my absentmindedness, particularly given what I was up to. I also remember thinking how terrible it must be for people if they stepped out of line in the slightest. The surveillance that took place during that period was quite frightening and I thought that this was how it must have been in Nazi Germany.

Final Comment

During discussions with the editor of this book I was asked to consider if I would do it again and if I feel it was worth it. I'll answer that below, but I would say that it is important for the reader to understand that in the UK many other people from all sorts of different political persuasions campaigned, picketed, demonstrated, disrupted sports events, leafleted, raised money through many means. They are often the unsung heroes.

Let me answer the former question in my own way. On my recent visit to South Africa mentioned above, it was refreshing to see the changes that had taken place. I met people who were supportive of the government, some who were critical and some, particularly young black people, who thought the change was too slow and not radical enough. None of that is particularly surprising. However, for me, the fact that I was in shops, bars and restaurants talking about such things was in itself a testament to the changes. The problem for the young is that they can't remember the past and don't realise the progress that has been made. This of course is inevitable but it's still worth us oldies arguing and sharing our positions and perspectives. This I did – when there was anyone willing to listen.

When I got to Cape Town I went to the dock to try to identify where my boat moored and where I dropped off the packages. What was once a quay was now called 'the Water Front' a sort of equivalent to Covent Garden in London. I recognised nothing except Table Mountain. There were shops, bars and restaurants full of tourists and young people of all races. It was good in many ways although I find the consumer capitalism that such things represent unattractive. I must confess a part of me wanted to explain to the young people what it was like on my last visits in the early 1970s – I felt a little like (and in that context probably looked like) a relic – so I went and had a beer at the Water Front instead. Even in the bars the atmosphere was one of people of different races mixing and getting along – a far cry from my experience in the post office described above.

I confess that quite a few of my political assumptions and beliefs have changed since my days as an ANC courier. However in the 1970s, it was easy for us ideologically. It was so clear that apartheid was wrong and that the policy of the ANC was right. Choices about taking action were easy and I am absolutely sure that had other friends and comrades at the time been in my place they too would have done the same. I was simply fortunate to be in a position to help. There are few political struggles that are as clear-cut as that. However, building a more just society in post–apartheid South Africa (or elsewhere for that matter) is a much more complex question. In my opinion, for what it's worth, while I do have some reservations about the policies of the Government, I think the ANC has done well. There remain problems and challenges ahead but no one ever said it would be easy to create a more equal society from that terrible system. I remain optimistic and have no regrets, on that score at least.

DURBAN 1971
Graeme Whyte

I remember sitting in a Durban beach front bar thinking about what an amazing day I had had, and how I had come to be there. I had spent the morning walking around town planning a 'terrorist attack' that would earn me several years in a high security prison if I were caught, and the afternoon learning to surf in the Indian Ocean waves, that rolled up on Durban's golden beaches.

They had these half size blow-up surfboards with two handles at the end. You walked out as far as you could and then you threw yourself just in front of a wave while holding on tight to the two handles. The beach had such a smooth gentle slope that you could travel for about forty yards on a thin skin of water. It was great fun and I was very happy pretending to be a tourist. It was a whites only beach of course, apart from a few young black girls who were there as nannies. Everyone was very friendly, the beach was immaculate, the sun and sea were warm, the beer was cool and you could begin to think it was paradise. Trouble is, everything I had seen in my morning walks reminded me it was really hell on earth.

I've never had any time for racism. As a boy, it always seemed a strange way of looking at the world and the people in it. My dad had a lot to do with that. During the Second World War he served in the RAF and spent a long time based in the Bahamas. He was a mechanic, but a very clever man who passed exams and was selected for training that took him to aircraft factories and air force bases around America, north and south. He travelled widely and was shocked by the racism he witnessed everywhere he went.

My dad was a Communist from the Fife constituency of Communist MP Willie Gallagher. He had never been out of the UK so going to America was quite a culture shock. It was full of surprises, but the racism was one of the biggest. He had quite a political view of the war and had opposed Nazi anti-

Semitism before it started. To see the same kind of stupid and often violent racism in the allied camp was deeply disturbing. My dad was also a musician who played bass in the RAF band. He also played in some of the big hotels along Miami Beach and met local musicians. Among his idols were the great black jazz stars whose talent sparkled in their playing and made all the talk of inferiority laughable.

His politics and his music forced him to confront the contradiction that was America in those days. Thousands of young men were leaving brutal racism at home, to go and fight it abroad. The very ordinary were heard routinely deriding the geniuses of music as their inferiors. It seemed an odd place. Even stranger was the fact that Americans were invariably so warm, friendly and hospitable. Those with Scottish ancestors loved to meet him and talk about 'home'. His RAF uniform was a key that unlocked doors everywhere he went and his description of himself as a simple mechanic was put down to modesty as drinks were ordered for one of the heroes of the Battle of Britain. Addresses were swapped and visits were promised as soon as the war was over. Yet, that warmth and generosity existed alongside the cold-hearted racism of the lynch mob. It was all very strange so he generally kept his opinions to himself and just observed.

One day, however, he decided to do something. Feeling very uncomfortable always sitting in the whites only section of the public bus, he sat with the black passengers to show a bit of solidarity. His protest didn't last long. Some white fellow travellers made it very clear to him that the consequences of his actions would be long lasting and very unpleasant. Musicians have to be protective of their hands and he wasn't a fighter by instinct so he moved. However, the feeling of frustration at being powerless in the presence of a great injustice never left him. I remembered him telling me that story as I sat on a whites-only bench in a Durban park in the summer of 1971. Like him, I had no choice about where to sit, but this time my protest would be heard.

Thanks to my mum and dad, I had grown up without racism

at home. I didn't know any black people, but also I had never heard anyone expressing racist ideas. Racism just wasn't part of my everyday life. My dad's stories had seemed to come from far away and long ago. So, I remember very clearly the first time I heard someone openly sneering at 'wogs' as he called them. The moment is clear in my mind. We were on a bus going home from swimming club. He was sitting opposite me and suddenly started talking about having a black family move in next door and how revolting that would be. It took me a minute to understand what was going on. I could hardly believe it. The spirit of the man who had ordered my dad out of his bus seat was alive and well and now sitting on a bus with me. I was stunned and confused. I couldn't look at him and didn't know what to say. I remember being puzzled for some time about that. Did he really mean it? If he did, how is it I had never noticed that he was an idiot?

At the age of 16 I joined the Young Communist League and at 18 the Communist Party. Given my background any other political choice was unlikely, but it wasn't a simple case of following blindly in my grandfather and father's footsteps. I felt no particular loyalty to the Soviet Union and knew very well how dissident critics of the regime were dealt with. I was inspired more by Fidel Castro and Che Guevara, Ho Chi Minh and the NLF. The war in Vietnam was the great injustice of those times and I felt very strongly the need to do something put a stop to it. The plight of black South Africans and the brave white opponents of the regime also moved me. I had been involved in protests and boycott campaigns. I was on the side of the poor and victims of injustice everywhere. When I was asked to go to South Africa I thought about it briefly and agreed to go.

I have sometimes wondered exactly why I went. It is very hard to understand your true motivation for the things you do in life. Sometimes you can understand things when time has passed. Occasionally, you need other people's help. Some things remain a mystery. Looking back, I can see a mixture of motives that led me to South Africa and to take such risks.

I can't say it was purely a political decision. I didn't sit down, make a cool assessment of that stage of the struggle and conclude that now was the moment for me to move from agitation, demonstrations and boycotts in Britain to direct action. That would be a simple, but not entirely honest explanation of why I went. Of course, it was largely a political decision. I had been an opponent of apartheid for as long as I could remember and wanted to do what I could to help bring it down. I wasn't simply an anti-racist; I was also a supporter of the armed struggle and wanted to help the ANC. It was a very difficult time and there were serious limits on what could be done by people living there. The repression of the opposition was ferocious with even prominent white Afrikaners like Bram Fischer getting life imprisonment for their opposition to the regime. There were compelling political reasons for people from outside going in to help.

Without a strong political conviction that this was the right thing to do, I would not have been able to justify taking the risk. I knew I would face a long time in prison if I were caught. I also knew that being interrogated by the police would be a very unpleasant experience. Ronnie explained this to me, but he also told me that the treatment of political prisoners was as racist as every other area of South African life and that I would not be treated as badly as a black prisoner. I held on to that and told myself it wouldn't compare with being arrested by the Gestapo and that I would probably cope. The danger was something to consider, though, and I didn't act impulsively.

Perhaps my age helped me to act on my political convictions. Like many 20 year olds, I also thought that bad things only happened to other people. They were caught – not me. I also couldn't really imagine what several years in prison would really mean. With the rest of a long life ahead of me, perhaps I thought I could afford the time. Now at the age of 55 and with a family to consider, I would not be so cavalier.

I certainly wasn't looking for glory or admiration. I knew I couldn't tell anyone. I think I knew I would be doing something special, but any congratulations would come only from me. The important thing was that I had been asked for help. I had to say yes or no and then live with that decision. Perhaps here there was something more than politics involved.

As a young boy, I had been brought up on a literary diet of boy's adventure stories. At different ages, tales of Scott, Shackleton, Magellan, Biggles, Thor Heyerdahl and all those who had battled and triumphed against the odds or died heroically in the process enthralled me. Being fact or fiction didn't matter to me. I felt the same emotions.

As I became more interested in politics, I also read about the French resistance, Italian partisans, Tito's communist guerrillas, men like Norman Bethune, Jean Moulin and others who had shown the same heroism and shared the same adventurous lives as my earlier boyhood heroes. I enjoyed their tales as pure adventure stories as well as political actions with which I agreed. I also felt that, as a Communist, I was part of a movement whose members had shown exceptional courage in the past, and in the present, and in some sort of way I was with them.

I knew I was being asked for help, but also being offered an opportunity. I had the chance to have a real adventure, to do something exciting and memorable. This would be an experience that few people would have and that I would look back on with pride and satisfaction. I also thought it would be a chance to take my place in a long line of people who had stood up and been counted. I felt that saying yes would put me with them and saying no would leave me apart. Nobody would ever know except me, but that was important to me.

So there wasn't just one reason why I ended up in Durban. The things I can think of are probably the most significant. Maybe there are other reasons too. The only thing I can say for sure is that I'm glad I was asked to go and very glad I said yes.

My involvement with Ronnie started when his contact in the YCL[57] asked me to consider going to South Africa on a

---

57 Bob Allen recruited Graeme; both were members of the National Committee of the YCL– Editor.

mission for the ANC, and to phone him in a couple of days if I was willing. I did exactly that and was then asked to choose somebody to accompany me. I thought about people I knew in the YCL and whom I could trust, and could get on with at a time of great stress. I finally settled on Denis Walshe, who I had known for a couple of years. I really liked him and felt he would be a solid, dependable person who I could imagine working well with. He thought it over, said yes and so the two of us started our preparations with Ronnie.

At first, I remember spending some time with Ronnie as he explained in detail the difficulties of life in South Africa for opponents of the regime. He put some flesh on the rather dry bones of my second hand knowledge. He introduced me to the clandestine life of the ANC and the Communist Party that brought home to me their difficulties and how much we could help by coming in secretly from outside. He showed me some books produced in the GDR. They were seemingly innocuous classics of literature, but half way through they turned into the works of Marx and Engels. We also had to be cautious in our meetings in case Ronnie was being followed. We met in busy places and had our conversations outside or in someone else's flat. Of course, I loved this. They were the sorts of little tricks I had read about in tales of the SOE in France. At this point, while I took everything very seriously, it was a bit like rehearsing for a play. It is easy and great fun because there is no audience. I knew that stepping out onto the stage would be altogether different.

Then Ronnie explained what he wanted us to do. Our main task would be to take into the country a suitcase with a false bottom containing thousands of leaflets printed on very fine paper. In the suitcase would be a large tin of sweets, also with a false bottom, containing the explosives and timers needed to make six small bombs. The bombs would be used to create a huge shower of leaflets that could be picked up by people nearby before the police arrived on the scene. The purpose was to provide the people with a call to arms from the ANC, and to let the people know that the struggle was not over, even with

Mandela and the other leaders in prison. Obviously, it was to be kept a secret that we had come from abroad to make it appear that, despite the repression, the internal organisation was still intact and capable of mounting such a daring operation.

We were also given hundreds of pre-addressed sticky envelope labels with which to post the leaflets before the day of the explosions. These we posted in small batches all round the town to avoid suspicion. Our third task was to take dozens of photographs of places associated with the black workers of the town, anywhere that they gathered in large numbers. We were never told why. Finally, we were to buy copies of all the newspapers that reported our actions the day after the explosions and bring them home.

Ronnie showed us how to construct the leaflet bombs. Showed us what tools and material we would need and how to dispose of them afterwards. He showed us how to paint our fingers with nail varnish to avoid leaving fingerprints. We had very detailed instructions about how to choose the bombsites and how to behave on the specified time and day of the action. This had all taken a few weeks and by the time we were due to leave I couldn't wait to get on with it.

The day before leaving, I found it difficult to sleep. My mind was jumping from trying to imagine what Durban would be like, to thinking about what would happen to all my stuff if I didn't come back, what prison would be like, what would my mum and dad say and what if I missed the plane. I had packed the suitcase Ronnie had given me and was impressed by the way the false bottom was disguised. When it was empty a suspicious person would probably spot it, but a customs man with no reason to be looking for it would not notice. The tin of sweets had been unwrapped then filled again and the cellophane wrapping put back so that it looked completely normal, even to me. I got out of bed a couple of times to look at them to reassure myself and then eventually fell asleep.

We didn't miss the plane and flew overnight to Nairobi then on to Johannesburg. Arriving there, I felt very nervous and hoped that the ANC security systems were all working. If there was an informer somewhere, this was probably where we would be taken. We had been told to go through immigration separately and, if anyone asked, my cover story was that I was a prospective immigrant coming for a visit. Denis went through first, I followed and told my story as naturally as I could. Then the man asked, 'Are you with our friend there?' and pointed at Denis. This made me very nervous. I thought if I say 'no' and he thinks I'm lying he would wonder why. If I say 'yes', he might ask why we had split up and be suspicious. I thought it best not to lie so I said yes ready to explain that I had stopped to tie my shoelace, the queue had moved on and I didn't like to push back in. I said 'yes'. He looked at me for a moment then stamped my passport and let me go. We were in, and my tummy began to settle down.

On our arrival in Durban we collected our luggage and as we stood wondering where to go a huge young black man grabbed my suitcase, swept it up onto his head and marched off towards the exit. I trotted along behind feeling uncomfortable about him carrying my bag while trying to look like someone who believed that this was the natural order of things. I was also desperate not to let it out of my sight and was relieved to get it back.

There were many other moments during my stay when I felt extremely uncomfortable about my privileged position and having to act the role of confident white supremacist. My worst moment was when we were out taking photos and looking for places to leave the bombs. We witnessed an altercation between a black man and a white man, which ended with the white man punching the black man hard in the face before strolling nonchalantly away. The black man sat on a bench holding his bloody mouth rocking backwards and forwards. I think he was crying. I could feel his dreadful frustration. We all knew there was nothing he could do. The white man was untouchable. I looked at him out of the corner of my eye and walked past as though I couldn't care less. That was hard. It did remind me of why we were there, though, and made me all the more determined to do a good job.

The realities of black suffering were not always as visible as that and for a white man Durban was a lovely place for a holiday. Since our cover story was that we were tourists, we had to play that role or we would have had nothing to talk about. Every day we went to the glorious beaches, sat in the park and strolled round the smart shops. The segregation was so complete that when we were in the city centre it was hard to believe that there was a black majority in this country.

In the evenings, we went out for a drink and to meet the locals. On our first evening out, we sat at a table in a small bar near the hotel where we were entertained by a young man with a guitar. As we went in he was singing 'If you're white you're all right, if you're brown stick around, but if you're black, oh brother, get back, get back, get back.' I was quite taken aback. It wasn't at all what I had expected. A few minutes later, we were hailed from another table. 'Come and join us,' said a man in his 50s. We joined his group and they became our regular companions for the rest of the stay.

I only remember two of them now. The older man, Wally, claimed to have been an RAF Spitfire pilot during the war. His stories sounded convincing so the claim was plausible. It seemed odd for such an enthusiastic supporter of apartheid to pride himself on having fought against the Nazis rather than for them. He was, however, a very jovial, chatty and generous fellow, and easy to pass the time with. The other one I remember was a young woman, different from Wally in many ways, but with the same easy sociability and generosity. Before we left, she invited us to go and stay with her parents who lived on a farm outside Johannesburg. She assured us that if we just turned up we could be sure of a warm welcome. It was all a bit spooky because I couldn't help feeling I was reliving my dad's experience in America.

We spent several evenings in their company and the conversation only touched lightly on anything political. They both had the same argument. 'They are like children. Without us to look after them, they would mess this country up the way they have every other African country without white rule.' I usually listened politely, and with genuine interest, but one evening they must have seen a flicker of something on my face because Wally said, 'Maybe you don't agree, maybe you're communists, are you communists?' I assured him that we weren't and to my relief the conversation moved on.

I discovered that Durban was a very easy place to spend some time and these people were typical in their generosity and hospitability. A real prospective immigrant with no politics and no curiosity could easily have lived in that cosy world and gone for long periods without seeing anything to trouble him.

We, on the other hand, had to go looking. Our leaflet bombs were for the black township workers so we had to be where they were. That meant the bus and train stations, the market, the beer halls and other places where white people just didn't go. I remember the shabbiness of those places with their grubby buildings, dirty trains and buses, the faded clothes, and the crowds. The transport was always packed, the streets were teeming with people and everywhere there were police cars with sullen policemen in the front, and vicious looking dogs in the back. If they stopped us, we would tell them we were just exploring and had got lost, but they never did.

They were scary places though. I remember passing two young black men who looked me in the face while shouting aggressively at me in their language. I felt very vulnerable. I felt my white skin was a provocation while at the same time my only protection, though not much if they decided to vent their feelings on me. I never felt so conspicuous as at those times and I worried that the police would be suspicious of us if they saw us more than once or twice hanging around in those areas.

We couldn't rush the job though. We had to choose litter bins that would be big enough to hold the plastic buckets with the leaflets. They had to be as near as possible to where the crowds gathered and on a route that wouldn't require us to double back on another one. We had to make a number of visits to those areas before we could settle on all six. Then one day we saw a police car parked next to one of our chosen bins, so we had to go round again to choose some reserves in case that happened on the day. When we had finally made our choices, we walked the route that we would take, to time ourselves. We had to set the first timer to give us long enough to get to the last bomb with 15 minutes to spare. I was greatly relieved when that part of the job was over.

Our next job was to make the bombs. It wasn't technically difficult but took a bit of time. We had to go to as many hardware shops as possible to buy the buckets, wood, soldering iron, glue and other bits and pieces that we needed. Then we had to turn our hotel room into a workshop.

This was where we made a big mistake. We had been out every day and had not found out what the staff routines were. I knew very little about hotels, and it hadn't occurred to me that the staff would have a key and could unlock the door and walk into our room any time they wanted to. I thought it might look odd if we spent a couple of evenings of our 'holiday' shut in our room so we decided to do it in afternoon as if we were having a siesta after a good lunch. We drew the curtains, switched on the light and got out all this stuff we had been buying over the previous few days and settled down to work. The air reeked of solder and the room was littered with leaflets and all the paraphernalia when, to my horror, I heard a key in the lock, the door opened and in walked one of the hotel staff.

She just stood and stared. We didn't move. We were all shocked. Then she mumbled an apology and left, but not before looking around the room in amazement. At first, we didn't know what to do. Obviously, we should have done that part of the job during the night, or wedged the door shut with a chair. I felt so stupid, but also very worried. I imagined her going downstairs to her colleagues with a 'Hey, you'll never guess what I've just seen.' I had no idea what she thought we were up to, but it was obviously something very strange, probably criminal, and certainly something well worth talking about. What if she told the management or a colleague who did? She might feel obliged to. If we were really up to no good and she had known all along and said nothing she could end up in big trouble. If what she had seen weren't enough for them to be straight on the phone to the police then a quick check of our room when we were out certainly would be. As the minutes ticked by, I became increasingly sure she would talk. Her job was just cleaning rooms and making beds. She would rarely have anything interesting to gossip about. The other staff would be very interested. We also had to consider that she would almost certainly realise who we were after the bombs went off. Even if she waited until we left the hotel, we wouldn't be leaving the country until the following day, which would give the police plenty of time.

We could leave straight away for another hotel, but that wouldn't stop her talking, and it would take the police five minutes to find out where we were.

We could just finish making the bombs and take them to a left luggage locker in the railway station. We could destroy our suitcases, get rid of the tools, clear up the room and then act as if nothing had happened, but that would take hours. Did we have hours? What if there wasn't a locker at the station? We could end up roaming the streets with our bombs looking for somewhere to hide them. Neither of us could drive so we couldn't hire a car and bundle everything in the boot. We could try bribing her, but there were no cash machines in those days and we didn't know how much that would take out of the cash we had left. She might just take the money and talk anyway.

At this point, the whole operation was in danger so we had to make a decision fast. We could not think of a foolproof plan so we had to take a chance. We could either do nothing and gamble on her not talking and spreading the news of what she had seen, or we could do something to keep her quiet and gamble on that working. Either way we would be taking a big risk.

I went out of the room and down the corridor to look for her. It was very quiet and I was worried she had already gone. Then I saw a cupboard door open and found her inside folding bed sheets. She looked a bit scared when she saw me. Maybe she had also been wondering what to do. She didn't know who we were. We might have been dangerous people. I considered threatening her or giving her the idea that we were police, or some kind of officials. Maybe a white man threatening to kill her would scare her no matter who she thought we were. I wasn't convinced, though, that I could frighten her. I was far too young to be any kind of senior police officer and didn't look remotely like a desperado. I dismissed that idea and asked her to come back to the room.

We had covered everything up so there was nothing for her to see and we sat her down and gave her one of the leaflets to read. She looked at it for a long time reading it carefully. This was it now. She might think this was her chance to win some favours from the authorities at our expense. She might think this was something really worth talking to her friends about. On the other hand, she might just agree to keep quiet at least until we were gone. Having once covered up for us, she would become part of the conspiracy and would have to either keep quiet or be very careful about who she told. She finished reading and then said, "You are fighting for us." I felt a great relief that she had understood what she had read and told her that she must not tell anybody anything. In a couple of days, we would be gone, but she mustn't tell anybody even then. She agreed, and then she left.

Now we could only wait. We finished making the bombs and tidied up the room. We put the tools and the bits of rubbish in a number of plastic bags and then went for a walk dropping them in different litter bins around the town. We kept going over what had happened and what we had done, and speculating about what might have been and what might yet be. We had a few drinks that evening, but I still felt scared coming back to the hotel. We had a good look around, but there were no signs of police outside. Everything seemed normal in reception and our room was empty and apparently untouched. It seemed that so far she had kept quiet. I slept badly thinking that they might come bursting into our room at around dawn. In fact I woke up about 8 o'clock feeling much chirpier. And thinking it was unlikely she would tell anyone now.

At last the day itself came. I was so relieved to have got this far and was desperate to avoid any more problems. We prepared our buckets very carefully. We had collected enough litter to cover each bomb to make it look like a bag of rubbish, and then we packed them two to a large plastic bag along with our towels and a change of shirt. I remember leaving the hotel feeling very conspicuous with these huge bags and expected that any minute someone would ask me what the hell I was taking to the beach, but nobody paid any attention to us.

Placing the first bomb was very scary. It was a big concrete litter bin about a metre across. I remember carefully setting the clockwork timer through a little flap we had cut in the side of the carrier bag, then carefully placing the bag in the bin so that it would stay upright. I think we had about an hour and a half to get all the way round and I could only hope it wouldn't be disturbed and found before it went off. We sat for a moment on the edge of the bin then wandered off to the next one. Everything went perfectly smoothly. There were no police by the bins, nobody else paid any attention to us, the timers all seemed to work perfectly and we were on schedule for them all to be set and go off at the planned time. At one point, we got on a bus, sat at the back and changed our shirts for ones of a very different colour. It might help to confuse the police if we had been spotted and a description put out.

There was only one hair-raising moment. It was the final bomb and we were running a few minutes late. Perhaps I was getting anxious about our luck running out and I rushed the setting of the timer. I was certainly very keen to be finished. For whatever reason, the timer switch slipped from my fingers as I was setting it. The mechanism started whirring and the timer dial started turning to make the connection that would set off the explosive. I just managed to grab it about a second before the thing went off in my arms. My heart really was leaping about inside me as I set it again, more carefully this time, and finally we were finished.

We had planned to be well away before they went off, but we couldn't help being curious. I think we had only about 10 minutes to kill so we hung around near enough to the last one to get some instant feedback. It made a fantastic noise and I was so relieved to hear it. I was still a bit shaky from my near miss so now I was keen to get out of the area. Within minutes, there were sirens going and police cars racing in all directions so we guessed the others had all gone off too. We made our way back to the hotel feeling pleased and excited.

I don't remember what we did that evening. It is strange that I don't remember more of the actual day. We had been working on this project for weeks and the build-up had been quite a tense time. Obviously the prospect of failing, letting down our comrades and being arrested had been on our minds all along. We had prepared very carefully when we were there and rehearsed the operation as much as we could. I was desperate to succeed when we came to the last day and perhaps the fact everything went so well made it a bit of an anti-climax.

I do remember lying in bed the following morning listening to the radio news. There was no TV in South Africa then. We were the main news item, and I learned that we had been part of a big operation with bombs going off simultaneously in three other cities. We had also filled the front pages of all the newspapers and everyone in the country was talking about us. It was a wonderful feeling.

After I had calmed down, I began to think ahead. We hadn't actually got away yet, and now an army of police officers was searching for us. If they suspected that foreigners were involved, they would have tight security at all the airports. Getting out might be harder than getting in. I was also worried that our success would count against us if we were caught. They might have been happier if they had foiled our plot. That might affect the way we would be treated? Since they now knew there were at least four groups of us, they might suspect us of knowing who the others were and go to any lengths to get that information out of us. I started getting nervous again.

We left Durban without difficulty the next day and flew to Johannesburg where we took more photos for Ronnie. Our suitcases were cleaned up so the remains of the false bottom weren't visible. We had been very careful to cover our fingers with nail varnish every time we touched anything associated with the operation so I felt we had covered our tracks well. I wasn't worried about the chambermaid. She wouldn't give us away now. My only concern was that someone might have seen us, and realised afterwards who we were. Maybe they had a description of us. Maybe an experienced policeman would smell a rat, however innocent we tried to appear. I think that evening at the airport was one of the scariest moments for me. I really didn't want to be caught now, when we were so close to getting away with it. Even after the plane took off, I couldn't completely relax. They could still call it back if they knew we were on board.

Only when we touched down in Nairobi did I really relax. We had done it and they would never catch us. I felt a mixture of great relief, satisfaction and pride.

It was strange being back home after my holiday. Friends asked me where I had been and if I had had a good time and I had no trouble looking them in the eye and lying. I had expected that it might be difficult keeping all this to myself, but I quite enjoyed having a secret. If the subject of South Africa came up I would join in and just wonder what they would say if they knew. When Nelson Mandela was released and the regime fell I wondered about telling people whom I knew would be very interested. I thought perhaps I should wait for permission though I wasn't sure from whom. Then as time passed what I had done belonged to a vanished world and there didn't seem to be any natural way to tell anyone. I couldn't just start a conversation with 'guess what I did once'. So, it just stayed with me.

In the grand scheme of things, what I did was very little, but I think in those very dark days Denis and I did something to keep the flame alive. I am grateful to have had the opportunity and very pleased I was able to help.

Graeme Whyte 30/12/2006

Denis Walshe

My journey to South Africa actually started in Vietnam. That is to say, a defining moment for my politics was meeting several female members of the Vietnamese National Liberation Front in Sofia, Bulgaria at the 1968 World Youth festival. The British YCL had run a brilliant campaign to raise money to buy bicycles, motor-bikes and medical equipment for the Vietnamese, to help them defeat the mighty American war machine. Ten of us took 123 bikes, one motor-bike and six boxes of medical equipment in an old red Routemaster double-decker bus from Southampton to Sofia to give to the Vietnamese. At the presentation it was clear how vital international support was for the struggle of the people of this war-torn nation. The young woman who received the equipment was unbelievably small and youthful, but she had shot down an American helicopter. As thanks she presented us with rings made from the helicopter. To me these young women were living proof that international solidarity was essential for those striving for liberation.

In 1971, I was 22 and had just finished my apprenticeship as an electrician. Most of my waking life was occupied with Southampton Young Communist League. Particularly at this time we were involved in the 'Stop the Seventies Tour' campaign, as whites-only cricket and rugby teams were touring Britain. To be in the YCL was to be anti-racist and internationalist.

Sometime in May 1971 my friend Tom Bell, General Secretary of the YCL, approached me with the prospect of going with Graeme Whyte to do ANC and South African Communist Party propaganda work in South Africa. I had no doubts, not least because the anti-racist feeling in my home had always been strong. From the time when my father arrived from Dublin to work, after having served in the RAF during the war, as an Irish immigrant the boarding house signs informed him: 'No Irish'. I was also acutely aware that it was British companies that made most out of the exploitation of the black workforce in South Africa. It seemed to me natural that it was our responsibility to disassociate ourselves from the activities of these companies in whatever way possible (boycotting Barclays Bank and South African fruit) as they did not represent the majority of British people. With these ideas vivid in my mind, I told Tom, without hesitation, that I would go. He stressed the danger and that secrecy was of the utmost importance. I was pleased to be told that Graeme and I had been vetted and approved for this mission by Jack Woddis, the much respected International Secretary of the Communist Party of Great Britain. At this point it would be true to say that I thought I was invincible, but just in case, I did tell my Mum and Dad where I was going, and why. They were totally supportive.

The next step was for Graeme and I to meet a man named Ronnie; if he had a second name, no one told us. The night of the meeting I came up to London from Southampton and we had to ensure we were not followed by BOSS, the South African secret service, or any of their representatives. BOSS was extremely active in London at that time and had even blown up the Anti-Apartheid headquarters there. Thanks to Graeme's experience as a train guard (he seemed to know London inside out) we got to the meeting by the most convoluted route imaginable and to this day I have no idea where we went or where the meeting took place. We arrived, the room was small, and Ronnie was calm and very clear about what needed to be done. We were shown an intriguing false-bottomed suitcase which was nine inches on the outside but only six inches on the inside. Beneath this false layer were to be 10,000 wafer-thin leaflets made of tissue paper, printed in the GDR (German Democratic Republic), which we were to smuggle into South Africa. They were written in several African languages including Zulu and Xhosa and closely typed to make maximum use of space. Ronnie then explained how to use the time-delay switches, leaflet launch-pads and explosive devices for the projection of the leaflets. These were to be thrown 30 to 40 feet into the air and be caught and carried by the wind; this was our method of distribution. The correct use of the timers was essential to ensure that each of the six explosions in Durban went off at the same time; they also allowed us time to make our escape. The timers were small plastic red clocks which were accurate enough for us to stagger the planting of each leaflet bomb. Ronnie then gave us a detailed explanation of how the devices and leaflets would be assembled into buckets and carrier bags to be triggered across the city. Ronnie told us[58] that this operation and five others were to be coordinated across South Africa and would take place at precisely 6 o'clock on Tuesday 10 August. Our job was to cover Durban. The leaflets were to be dispersed in densely populated black areas but also for maximum coverage in the main white high street outside the offices of the *Durban Star*, the city's main newspaper. We had no idea who would be doing the other cities, comrades from South Africa or another part of the world. The aim was to make a massive impact across South Africa.

Obviously an international operation like this was going to be expensive. Ronnie made it clear that money was tight – so tight that we needed to bring back anything left over. A couple of days before we left, Graeme and I collected our suitcases and tickets from the YCL's national office. The cases were so big we looked like we would be on holiday for three months. We flew out of Heathrow on 2 August; fortunately airport security in those days both in London and Johannesburg was not like today – no ultra violet screening to show up our false bottomed suitcases. We found the hotel recommended to us and spent the next three or four days checking out sites to explode the leaflet bombs. Being in the country I was struck by how successful the international campaign to isolate the apartheid regime of South Africa and show solidarity with the ANC had already been. Clearly the impact was being felt in South Africa as even the pubs had collection boxes for a campaign to: 'GIVE HAIN PAIN'. This was a hate campaign against Peter Hain, then a Young Liberal, because of his very effective role in challenging

---

58 Ronnie Kasrils writes: I doubt I would have told Denis that there would have been simultaneous actions in five other cities, but of course I would have stressed the need to keep the time schedule which would have certainly created that expectation.

racially selected South African sports teams in international competitions (Stop the 70s Tour Campaign). Clearly our attempts to isolate apartheid internationally were having the desired effect. Though this gave us hope, it reinforced the bleak realisation that if we were caught we wouldn't get much sympathy here.

South Africa dazzled us with its beauty, climate, riches and people, from the vibrant Indian Ocean to the awesome landscape. In contrast to this magnificence stood the shocking reality of racism and segregation, immense wealth at one end of the spectrum and absolute poverty at the other. Park benches that did not allow black people to sit on them, buses that black people were not allowed to get on. This bizarre scene was all the more sinister for appearing to be totally normal and acceptable; there was the Barclays Bank DCO, the Prudential Assurance – just like being in London.

In the meantime, we found several spots in the train station, bus depot and market place, which would be ideal for the leaflet bombs. There were hardly any whites and thousands of black workers passed through at rush hour, returning to their homes in the townships. On our reconnoitring trips we were religiously ignored. People here were obviously unused to seeing or speaking to white people. Being white, we were clearly out of place and all the more conspicuous thanks to our furtive glances over our shoulders. We spent time rehearsing stories of being lost tourists; our cover story.

Having chosen our sites, the 10th was rapidly approaching. We bought the bags and buckets and planned to open the suitcases the next morning. This was the first day that we had stayed on in the hotel after breakfast. We cut open the false layer of the suitcases and removed the densely packed leaflets. We spread them out before packing them into the buckets we had, so that they would be more easily caught by the wind when exploded. This meant that our beds, the floor and any surface space left in the hotel room were covered with 20,000 leaflets. The magnitude of what we were doing still hadn't hit us; this was just a job to be done. Fumbling with the time switches in the buckets was all that concerned us.

Then the door directly in front of us opened. Genuine confusion soon gave way to sheer alarm. This must be the South African police, with a room full of leaflets and timers, and it wasn't looking good. Our relief to realise it was a young black woman, our chambermaid, was short-lived. She looked as confused as we did. How was she ever going to clean this room? She just stood there, taking in the scene. Our minds were racing. We tried to explain by thrusting a leaflet into her hands and telling her that we were supporters of the ANC and despite her lack of English we continued to tell her about our work for them. She never said a word and shock had rendered her face expressionless. We desperately hoped that our hurried words about ideals, and solidarity salutes, were falling on fertile ground. This was the first jolt of genuine fear that I had felt and all the moments of nervous glances in crowded markets and secret meeting places took on a new significance. The possibility of discovery and failure loomed large.

Finally we told her that we would tidy the room. She left with a leaflet, and we were left stunned. We packed everything into the suitcases, locked them and knew that we had to get out with our passports as soon as we could. Walking through the lobby of the hotel we were as unconvincing in our attempts to look casual and unflustered as we were at impersonating lost tourists. We sat just inside the door of a bar near the beach. Should we abort this operation, or not? After this drink would we be heading back to the hotel or the airport? We ran over our options. Would the chambermaid shop us? In our wisdom we had actually given her the evidence, but at the same time we worried that she was now in a very difficult position herself: if she kept quiet she became an accomplice.

Possession and even reading leaflets published by the ANC was illegal under South African law, a fact she was no doubt well aware of. Invincible wasn't in the vocabulary now. Since neither of us frequented hotels often, the fact that they were cleaned during the day hadn't even occurred to us and our inexperience for this task seemed glaringly obvious. After all of the efforts of the ANC, from the money to the trust they put in us, had our lack of attention to detail jeopardised what we had all worked so hard for? As we talked this over, I was struck by Graeme's clarity and sheer bravery. We decided to go back to the hotel.

On our return everything was the same as usual; our worst fears were not realised. That evening we rapidly prepared the six buckets which we stored in the bathroom ready for explosion the next day. This was probably the most frightening night of my life – we didn't sleep a wink. Not only had the operation to be successful but also we had to avoid being caught in the process. We had the added fear that we may have been tricked into a false sense of security and were going to be caught in the act. By the next morning, having not been arrested, we decided that the chambermaid was our comrade and bought her the most expensive watch that we could afford. After breakfast we completed our preparations and gave our chambermaid the watch. She was very pleased and we kissed her goodbye.

That afternoon we set about positioning the leaflet bombs and set the timers with varying times, from 45 minutes down to 15 minutes, as we rushed about town putting them all in place. The last one we strategically placed outside the *Durban Star*. From the far end of the street we waited and watched our device explode with a massive bang as thousands of leaflets cascaded over the high street. We were jubilant. It felt like we had succeeded, and that evening we had a very low-key celebration in a whites-only bar.

We had arranged to fly home the next morning, firstly to Johannesburg, then to Rome. We just had time to buy the *Rand Daily Mail* before we left; and we were delighted to see the whole of the front page was covered with the story crying out in bold type 'PAMPHLET BOMBS BLAST AGAIN'. It described how '*Thousands of subversive pamphlets were scattered in the major centres of South Africa last night when at least 11 home-made time bombs exploded in Johannesburg, Durban, Cape Town and*

Port Elizabeth.' It was reported that the blasts had gone off simultaneously in the rush hour as workers streamed home, and, as planned, nobody had been hurt. The paper described how the police rushed around in an attempt to confiscate the leaflets. I am pleased to report that they failed to stop the ANC having a voice and we were both exhilarated and relieved to be going home.

These ANC leaflet blasts were reported across the world, and I have since been told that exiled South Africans and anti-apartheid campaigners were encouraged to see that, despite its leaders and members being murdered, jailed, banned and exiled by the regime, the ANC was not crushed and was fighting back, making its voice heard.

On reflection, the courage, determination, but most of all the political will to create the broadest possible movement, embodied by the ANC's strategy at home in South Africa and internationally, laid the basis for the destruction of one of the most cruel, undemocratic and hated regimes of the 20th century. It also formed the sound basis for the construction of a free and democratic South Africa.

In Britain, a symbol of the success of isolating racism in South Africa has been how the Tory Party has gone from Thatcher's branding of Mandela as a 'terrorist' to Cameron's assertion that she was wrong. Whilst personally, since the defeat of apartheid, in our house we have happily re-educated ourselves into buying South African goods rather than boycotting them (although we still have to remind ourselves it is okay sometimes!).

To this day I don't know the name of our chambermaid, but I often think there were three of us on this mission – what a star she was!

Steve Marsling

I was born in 1951 in South London, just south of the Elephant and Castle. My family lived in various council estates around that area. We were not a particularly political family but both Mum and Dad were strong trade unionists and I guess without knowing it a class consciousness rubbed off on me.

Like the rest of my mates, I took and failed my 'eleven plus' exam and left school at fifteen. I had various jobs and slowly but surely came to the conclusion that working-class people made the wealth for others but saw precious little of it themselves. It also seemed to me that the Labour Party was always too busy trying to appease the bosses rather than fighting for the rights of working people. It is that background that led to a chance conversation in a pub near the Oval. To cut the story short, it wasn't long before I joined the Young Communist League. I was around 18 at the time.

I was a member of Brixton YCL and soon immersed myself in studying and selling *Challenge*, the YCL newspaper. At some time in 1971, Bob Allen, the YCL London Secretary, asked if he could speak to me privately. He said the South African Communist Party needed two people to go to South Africa and carry out some work for the Party and the ANC. He asked me if I was interested and did I know of anyone else. I said yes and asked Sean Hosey.

A little later we both met Ronnie Kasrils and he told us that we would be taking some letters; but more importantly we would be also taking out explosives to detonate various leaflet bombs – the idea being that the bombs would blow the leaflets up in the air and people could pick them up on their way back to the railway and bus stations before the police had time to confiscate them.

We were trained in how to handle the explosives which were hidden under a false fibreglass bottom of a suitcase. Training always seemed to take place after an Arsenal home match. Ronnie Kasrils was a passionate Arsenal fan! We were well trained and nothing was hidden from us. It was explained fully what would happen should we be caught, i.e. a minimum five year sentence under the Suppression of Communism Act. We also knew that we would undergo various tortures before being brought to trial.

My hatred of apartheid and all forms of racism came from my firm belief that the ruling class always had it easy when the working class was arguing among themselves. 'Divide and rule' has always been a highly effective weapon to stop united action.

Arriving in Cape Town in August 1971, we stayed in a small hotel and had instructions to 'blend in' and sightsee – so that meant Table Mountain and Cape Town Races. After breaking through the false fibreglass bottom of the suitcase we began to assemble the explosive devices. The explosives were to be triggered by attaching them to a parking meter timer. For those not in the know, these timers were removable gadgets which reminded people when it was time to return to the meter. We discovered a problem with one of these gadgets: – it seemed to have a life of its own and would often, during practice, spring back to the 'time up' position, but we decided to go ahead with it anyway.

We had been unlucky with the weather. Cape Town in August can often be cloudy and rainy and for most of our week there it was exactly that. The plan was that we would don large raincoats and hide the small buckets, containing explosives and leaflets, underneath the coats as we made our way to the bus and railway stations during rush hour. Of course as luck would have it we woke up to find Cape Town bathed in sunshine and not a cloud in the sky! So two idiots in ankle length macs made their way past people in vests and shorts hoping we could pass ourselves off as eccentric Englishmen! (or Irishman in Sean's case)

The first two bombs were laid and the timing devices set. However, on the third, the dodgy timer decided to play up. As I wound the timer back, and set it for 20 minutes, it immediately started to go off! I managed to get my finger nail between the timer dial and the detonator. I moved it back slowly and it stayed. I looked up at Sean, who had turned white! I was shaking like a leaf as I realized how close I had been to becoming a one-armed socialist. The action was purely instinctive as I am not normally hero material. I think we laid six bombs in total of which five went off. We spent that evening watching Cape Town play football.

The next morning we were due to fly back to London. We were delighted that our actions made the front page of every newspaper we could find. It was reported that the police were lying in wait for us as they were expecting something like this to happen. Missing two raincoats on a summer's day does not say much for the intellect of the South African security forces. When we got to the airport we were told there was no flight back to London! We had to fly to Salisbury, Rhodesia, and then catch a London plane from there. We realized that under Ian Smith's regime we were not safe until we left Rhodesia. We were somewhat taken aback to find it was headline news in that country too! Sean insisted we were not safe when the plane made a fuel stop on the Cape Verde Islands, as this was part of the fascists' colony of Portugal under the Salazar regime. However, I thought Sean was stretching a point when insisting that the plane could be forced to land over Franco's Spain!

When we got back, Ronnie's face was a picture. He was so happy! I then told him I was going to Teachers Training College in Reading. A short time later Ronnie got in touch. He asked if I would be interested, once I had qualified, in teaching in South Africa and acting as go-between for the movement. I agreed. Later Ronnie was in touch again. There was an urgent job on. Some money had to be delivered to a drop in Durban (I think) and could I do it? I said yes. But when I thought about it, there was a problem. I had exams coming up and I would have to explain a week away from lectures. I told Sean, who was working for Granada TV at the time and he said he would go as he was owed leave and this time the sunshine was guaranteed! Ronnie was OK with the change.

Sean was to send me a cryptic postcard which would let me

know everything was OK. Just before he left we went to watch Crystal Palace. They lost, which pleased both of us. It sounds daft now, but I remember feeling a bit envious of his week in the sun – after all there were no bombs involved, no dodgy technical stuff, just some money to be dropped off and a sun tan to be had. I arranged to meet him in a fortnight.

No postcard arrived that week. I contacted Ronnie. We both feared the worst – or Ronnie knew; I cannot remember. Ronnie asked if I knew Sean's landlady well. Luckily I did. I went round and cleared out any personal stuff that the South African secret police (BOSS) could use against Sean. Ronnie guessed they would send someone to Sean's place posing as his friend. He was right! Within a matter of hours BOSS came calling. I told the landlady to say that he couldn't stay and that someone she knew had already been in to clear the room. (I didn't want her place broken into; she was a good person and didn't deserve that.)

I came back home and just broke down. A good friend of mine had taken my place and had walked into a trap. Ronnie said they had just got lucky and cracked the code by accident.[59] Your rational self says you're not to blame but your emotions tell you that is a lie. There was his family to face (they were a Communist family and were brilliant, a tower of strength) and the thought of what he was going through was hard to cope with.

Sean had to endure 13 months solitary confinement before being brought to trial. In that time he was brutally tortured, yet when asked to renounce the ANC in court, in exchange for his freedom, he refused. He always had bottle. His incredible bravery was an example to us all. As for myself, I was followed and had a few dodgy phone calls. Apparently they found my signature on something. If Sean hadn't taken my place, I would have been done for both visits and received a likely sentence of

---

59 Sean was caught not by accidental cracking of a code but unfortunately because the comrade we sent him to meet had, unknown to us, been captured. Under torture he had revealed the secret method of communicating with us in London and the SA security police had led us on. – Ronnie Kasrils.

ten to fifteen years. Sean was found not guilty of our adventure but guilty of the most recent offence and sentenced to five years.

I spent my time working with Sam Ramsamy in the South African Non-Racial Olympic Committee and Aziz Pahad of the ANC as well as the Anti-Apartheid Movement. When Sean was released the family had a big party in his home town, Coventry. It was very emotional. We went away to St Ives in Cornwall for a week and had a good laugh but I guess we both felt a bit awkward.

I don't regret my time in the Communist Party. In so many ways it was the making of me.

Sean Hosey

As a young man of 22 I had been living in London for 18 months. I had a flat in the house of an Irish family in the Islington area, just round the corner from Arsenal's ground at Highbury.

My family and I had immigrated to England in 1960. I had come with a head full of catechism and an acute sense of Irish repression which, on reflection, was probably partly historical and partly romanticised.

My parents were staunch socialists and were active in the Communist Party in the Midlands. I followed in their footsteps and joined the Young Communist League when I was fifteen. I also supported the anti-apartheid movement. I had continued these allegiances when I went to London.

It's important to remember how strong feelings were against apartheid at that time. It was not just the political left, who were also deeply engrossed in the anti-Vietnam War campaign, who were involved in the anti-apartheid movement. Campaigns against South African produce and the whites-only South African sporting teams were widely supported.

Church clerics criticised apartheid from the pulpit regularly and middle-class housewives shunned South African fruit in supermarkets. Several ministers in Labour governments over the last ten years were prominent in the campaigns – Peter Hain, Jack Straw and Charles Clarke to name but three. Everyone had heard of Nelson Mandela.

I had made some good friends in London. One of those was Steve Marsling, a slightly cheeky chap who lived with his dad in the Elephant and Castle area. Steve has described in his section how he had been approached by Bob Allen, who at that time was secretary of the London District of the YCL, and in turn asked me if I would be interested in going to South Africa to disseminate anti-apartheid material.

I did think about it but it didn't take me long to agree. Of course part of me saw the adventure of it, going to South Africa to the exotic sounding Cape Town. Remember, I was still only

22. But by far the predominant reason was the moral one. Anything I could do to dent the apartheid regime, however small, had to be the right thing to do.

I recall a conversation I had with Steve about the dangers that faced us if we were caught. We knew that it would not be a holiday camp because our 'handler' Ronnie Kasrils had explained in some detail the sort of treatment we could expect. However, we focused our thoughts and plans on doing the job successfully. We perhaps didn't understand or realise what the impact would be for our families and friends if that were to happen. That was something I was to learn later. However I also later learnt about the fantastic support they were to give me and that they endorsed my actions.

Obviously we had to be secretive about what we were up to and that included my family and girlfriend at the time. Our training and preparation at the time was also quite surreal, taking measures to ensure we were not followed, the use of false bottomed suitcases, understanding the extent of police and security police networks in South Africa, planning how to act the part of carefree tourists in Cape Town and how to handle low grade explosives.

Steve has explained how we took leaflets and small explosives in false bottomed suitcases into South Africa. It's important to point out that the explosive material was little more than medium firework strength, enough to lift a small platform of leaflets from a bucket 30 feet or so into the air. The African National Congress, in its liberation struggle, never adopted indiscriminate anti-civilian tactics. What we took in could do no damage to people. What we wanted to do, and spectacularly succeeded in doing, was to dent the arrogance of the South African police state and encourage the anti-apartheid movement within the country.

If I had ever had any doubts about what we were doing they quickly disappeared on arrival in Cape Town when I saw the 'Blankes' only, (whites only), signs all over the city, even on park benches; blots on the landscape of the very beautiful Cape Town perched beneath the hugely atmospheric Table Mountain.

Another episode reinforced this apartheid reality check. Whilst we were preparing to carry out our mission, Steve and I had befriended a couple of young women and arranged to have a meal with them in a restaurant. In the middle of our meal a uniformed policeman entered. Both the girls froze. They later told us that they were officially classed as 'coloureds' and were in a whites-only restaurant. If the policeman had asked for their ID papers they would have been in serious trouble. So would we have been, with Ronnie, for unknowingly compromising the achievement of our task!

We had six bucket devices to place in central Cape Town, near the railway station. They needed to be timed for 5 pm to coincide with the trains taking black workers home. We had identified our spots in advance. However, when the day came to actually place them we were nervous. We had been told that the security police were on high alert and would be vigilant. In the week we had been in Cape Town preparing for the big day the weather had been poor. We had purchased large raincoats so that the buckets could be reasonably concealed. However, D day turned out to be fine. It was still a little chilly, as August in Cape Town often is, so we could justify the coats. A couple of large bags from a fashionable shop completed the disguise of our packages.

Access to the timers was via a small cut-out section at the side of the bags. One of the timers had been slightly malfunctioning during testing at the hotel. We had not set the timers on our six devices, in case they malfunctioned before we had placed them. The plan was to quickly and discreetly set them at their placement points and then get away from them. The first three went to plan. However, the fourth one, the dodgy one, immediately went to the 30 second mode with its familiar buzzing tone which we immediately recognised. Steve reacted quickest and managed to disconnect the device with a couple of seconds to spare.

We then got well away from the area and awaited developments. They were pretty spectacular. Every South African newspaper had screaming headlines about the leaflet bombs. Unbeknown to us there had been similar shows in all the major cities. Even better, they had all gone off at precisely 5 pm. It looked like a well coordinated operation and it had made its mark.

We kept a very low profile for a couple of days and then flew out of Cape Town. Having carried out a reasonably professional operation we nearly blew it at the last moment at the airport. Thinking we were late for the plane, we started running on the airport foyer and were quickly confronted by three policemen toting machine guns. Putting on a couple of village idiot performances got us out of that scrape but neither of us properly relaxed until we were well up the African continent 35000 feet up in the air!

TONGAAT AND DISASTER

Just over a year later, Steve told me there was another job to be done. I met up with Ronnie surreptitiously in St James's Park and he outlined the mission. On the face of it, taking some passbooks and money to some comrades in Durban seemed a far simpler mission than the previous one. But it was to prove very much the contrary.

Using the tried and trusted false bottomed suitcase method, I flew to Durban with four false passbooks and a few thousand rand. I was to meet my contact at a small town called Tongaat just outside Durban. All I had was a description of the man: small and stocky, wearing a hat and glasses. A successful exchange of passwords would mean I would hand over the passbooks and money to him. As I subsequently discovered, that man was Petrus Mtembu who had been captured and tortured before I even left England. I was walking into a carefully prepared trap.

Arriving in Durban I was confronted with a very hot and fashionable resort. I had a couple of days before the handover, so I made the most of the sunshine and great beach. I managed to get quite badly sunburnt on one of my arms which developed into blisters. I came to bitterly regret this later when one of my interrogators thought it fun to rub the sole of his shoe over the blisters.

What was to prove my last day of freedom for nearly six years began with a short sedate train trip from Durban to Tongaat. Ironically I bought a return ticket.

Tongaat at that time revolved round the sugar industry. Mainly an Indian town, it is near the aptly named crocodile creek. Other sorts of manhunters were waiting for me!

The walk from the station to the place of exchange, the Post Office, was hot and sultry. I was feeling relaxed, nothing of any consequence caused me any concern. I carefully approached the Post Office and there was my contact, a short and stocky black man wearing a hat and glasses. We quickly exchanged passwords and I gave him the parcel. I still felt completely relaxed and started to walk away. Then came the words that would stay with me for a very long time. "Hold it boss." My first thought was, why would a comrade be calling me boss? It was a term, after all, which denoted the subjugation of black South Africans. The reason became quickly apparent when I turned round and was faced by four black men displaying a considerable amount of firepower, all of it aimed at my chest.

Within minutes a posse of white security police had arrived and I was whipped off to security police headquarters in Durban. I tried desperately to keep my wits about me and not to crumble. One thing was obvious. One of the men with a gun had been my contact. It was safe to assume that I didn't need to try to hold out on that front. It was obvious that either he wasn't the comrade I was supposed to meet or he was a double agent. How else would he have known the handover arrangements? Knowing that helped me, in a strange sort of way.

What followed was eight months of solitary confinement and interrogation. Ronnie had given me some indication of what to expect if I was caught. Suffice to say that all his warnings, plus some, did happen. Many other comrades have described that process and many never got to tell their tales. However, a most peculiar element in the early stage of that period was an obsession that a couple of the senior security police had with Harold Wilson.[60] They seemed to believe that I knew something of Wilson's visit to Moscow and were convinced that he was an agent of international communism. Now this was both laughable and frightening. But I wasn't in a laughing environment and if they genuinely believed their paranoia then it was extra interrogation time and a few more beatings for me. Eventually they dropped it.

I was taken by light aircraft on an odyssey of security police headquarters in Cape Town, Blomfontein, Jo'burg and finally Pretoria. I think they wanted to show off their international captive.

Throughout that time my only objective was to get through to the next day. I was in limboland and had no idea what they were going to do with me. At best I hoped they would just deport me. But eventually, in May of 1972, I was brought out of my cell to an interview room where I met George Bizos, a well-known lawyer who had represented many comrades over the years and had been on Nelson Mandela's defence team. He showed me a lengthy-looking charge sheet and I realised it could be some time before I left South Africa. George proved to be a very good lawyer and was very supportive to me during the trial period, which was to last for more than three months. A number of interviews were held in the adjacent 'awaiting hanging' wing where at any one time there were up to a hundred condemned men awaiting execution. Hanging day was Thursday, when usually eight people were hanged at the same time. I learnt much later on that our prison doctor would occasionally administer a fatal injection on the occasions the hanging rope had not completed its task. I asked him how he squared that with his Hippocratic Oath. I seem to recall that I got a couple of days without food for my impertinence!

George and I had a meeting one Wednesday before a hanging day. It was the practice to notify the unfortunate

60   British Prime Minister – Editor.

eight of their fate the day before with a decree from the State President, introduced with the preposterously inappropriate word 'Greetings'. The practice then was for the other prisoners to start singing to help the condemned through their last day and night. I have never heard such soulful and moving singing in my life – a wonderful harmony of the hopeless in support of the lost. George was visibly moved and upset. He asked that our subsequent interviews be held at Pretoria Central.

I only met my fellow accused on the first day of the trial in Pretoria. They had also been through hell and the black comrades had taken more of a physical battering than I had. Poor Alex Moumbaris had tried to take his own life. It felt slightly weird seeing the real Petrus Mtembu. He had been caught and tortured. With the information they had obtained, the trap was set for me.

Shortly afterwards I had a great surprise when my dad visited the prison and told me he was going to stay for the trial. At that time we did not know it was going to last for three months. With great support from all of my family and lots of supporters at home, as well as financial help for my defence from International Defence and Aid, the finance to do this was found.

Early on in the trial there was a surprise celebrity attendee at the trial, the actor David Tomlinson, who was interested in jurisprudence and attended trials around the world. I was able to have a brief discussion with him. He was amazed that a state witness against Theo Cholo admitted under cross examination that he had turned state witness after he had been tortured. I could hear him tutting in open court. The judge, Boshoff, gave him a withering look and I thought he was going to chuck him out of the court.

The Terrorism Act was an effective catchall for anything that threatened apartheid supremacy. Any breach carried a mandatory minimum sentence of five years. Eventually Boshoff found me guilty of attempting to embarrass the administration of the state. He couldn't convict me on the Cape Town charges but there was no way out of the Durban issue.

George Bizos thought it was worth an appeal, but I never held out much hope, and so it proved.

My five years in prison were to bring me into contact with a number of inspirational and supportive comrades such as Bram Fisher, Dennis Goldberg, Dave Kitson and John Matthews, who were all serving life or very long sentences.

There are many stories to be told about that time but that's for another time.

Sean Hosey, October 2007

On his release and return to England, Sean Hosey was awarded a scholarship by Warwick University to study for a master's degree. Finding that the students had named their union bar the 'Sean Hosey' bar, he persuaded them to rename it the 'Cholo' bar in honour of Theo Cholo who was still in prison at that time. – Editor.

Mary Chamberlain

In 1971 my then boyfriend, Carey Harrison, was approached by an old Cambridge friend of his, Katherine Levine, to help the ANC cause. At the time, both of us were members of the Communist Party. Katherine put us in touch with Ronnie Kasrils and we were duly vetted by both Ronnie and Joe Slovo. The plan was to 'emigrate' to South Africa with our 'household effects' packed in old tea chests with false bottoms containing ANC and SACP literature which we would then distribute. The ANC presses had been smashed and our role was to distribute the small histories of the South African Communist Party, documenting its part in the anti-apartheid struggle and a comic book published by the ANC which explained how to resist the regime, with force if necessary.

We married in October 1971 and sailed for South Africa in the spring of 1972; we rented a flat in Cape Town, and over the next few days packed the literature, stamped and posted it from every post box in Cape Town, over 5,000 packages from memory. We left immediately afterwards. I feel honoured that the ANC trusted us on that mission. It remains my proudest achievement.

Roger Allingham

I come from rural Hertfordshire and was born in 1945. The nearest villages were Wheathampstead and Kimpton and the nearest towns were St Albans and Luton. My father was a sheet metal worker who was never active politically, though he voted Labour. My mother was the daughter of a Swiss farmer who settled in England just prior to the Second World War and was also apolitical.

I first became active in the youth section of the Labour Party but then in about 1964, when disillusionment set in, I helped form a YCL branch in Hatfield with the help of Phil Bird, the YCL District Secretary. This venture was guided by veteran communists in Hatfield (including Ron Halverson, a veteran trade union member) and it was not long before I joined the CP.[61] We were part of the South Midlands District of the CP and Tom Mitchell in Luton was the District Secretary. When Phil Bird gave up as YCL District Secretary it was Tom Mitchell who persuaded me to take his place and I remember spending a lot of time on cold winter nights travelling around the South Midlands talking to small groups of Young Communists. Tony Chater was at that time lecturing at Luton Technical College and was on the South Midlands CP District Committee. Later, of course, he went on to become the editor of the *Morning Star*.

I guess I was one of the generation of the 'upwardly mobile' from the skilled working class in that period. With the 'O' levels I obtained at St Mary's Secondary Modern school in Welwyn and the odd 'A' Level in Economics and British Constitution which I studied on night courses, I managed to get into Balls Park Teacher Training College in Hertford, as a mature student. Steve Arloff, who was active running the Stevenage YCL branch and had a background in building workers' trade unionism, had already gained a place there and suggested that I join him to get into higher education. Three years were spent there at the height of the student uprisings in Europe (Cohn Bendit aka

61 CPGB – Editor.

'Danny the Red', Tariq Ali, etc.) and I was very active in student politics, forming a Marxist group and later broadening the base to a Socialist Society. My best friend was John Croll who had a greengrocer's shop in Puckeridge and he made frequent visits to socialise with students at Balls Park. With a father who was a staunch CP member of the 'Stalin' school, John was also very committed to communist politics. He travelled to Covent Garden fruit and vegetable market twice a week to purchase cheap fruit and vegetables for his shop. I joined him on many trips, leaving in the evening, drinking all night in London pubs, and then sleeping at the house of his South African cousin, Ann Nicolson, before going off in the early hours of the morning to Covent Garden Market, then back to Hertford and study! Often I met and talked to Ann Nicolson, Silva Neme and Jean Middleton and they influenced me a lot. Ann was living in London after serving time in a South African jail and her co-accused, Silvia Neme and Jean Middleton, were also living in London. They were all active in the ANC in London and I had a lot of contact with South African exiles.

Leaving Balls Park College I managed to gain entrance to Pembroke College, Cambridge, and gained a Bachelor of Education, with History as a main study. Here again I found myself at the heart of student politics with a very active CP branch and broader Socialist Society.

After College I spent three years teaching in Stevenage at a Comprehensive school, then a year in Brecon, Wales, running the water section of a young people's holiday adventure camp for PGL Ltd. Then it was some eight years working for the London Borough of Hillingdon as a Youth & Community worker running a water activities centre for young people on a disused gravel pit. It was in 1984, whilst working there, that Ronnie Kasrils recruited me for the MK work in South Africa. At that time I was not politically active, due to work and family commitments, though needless to say I was politically committed in support of the South African anti-apartheid campaign and the ANC armed struggle. In 1984 Jean Middleton, who was editing *Sechaba*,[62] approached my friend John Croll on instructions from Ronnie Kasrils to recruit him for underground work in SA. He had commitments at that time that but indicated he knew someone who might 'help'.

John approached me and a meeting was set up in a London pub with Ronnie Kasrils, Eleanor Kasrils, John Croll and myself. We talked at length and by the end of the evening I had agreed to give up my work and move to Southern Africa to undertake underground work. I felt honoured to have been requested to carry out such work and felt it my 'international solidarity duty' to respond to the call. At that time I was single and therefore felt I could undertake the work. Ronnie gave 'evening classes' in a house in London on the methodology of secret cell work and explained that it was of the utmost importance that no one should know of my activities. A 'legend' or story was constructed for my family (mother and siblings) of going to explore in Botswana.

Initially I was to be deployed in Gaborone running a safe house, but when the time for departure came Ronnie had redeployed me to South Africa. They wanted a 'safe house' set up for a planned attack on a South African military base (code named 'Uncle Barney') on the Golden Highway south of Johannesburg and next to Soweto. I set up the house with Susan Westcott in Henley on Klip which is about 60 kilometers south of Johannesburg. Susan went back shortly after the house was set up, and I was left to look after the house on my own. Life was then spent with the legend that I was a 'writer' and collector of Africana books (early books on South Africa). My work, under the direction of Ronnie, was to carry out surveillance of all South African military establishments in the vicinity of Johannesburg, Vereeniging, Sasolburg, and the Vanderbijlpark area. Through reconnaissance I drew up maps of all the military establishments in the area together with information about high ground that

---

62 *Sechaba* (nation) was the official magazine of the ANC, published monthly and mainly circulated outside South Africa. – Editor.

would be suitable for use with mortar attacks, and had meetings in Botswana and Zimbabwe with Ronnie Kasrils to pass on the information. Except when on debriefing visits to neighbouring states, I used the system of book coding to send secret messages, hidden inside greeting cards, to neutral addresses in England. These were duly passed on to Eleanor Kasrils, who passed them on again.

The proposed attack on 'Uncle Barney' was delayed many times and eventually I abandoned the safe house in Henley-on-Klip and found a new one near Eikenhof, also south of Johannesburg but closer to Soweto. This house was a cottage on a farm. The owner of the farm had a brick company close to Soweto and never came near me. Whilst briefing Ronnie Kasrils in a neighbouring state, the plan to infiltrate a special cell into the country was explained to me. We discussed three ways of infiltrating the cell. Firstly they could enter by train from Botswana using false passports. Secondly they could enter by 'jumping the fence' in Botswana, or thirdly they could fly into Lesotho and then make their way across the Lesotho highlands to the Drakensberg mountains and thence into South Africa.

I went back to South Africa and researched the Lesotho option. The main problem was that the infiltration would be in winter time and we were worried about the possibility of cold and snow in unfamiliar terrain. I also researched the border roads between South Africa and Botswana. At the same time I moved to a new flat in Rosettenville, a suburb of Johannesburg. Eventually the option of jumping the Botswana fence was chosen, and I was called to Gaborone to meet the group. We agreed on an exact date, time, and place that I would rendezvous with them on the border and agreed coke can signals to be left on the road. The place chosen was some kilometres east of Bray, which is a small border post.

Everything went like clockwork and I picked up the group, which consisted of Damien de Lange, Susan de Lange (only married later), Ian Robertson, Hugh Lugg & Paul Annerson. The group was settled into the cottage at the farm and I went back to the apartment in Rosettenville. In a briefing meeting before I departed for Rosettenville we agreed on danger signals, to be shared if one of us came under surveillance, and rendezvous places. Our training came in very useful in this respect, because the very next day I came under surveillance. Having left the Rosettenville apartment the next morning, I carried out a number of standard checks to see whether my kombi was being followed. This consisted in driving a roundabout route whilst switching lanes and making turns suddenly and also running traffic lights to see if anyone was following. Everything seemed OK but as I started to drive towards Eikenhof I noticed an old model grey Peugeot with three black men and one black woman. I indicated I was turning left and they pulled over into the same lane some few cars back and also indicated left. I drove straight over and saw them turn left. I turned off the main road and stopped in a side street. After some delay I then saw them driving past. They had obviously realised their error in losing me and were retracing their steps trying to find me.

Now the cat and mouse game started! I abandoned my visit to the cell at Eikenhof (training instructed that the main thing is to buy time for other comrades so they can go to ground), and went to a local shopping centre where, from a public box (checking no surveillance), I made a short coded call to alert comrades that I was under surveillance. Then I took my dirty laundry to a launderette for washing. By the time I left I could see my tail had by now found me again. I led them around various normal places during the day and then retired back to my apartment in Rosettenville. The next day I was expecting a tail but not as heavy as it turned out to be. During that day I counted five different cars following me around Johannesburg, with mostly white occupants, as I continued with a normal day of activities of shopping and visiting the bank. One couple followed me into the bank (we were trained to use reflections to see who was following). At one point I went into an underground car park at the Carlton Centre, a shopping centre in downtown Johannesburg. They froze at following me into the underground car park and were confused. Realizing that I was not being tailed I quickly left the mall on foot and walked around Johannesburg, checking that I was not being followed. When I returned and left with my Kombi the tails were back!

The next day I tried the same trick using the underground car park but they had reorganised and picked me up on foot straight away. The following day was the first of the prearranged meetings with the cell if we had trouble. Signals had been worked out in advance to indicate whether it was safe or dangerous to approach. The first meeting place was in an Africana bookshop in downtown Johannesburg that was a rambling old house. I went to the shop and browsed on the second floor for some time, but my comrades did not show up. As I went down the stairs I bumped into one of my 'tails' coming up the stairs. He stopped and very self-consciously looked at a picture on the wall whilst I walked down and out of the shop (we had been taught that tails are conscious about their work and instinctively act guilty if confronted!).

The next day I went to the fall-back rendezvous meeting place, which was a restaurant in the split level Carlton Centre. I took a table and laid a magazine on the table indicating it would be dangerous to approach me. During the course of the next half hour I saw my tails walking round and round the split levels and my comrade friends also walking the split levels! The tails were being tailed by my comrades! Abandoning a chance of a meeting, I left the restaurant and walked into the connected Carlton Hotel to get a lift to the car park. I entered the lift on my own, but was very surprised when Damien de Lange suddenly jumped into the lift with me. He said he used the opportunity, when the tails stopped following into the hotel, to contact me. We had a hurried meeting as we travelled up to the top floor on the lift. He said surveillance on me was very heavy and I must get out of the country. I gave him as much money as I had on me, as I knew the cell was short of money at that time. Then he got out at the top, and I went down to the car park in the basement.

When I left the car park my tails were back. The next day I went to the British Consulate in downtown Johannesburg and requested to see the British Consul. The clerk behind the glass screen disappeared and then came back and wanted to know on what grounds I wanted to see the British Consul. I explained that I was being followed and wanted consular assistance. The clerk disappeared and when he returned said the Consul would not see me. I then said I would sit in until he did see me and took a waiting room chair. This had the desired effect because when the clerk disappeared again he returned with the Consul General. I was shown into a room and the Consul General (Mr Dove) wanted to know what I was doing in South Africa and what the story was. I maintained that I was looking to set up a business and was being followed. He looked at my passport and wanted to know why I kept visiting Botswana. I said I had a girl friend there, and he said 'please don't take this amiss, but if she is black, this is probably the reason you are being followed'. Then he said, 'What do you want me to do?' I explained I want to leave the country but I feared that I would be prevented from doing so. He said, make a booking for your flight and advise me on the flight details. I left the building and made a flight booking and returned again to the Consulate. He then gave me his personal home number and told me to phone him from the departure lounge when I left, explaining that if I did not make the call they would follow up with the South African authorities on my whereabouts.

After the visit to the British Consulate I felt reassured that someone would take steps if I was arrested. I had a few days to kill before my flight, so I entertained my tails by taking them to places of interest. On one particular day I went to Johannesburg Zoo. To me it was hilarious walking around looking at animals, and observing tails all over the place watching my every move. At lunch time I took a seat at the Zoo restaurant. It was not long before I recognized three of my tails together with two young children taking up a table near me. The children were seated with their backs to me and at the end of the meal, as I paid the bill and moved to leave, the children turned round to look at me. (Presumably the tails had said that I was leaving, and the children were not yet trained in how to react!). Leaving the restaurant I walked up to the Rock Art Museum which was at that time an open air museum within the grounds of the Zoo. You could hire a portable tape cassette to take round the exhibits that told you all about a particular rock painting. Walking around with my cassette player I was surprised and amused to see one of my tails also walking around with a cassette recorder to his ear. They were really convinced that I was going to meet someone.

On the day of departure they followed me to the airport but I checked in and got through to the departure lounge without problems. Paranoia had set in a little and I kept scrutinizing the other passengers on the plane, even looking at reflections of people in windows when back in London. On linking up with Eleanor Kasrils I was debriefed on the whole story. She told me the cell had not been detected but was very short of money. It was arranged that a girl friend would courier money out to them. Miraculously, the cell survived for a number of years. Infiltrated in 1986, they carried out espionage and then an attack on a communications tower at Linksfield Ridge, Johannesburg, during or about late November 1987, and an attack on a military bus transporting South African Air Force personnel at Benoni on or about 1 March 1988. Unfortunately they were revealed to the South African security forces in 1989 when a member of the cell[63] gave them away. At that time they were living on a smallholding at Broederstroom near Pretoria and they became known as the 'Broederstroom Cell' in court.

My return to England marked the end of the first phase of my MK activity. The next phase started when I went to Zambia. I stayed on an ANC farm north of Lusaka and was given a new identity and got to know Peter Smith,[64] another Englishman who was there. Then I joined a new safe house in Gaborone, Botswana, with Peter. We made a detailed exploration of the

63 Betrayed by Hugh Lugg, the other members of the cell were sentenced to very long terms of imprisonment, cut short by the ANC victory. – Editor.
64 See Peter's story elsewhere in this book. – Editor.

Botswana border fence with South Africa from Lobatsi, in the south east of Botswana, to the south western border with Namibia, a distance of hundreds of kilometres in an area of the Kalahari Desert that was bush, thorn and sand. Here we met up with comrades from South Africa many times and supplied them with arms and ammunition, by literally handing the stuff over the fence. The fence was nothing more than a cattle fence not more than waist high. We discovered that every kilometre there was a special fence post surrounded by a protective ring fence. These were the border marking posts and the South African government, when constructing the fence, had conveniently put a marker disk on the top with a number. A rendezvous with a group inside South Africa was thus very easy. We just sent a coded fence number and, no matter how remote the place, the comrades could easily locate the meeting place anywhere on the fence that was hundreds of kilometres long in the desert.

My later work for MK involved training in Cuba to be a Master of a Sea Going Vessel, with the intention of opening up the sea border of South Africa for struggle, but towards the end of my training the political situation was changing. I listened daily in Havana to the South African overseas broadcasts of news on short-wave radio, and they announced they would be staying on the air longer than the normal broadcast for the release of Nelson Mandela from prison. Nelson was due to broadcast a speech from Cape Town City Hall and I waited and waited for that speech. It was frustrating because the short-wave signal got weaker and weaker and Nelson was delayed for longer and longer in making that speech. Happily, however, I did hear the very, very faint speech whilst in Havana!

Returning to South Africa, I was redeployed on the importation of arms using a safari truck carrying tourists because at that time it was still not clear that a peaceful negotiation for a transition of power could be negotiated. We continued to stockpile arms that were later officially handed in when we moved to a settlement.

After the settlement, I integrated into the new South African National Defence Force. Then began a new chapter, playing my part in building the new South Africa. My role was to help oversee the transformation of the Defence Force into a law-abiding organization under democratic control, with military personnel that reflected the demographics of South Africa. I was awarded the ANC Decoration Medal Gold for my military services in MK and held several senior positions before retiring in 2005.

Since retirement I am now actively involved in community development, running skills training courses for young unemployed people, and primary health care services in local townships where I live. I am married to Stella, a South African, and have two small children called Emily and Sipho.

Roger was granted amnesty by the Truth and Reconciliation Commission. The official record of this decision is given below. – Editor.

AM 6209/97)

DECISION

The applicant, at all times material hereto, was a member of the African National Congress (the ANC) and Umkhonto weSizwe (MK).

From 1986 he was involved in intelligence gathering. He conducted surveillance and other acts of reconnaissance in respect of military installations, camps and bases throughout the country. He passed on information gathered in this way to his commanders in MK for use, at their discretion, to further the aims and objectives of MK.

He was also, from 1987, involved in the transport of weapons of war from both Botswana and Zimbabwe into South Africa.

He, at all times, acted under the general Command of his commanders, Ronnie Kasrils and Aboobaker Ismail.

We are satisfied that the applicant acted with a political objective and with the intention to further the aims of the ANC in its struggle against the government.

The applicant is accordingly **GRANTED** amnesty in respect of the gathering of intelligence and passing information on to MK and the unlawful possession, transportation and handling of weapons of war.

SIGNED AT CAPE TOWN THIS THE 23RD DAY OF JANUARY 2000.

'AFRICA HINTERLAND'
Stuart Round

The time comes in the life of any nation when there remains
only two choices – submit or fight. That time has now come to
South Africa. We shall not submit and we have no choice but
to hit back by all means in our power in defence of our people,
our future and our freedom.
Nelson Mandela

In 1986, when this story begins, the oppressed people of South
Africa were rising up in their thousands in an attempt to make
the country ungovernable, which often resulted in crowds of
unarmed civilians being fired upon by the police and army. The
choice Nelson Mandela had outlined so succinctly for the nation
was being mirrored in the life of each individual, and it was a
tough choice; the apartheid state routinely arrested, tortured,
imprisoned and murdered its political opponents.

At the same time, five thousand miles north in a kitchen
in Finchley, North London, I sat facing my own dilemma.
That I was in Finchley was not insignificant, for this was the
constituency of the then Prime Minister Margaret Thatcher,
placing me inside the belly of the beast; at least that was how it
felt to me at the tender age of 18 years old.

I was raised in Nuneaton, a small town in the Midlands,
by entirely non-revolutionary parents on an aspiring middle-
class suburban estate, detached houses, drives and gardens –
not wealthy, but far from the industrial working class, and a
world away from a South African squatter camp. Brought up to
believe in Queen and Country, I took great delight in learning
about the British Empire at school, and all that had made
Britain 'Great', and was imbued with more than my fair share
of national pride. I was taught that 'British' equated to 'best' in
everything, especially values – that to be British meant to stand
up for fairness and what is right. This is best exemplified, so
the story goes, by the notions of fairness, honesty and decency

embodied by the laws of that most English of games, cricket.

It wasn't just the sky high unemployment that faced me as I left school, nor the industrial decline of a nation once celebrated as 'the workshop of the world', nor was it just the polarisation of rich and poor of the Thatcher era that spurred me into a burgeoning sense of class consciousness. It was a growing sense that the ideas of 'freedom and democracy', watchwords of the cold war, had in fact been hijacked and were being used to push the world to the brink of destruction. One sunny morning, aged just sixteen, I was awoken in my bed by the sound of a nuclear air raid siren. It turned out to be just a test gone wrong, but at that moment as I looked out of my bedroom window I saw a world that was about to be destroyed forever.

Perhaps that was what made what was happening elsewhere around the world real and immediate to me, what made me take notice of the ruthless and murderous fascistic regimes being created and supported in defence of 'freedom and democracy' from Chile to Israel, Indonesia to Iraq, and worst of all in Africa. Perhaps that one moment where the comfort and safety of my sheltered world was shattered was all that was needed to make the illusions that surrounded me fall from my eyes. And once they began to fall, they fell very quickly. It wasn't long before I could see that my country was in fact built almost entirely on the suffering and domination of others. Starting with the Welsh, Irish and Scots, the rulers of England then went on to dominate the world. The justification for this at the time was that the Empire brought civilisation to otherwise savage and primitive people, and glory to God, Queen and Country.

That British ways and British people were superior was considered self evident; as Cecil Rhodes – one of the architects of southern Africa, 'father' of Rhodesia and founder of South Africa's Diamond Trading Company – once said, 'Remember that you are an Englishman, and have consequently won first prize in the lottery of life'. This was an expression of the same belief in the God-given superiority of European civilisation which was reflected in the minds of the white South Africans who had constructed and still viciously defended the apartheid system.

However, I found it as hard to see the superiority inherent in the brutal oppression of black South Africans as to see how civilisation had been edified by the suffering of the millions of African slaves on which Britain had built its wealth. It was as hard to see the 'fairness, honesty and decency' of Boers shooting unarmed children in the streets of Soweto as it was to see glory in the British concentration camps used against them in the Boer War. From America to Australia, India and Africa, European colonialists had invaded and, where practical, committed genocide against the indigenous populations. The real motives for this were glaringly obvious to me; nothing could stand in the way of profit. The extraction of raw materials from foreign lands, along with the exploitation of both foreign and domestic labour, was intrinsic to that process. In South Africa this was characterised by the ANC as a process of 'internal colonialism', where the white elite established protected enclaves inside the colonised country which, unlike other countries further north, offered a temperate climate more suited to European comfort, health and, importantly, agriculture.

To me, the only self evident fact was that it was white people who had behaved most like savages, and that the British Empire by definition, and now apartheid, was simply not cricket at all.

The ANC, legitimate representatives of the South African people, had declared an armed struggle to overthrow the apartheid state, and as I sat in this kitchen in Finchley, I was being asked to help. 'It could be dangerous', they told me; the implications were terrifying.

It was a defining question. Was I prepared to die for my beliefs or, if need be, to kill for them? Was I the sort of person who submits to fear, and if so, how much fear and how much was I prepared to surrender? Was I prepared to live my life as someone who did nothing in the face of injustice?

If ever there was a situation to test one's ideals, it was this. I had always believed that it was a good idea to beware of ideologies that result in killing people in the name of some higher cause. Even with right on your side, how could sending projectiles of molten hot metal through flesh and bone serve humanity?

However, the situation in South Africa was immediate; people were dying and suffering horribly every day and the longer apartheid continued to exist, the greater the death and suffering would be. From the level of violence as witnessed daily on the BBC evening news it was clear that those who were benefiting from the injustice of apartheid were prepared to defend their privileges at any cost, and that such was the dichotomy in South Africa that peaceful compromise appeared beyond reach.

To have the option of remaining a spectator, sitting on the sidelines theorising and cheering the good guys on, seemed like a luxurious indulgence when compared to the choices being faced daily by South Africans themselves, a luxury possibly to be paid for in more of their lives lost and wasted. Inaction was complicity in this crime, so I decided that it was time to get involved, if necessary to fight, and if required, to get my own hands dirty in the process. So, full of youthful bravado, and perhaps a little over eager to please, I gave my considered response, 'If you would like me to drop a bomb in a waste bin in Johannesburg then that is what I will do.' A ripple of surprise crossed some of the faces present, who, I can now tell you, were members of a committee known as 'The London Traders', made up of ANC exiles in London, members of the National Executive Committee of the ANC and ANC field commanders. The man conducting the interview was a Mr Mannie Brown, who seemed very pleased with my answer. 'We don't quite need you to do that,' he explained, 'but we do need help getting equipment into the country.' In his early sixties, Mannie was a wily character with a cheeky glint in his eye, although it would have been a serious mistake to confuse this simmering sense of fun with frivolity.

He too was facing a very serious decision, whether or not to entrust a vital new operation to the untried and untested hands of a teenager who didn't even hold a driving licence, where failure would mean the loss of both the operation and the operative. He decided to take a chance. 'How would you feel about going on safari?' he asked.

Over the next few weeks, in between driving lessons, I was introduced to the operation. The London Traders had set up an overland safari company in Greenwich, London, called Africa Hinterland – the name had been chosen deliberately for its Germanic ring. An office had been opened and manned, and a tourist brochure produced.

Mannie took me to see the truck, a 10 tonne 4x4 Bedford M-Type, as used by the British Army, which was being customised in a field near Ipswich by 'Jimmy', aka Rodney Wilkinson. Rodney was a colourful character, solely responsible for the 1982 bombing of the Koeberg nuclear power station, just months before it was completed, who then went on to conceive, design and build the Africa Hinterland truck, producing a work of pure genius. Using sloping panels covered in black rubber to throw the eye, he had designed a safari truck that concealed two vertical channels under the seats, just 4" wide, running the length of each side. Within these, one tonne of small arms and ammunition sealed in a special plastic wrap and housed in hand built wooden boxes could be concealed and transported through the border, and then be delivered to wherever in South Africa they were required.

I spent just three days with Rodney learning how to access the compartments, and undergoing a crash course in counter surveillance, how to spot enemy agents, escape routes out of the country, discreet communication codes, and maps of Cape Town where the first dead drop was to take place. Fortunately, I can be quite a fast learner, especially when my life depends upon it.

The journey would begin in Nairobi, Kenya, and follow a 7,000 mile route through game parks and along the coast of East Africa before heading down past Mount Kilimanjaro, through Tanzania and into Zambia. In Lusaka, capital of Zambia and headquarters of the ANC, under the guise of a 'service', the truck would be taken and loaded with the 32 wooden boxes, each containing a combination of AK47 assault rifles with corresponding 7.62mm ammunition, Makarov 9mm pistols and ammunition, hand grenades, tins of TNT and assorted Limpet Mines.

From Lusaka the truck would head to Victoria Falls and cross into Botswana, before heading to the South African border at a tiny crossing near Francistown called Parr's Holt (Stockpoort on the South African side). Through Johannesburg, across the Drakensberg Mountains and along the Garden Route, the trip was to end in Cape Town, seven weeks after it began. My role, Jimmy explained, was to accompany another driver on the first trip, but as a passenger and without his knowledge. This driver, as far as I am aware, has still never publically declared his involvement with this mission so I won't name him here. My task was to keep an eye on him, assist him where I could, and importantly to check out the other passengers as possible spies. Once safely through the border I was to reveal myself to the driver using a code phrase, and disclose the location of the delivery which we were to expedite together. We were then to hire a van and a scout car, load the boxes into the van which would be delivered to a prearranged location bearing certain signals to indicate to the internal cadres that it was safe to approach – these had amendments that indicated danger should we have been compromised along the way. The van would be collected using a key stored in a magnetic box under the wheel arch, emptied and returned, whereupon we would drive directly back to Nairobi and prepare to do the whole thing all over again.

While the last preparations for the operation were being made and the vehicle was being shipped to Mombasa, Kenya, I headed off to Europe with my backpack and tent and spent a couple of months hitch hiking, grape picking and generally trying to grow up. That in itself was an experience, but finally, with a few stamps in my passport and some stories to relate to the other passengers, I headed back to London for my final briefings.

And so it was that in February 1987 I landed in Nairobi and

made my way to the Grosvenor Hotel to rendezvous with the truck and 14 other passengers. I had begun to develop a legend during my trip around Europe, and now continued to develop a persona free of political thought, which, now aged 19 years, naturally gravitated towards drinking, chatting up girls and having a good time. I was having the time of my life in fact, and given the uncertainty of how long my life would now continue this was a welcome relief and seemed entirely appropriate.

However, as the journey progressed I steadily became more concerned that one of the other passengers was more than just a tourist. He fitted the profile of a spy that I had been told to look out for, a macho type, a keen photographer, with a military bearing and a huge moustache! This passenger expressed a great deal of interest in the vehicle, one time asking if one side of the outside storage lockers was deeper than the other, because the tent wouldn't fit back in. It wasn't. I quickly discovered that the tent pegs were stuck at the bottom of the bag. He kept asking lots of questions about the company, who the directors were and why had they set it up. One evening, when drunk, he started to tell me about a Mauser pistol he had handled that had once belonged to an officer of the Waffen SS!

When we arrived in Lusaka I made my pre-arranged meeting with Jimmy and he took me to a secret meeting with two of the field commanders, Phil, aka Muff Anderson and her partner, who I was to call Tony. Also present was the new head of the ordnance section of which I was now a part, Rashid, who had replaced Casius Maake following his assassination in an ambush in Swaziland.

Had I any remaining illusions regarding the seriousness of the situation I was now in, over the next half an hour they were to be thoroughly dispelled. Following my report, the prevailing consensus during the ensuing discussion was that this individual should be arrested and removed from the trip, whereupon he would be sent to a camp in Angola. His fate then would have been dire indeed; my suspicions were about to cost this man his life! However, not only was I not sufficiently certain of the accuracy of my analysis, even if he was an apartheid spy there was no reason to believe that he had seen anything to raise his suspicions. And furthermore, to 'disappear' him would have confirmed the nature of our expedition to his commanders as clearly as sending them a telegram, surely attracting much more attention. So I argued against this, and in view of the fact that I was the 'man on the ground', rather reluctantly the others agreed.

As I left this meeting, it occurred to me that if I was wrong about this, my unknowing comrade and I would pay for this mistake with our own lives, and – as may in fact have proved to be the case – that by allowing him to continue his activities, in future other comrades might also pay as severely. Nevertheless, viewed dispassionately, I was sure that this was the correct tactical decision to take. We would be subject to all sorts of scrutiny before our mission was complete, and we had to be able to withstand it or else we would in any case fail.

The political situation throughout the southern African region was incredibly tense, and the entire country was on high alert as during the preceding weeks there had been several South African attacks on ANC positions in Zambia. So, through the various Zambian army checkpoints and searches, now loaded with a full cargo, the truck made its way out of Lusaka and headed south towards Livingstone, the location of the famous Victoria Falls. After a couple of day's rest in Livingstone we would head beyond help into Botswana, and then on to the South African border itself.

As I lay sunning myself by the side of the pool at the Livingstone Intercontinental Hotel, sipping on a beer and contemplating all that was to come, I noticed Phil and Tony playing with their child just across the pool. This immediately struck me as strange; they had said nothing about following us. Being careful to ignore them in front of the other passengers, I went for an ambling walk up the road back towards the campsite, and sure enough after a couple of minutes a car pulled up beside me, and I dived into the backseat and lay there as we drove away, out of sight of any watching eyes.

The mission was off! The Soviet Embassy in Harare, Zimbabwe, had intercepted South African radio traffic advising all border posts to be on the lookout for a safari truck with a blue tarpaulin! This had to be us, and Rashid had decided to abort. At that moment it seemed as if all the months of training and preparation, all the weeks of travelling, had come to nothing and had been a total waste of time.

The passengers were duly informed by the driver that, due to the unstable nature of the region at that time, the directors of the company had decided not to proceed into South Africa. Africa Hinterland was one of a very few companies still travelling into South Africa – most trips terminated in Harare, as due to sanctions against apartheid, particularly in Tanzania, there were all sorts of difficulties travelling back north which necessitated duplicate passports for the drivers and duplicate carnets for the vehicle – so this was a very plausible excuse.

A couple of interesting things happened at this point; my spy 'mate' passenger reported to me that he had seen a South African guy snooping around our truck – he even said that he wondered if this man was a South African spy. He then immediately transferred himself onto one of the other trucks which happened to be in Livingstone at the same time, which also had a blue tarp, and continued his journey south with them. My interpretation of this was that he had in fact met with his own commander, and was covering himself with this dubious story of a suspicious character hanging around the vehicle in case he had been observed, and that he had then been given instructions to check out the other vehicles on the same route. This was the last I ever saw of him.

Unknown to me at this moment, the real cause of the alert was most likely rooted in London. Jimmy, who was well known for enjoying a drink or two, whilst drunk one night had left a briefcase in the back of a taxi with the full details of our operation inside, including diagrams of the vehicle! On pain of death, he had managed to recover it, but perhaps not before some of the information inside had been seen and found its way to the enemy. Whether this was what had prompted the initial interest of the security forces in us or not, it seems that by aborting our mission for the reasons given we had gone a long way towards convincing our spy of the innocent nature of our expeditions.

As my return flight was already booked from Johannesburg, there was nothing else for me to do but to venture into South Africa alone, and then to fly back to London. Thus, I got my first view of South Africa. I had expected to find that white South Africans were all monstrous fascists who despised black people – I was quite surprised to discover that mostly this was not the case. I, a white man, was welcomed with the utmost hospitality and found that for the most part white South Africans were very much like the people back home. The forms of racism were different – amongst the UK's racists there was a strong element of hatred, in South Africa the racism manifested itself more as a highly developed form of paternalism. However, far from making me doubt the choice I had made, the similarities I saw rather made me view my own country with fresh eyes, and what I saw was not flattering.

When I got back to London, a debate was raging about what to do next. In the end, a dummy vehicle – still with a blue tarpaulin – was sent through the border and crossed unhindered. The mission was back on!

This time, I was to head straight to Cape Town to wait for the truck to arrive – it would have been implausible to go for a second trip with the same driver. This gave me a good opportunity to reconnoitre the routes and explore the camp sites in the area to find the most secluded one to make the transfer of the boxes from the truck into the van.

Eventually, the truck arrived. I met the driver outside the bank where he had been instructed by London to pick up some money; of course he recognised me instantly and howled with laughter. Still, I delivered the required lines; question, 'Where are you from in London?' answer, 'Finsbury Park', reply, 'Do you drink at the "Sir George Robey?"'

Even though he had successfully traversed the border we didn't necessarily feel any more secure. All the time checking for tails and searching the vehicle thoroughly for tracking devices we headed to the campsite, and late in the evening dismantled the seats and transferred the boxes into the van.

With me driving the scout car and him the loaded van, we reached the dead drop and parked, and then began six hours of waiting. The tension was palpable, reaching a pinnacle as finally we returned to the drop site and, observing the correct alterations to our signals, cautiously approached the vehicle. After a couple of drive-bys all looked clear, so we picked up the van and headed back to the campsite. The relief was immense, although we still had to get out of the country.

I headed back to the airport as he began the long drive back to Nairobi. Step by step, through immigration and customs, as the wheels of the plane left the ground, and then finally as the aircraft exited South African airspace, I was filled with the greatest sense of exhilaration I had ever felt in my life. We had done it!

We had planned to drive the next trip together; the need for secrecy between us now diminished following the first successful delivery. However, unplanned events in his life meant that I was to drive the next safari alone; this time he would fly into Cape Town to meet me. This seemed pretty daunting, the truck was huge and the roads dangerous and difficult. Mannie expressed great faith in me, which was reassuring as I had probably more confidence in his judgement than I had in my own.

I was right to feel daunted; still only 20 years old I was the youngest person on the truck! I grew a beard, which aged me a few years, and then lied to the passengers about my age. This was without question the most challenging and difficult experience of my life. Driving up to 18 hours a day, followed by whatever maintenance the vehicle required – all of which I had to learn on the hoof. Bluffing my way through questions I didn't know the answers to, dealing with checkpoints, border crossings, sick passengers, angry rhinoceroses and belligerent elephants. I managed to almost drown myself when I fell out of an inflatable raft in the middle of rapids on the Zambezi, scary enough until when finally I surfaced I observed 10ft Nile crocodiles sunning themselves on the rocks not more than 20 yards from where I floated in the water waiting to catch a life-line from the boat and be hauled back onboard. Not to mention the apprehension at the South African border crossing that was looming nearer with every passing day. In such an environment, it was almost inevitable that I ended up forming a relationship with a female passenger, but then it became incredibly difficult to lie at night in someone's arms but not be able to share my deepest fears. It was almost impossible to drag myself away from the warm, naked embrace of a beautiful girl and deliberately put myself in harm's way, potentially to face capture, torture and death. Nevertheless, that was what I did, and seven weeks later I once again saw the now familiar sight of Table Mountain in the distance on the final run into Cape Town, and once more we went through the same routine of delivery. This time I drove the truck back to Nairobi, a journey of 3,000 miles in five days, and again, as I watched Parrs Holt disappear in the mirrors behind me, that same sense of utter elation, deliverance!

Over the next couple of years we managed to recruit new drivers: Jo Lewis, Mike Harris and Menno Schreuder. Duly trained in how to run a safari and all the extras that went with it, they did an excellent job. Eventually we relocated our base to Johannesburg and started running a round trip from there which could be done with much greater frequency. Once this was underway I felt that the operation was in very good hands and, after five years, tired to the core and really quite burnt out, I retired from my life as a gun runner. The operation continued up until 1994 when finally the first properly democratic elections in South Africa returned an ANC government with a massive 65 per cent of the vote, and Africa Hinterland was wound up having moved around 40 tonnes of hardware into South Africa. I firmly believe that it contributed to the final realisation by the apartheid state that to continue would result in their total destruction at the hands of a popular uprising.

There were many scares along the way, too many to go into here, but ultimately we all survived, the operation was never discovered, and every load that went into South Africa was delivered on time and to where it was needed. For me, this was the greatest of our achievements, to have survived intact, although not entirely undamaged. The psychological scars of such an enterprise take a long time to heal, and even now I still dream of that truck, and I guess I always will.

Sometimes, I think of the comrades tortured and killed, those who resisted interrogation and those who didn't, and I wonder at how easily that could have been me. At other times, I think of the people blown apart, killed, maimed, shot or injured by the weapons we supplied, their families and loved ones, and wonder at how expensive was the price of freedom.

Today, South Africa is free, and people can now grow up and live their lives to their full potential regardless of the colour of their skin. Because of that, South Africa, I am proud to bear my scars and to carry my share of guilt – that is my gift to you.

ON HIGH HEELS
Lucia Raadschelders

'Where, quasi-land?' This was one of the first questions my husband-to-be asked me when I tried to convince him to marry me. 'Is it really a country? I thought it was a homeland.' Having dealt with his first shock that I was not really asking him to marry me out of a secret love for him, but only wanting to borrow his surname, all the other questions started to come. He had heard of Swaziland but he didn't think it was a 'real' country. Sorry Swaziland. But we are back in 1986. Swaziland was not only dependent on South Africa economically but was also a country where the South African military and intelligence were free to come and go without repercussions by the Swazi government.

I was on a roller coaster. I had resigned from the Dutch Anti-Apartheid Movement (Dutch AAM) a few months earlier because I really didn't feel like organising another demonstration, fundraising event or whatever where always too few people showed up. I wanted to contribute more but had no idea how to give 'hands and feet' to this feeling. I had a vague notion of maybe writing a book about women in South Africa or to go there to make a documentary. I had this secret wish to go to South Africa, despite the boycott. I wanted to see and feel for myself and connect with people that mattered.

And it just fell into my lap. Cycling home after an evening at Conny's[65] house I couldn't believe my luck, so to say. She had given me time to think about her proposal but I had already made up my mind. To whom could I give my bike; what to tell my family and friends; what to do with my flat?

Conny had asked me if I would be prepared to go to Swaziland to assist the ANC underground by running a safe house. It would mean that I couldn't tell anybody what I was going to

---

65 Conny Braam was chairperson of the Dutch Anti-Apartheid Movement and was, secretly, involved in the recruitment of people, mainly from the Netherlands, to do all sorts of work for the ANC underground. She also played a big role in the recruitment for Operation Vula. She published the book 'Operation Vula' on her involvement – see Appendix 4.

do and we had to come up with a cover story. I had to change
my name, get a 'real' profession and lead a double life. I had
to disappear from the Dutch AAM scene in Holland without
raising too many eyebrows.

I had no idea what this really meant and probably only
understood by the time I had to leave Swaziland again, about
two years later. But this was the 'more' I was looking for. South
Africa was in my blood and it just would not let me off the hook
that easily. I had never been there but I had met many ANC
comrades through my work with the Dutch AAM and shared
love and pain with them. At that time I hardly had friends
outside the Dutch AAM circle of people and it had become my
life.

So, there I was, so excited but frustrated at the same time
since I could not share this with anybody. I felt bad towards
my sister Jacinta, pregnant at that time, and I had asked her if
I could play a substantial role in the life of her child. I didn't
want children of my own but would love to have a child more
prominently in my life and I felt this was the right time. I don't
think Jacinta and I reached any conclusions but I did feel I had
committed myself during our holiday together in Barcelona,
just before Conny approached me.

The first step was to get rid of my surname, Raadschelders,
since it is too recognisable. I didn't think this would be a
problem. I knew exactly which friend to ask to marry me just to
give me another surname – a very dear friend. I was so wrong.
Although he supported me absolutely at a political level, he was
too concerned about my safety and wanted to be involved in a
way that was not possible. It was quite emotional and I think I
didn't realise how close we were. What a fantastic friend to have!

OK, I had to look for somebody a bit less close to me. And
there was Tom (not his real name). We were living in the same
squat in Amsterdam, an amazing place in the eastern part of
the harbour. I knew him as a neighbour and as somebody
with whom I shared the same political beliefs. He was single
and still studying to become a medical doctor. I was nervous

when I made an appointment with him. I did not know what response to expect but I was sure that, whatever the outcome, he would keep his mouth shut. How do you tell somebody in Holland that you are going to work for the ANC underground in Swaziland; isn't that something out of a spy novel? I had had some dealings with Tom because of the NGO he worked for: investigating pharmaceutical multinationals and exposing the dumping of medicines in the developing world. I had consulted him on Depo Provera and the forced use of it in SA. I knew he supported the ANC. I was a bit taken aback by his response. He raised issues I had not thought about. He wanted to think about my proposal for a couple of days and he soon agreed to marry me. We discussed the possibility of him joining me in Swaziland after finishing his studies. It was in his mind anyway to go to a developing country and it would be fantastic for my cover (and for me!). I felt so relieved.

We had a quiet 'wedding' with two of Conny's friends as witnesses. It did feel strange, and we had a failed attempt at some sort of celebration, but I was not in the mood. All of a sudden it was getting serious. With marrying Tom my cover started to grow: the wife travelling ahead of her husband to set up home; he to join after finishing his studies; the brand new doctor eager to offer his services. He had only one exam to go and since I had just left a job I had the time to come earlier. The first hurdle was taken. I had a new name and could apply for a new passport.

The next step was informing family and friends. But inform them of what? Of course they did not know of my marriage so I needed another story for them. That was easy. I was going to travel in Southern Africa for a couple of months, wanting a break after my work at the Dutch AAM and starting in Swaziland. I would just extend my stay again and again. I would have to find work to supplement my meagre savings. I was not completely happy with this cover. If you know me, you'd know that I am not really the type of person just to go and travel on her own for months without any specific plans. But this was the best we could come up with.

Changing my appearances was the easiest part. Contact lenses, a perm, a visit to the dentist and a change of wardrobe. It is so easy to change your outside. I had to throw out my purple coveralls and boots and try to walk on heels and in tight skirts. Oh my God, this is not me. I don't know how to behave in these clothes. What will my friends think? My story of other norms in Southern Africa, women wearing skirts and having the need to adapt sounded flimsy in my own ears. Getting paranoia already? I found it difficult to be in my old world preparing for a new one. But I had to change and disappear from the scene.

How does one do that? Especially since most of my friends and acquaintances were connected to the Dutch AAM in one way or the other. One thing was not to go to events organised by Dutch AAM anymore, as if I had lost interest and wanted to pursue my own thing. It felt like disowning me. I might be wrong but it looked amazingly easy to 'disappear'. Just don't go to rallies for a couple of times and people forget about you. To others, closer to me, I would also say that I didn't want to jeopardise my trip, secretly including a visit to South Africa, and I didn't want to jeopardise a visa to SA. That seems to do the trick. Friends close enough to me but not knowing what I was really up to, acknowledged silently my commitment: 'If Lucia goes to a place like Swaziland she will have a reason to do so and we should not question her'. Thank you dear friends! For friends outside the Dutch AAM it was much easier: after having worked at the AAM for a number of years I just wanted to visit the region, meeting friends, and I would look for work when my money was running out. I had funds to carry me through for about three months. The 'agreement' with Conny was that I would go for at least one year. I remember that there were a couple of solidarity events during my 'disappearing act' and I really felt so bad and felt left out in the cold, especially when friends did comment on my absence – no matter what Conny was saying to make me feel better.

I told my family the same story: wanting to have a break, travelling in the region, keeping the time-frame vague.

My mother did not like this at all but I had always been the 'different' one in the family and she had no choice but to accept. I was concerned about my family but how does one reconcile political ambition clashing with family ties? Because, don't be mistaken. I made this choice in my own interest. I took this decision because I wanted to contribute to the struggle and be much more involved than the AAM could 'offer' me. It was the 'more' I was looking for.

To prepare myself for a new profession I taught myself touch-typing since the idea was that I should try to get a job as a secretary or something in the hospitality industry. My farewell present from the Dutch AAM, an electronic typewriter, turned out to be very handy. I wonder if Conny had 'targeted' me already at that time!

I had left the AAM in December 1985 and was unemployed. Conny was having problems funding everything and I went to work as a cleaner in somebody's house for three days a week, a huge renovated house in the posh Concertgebouw neighbourhood in Amsterdam. What a bore. But at least it provided me with the cash to buy a ticket to Swaziland as well as a new wardrobe and some jewellery. Conny taught me how to use make-up. She also organised some fantastic testimonials for me which gave me an employment history in the Netherlands to assist me to find a job in Swaziland. Besides my work with the AAM I had only worked as a volunteer in the Peace and in the Women's Movement and we had to invent a work history. All the testimonials were by companies that existed and could be checked and would vouch for me. Conny had an incredible network of people assisting her in all sort of things.

The time had arrived. I had to pack up my belongings. I was lucky to be able to sublet my flat for one year, the maximum the corporate body would allow. I stored some of my books with my sister Trees. I destroyed my diaries – just in case. Jacinta came to my flat with her newborn daughter Eva, a few weeks old, to say goodbye. The feeling of being on a roller coaster was gone. The uncertain future was about to start and I did not feel ready for whatever I was going to do; doubts about if I would be able to cope on my own, if I could 'deliver' and clinging to the idea that Tom would join me. I must have been mad. I had no farewell party, I just left quietly in October 1986.

The plane landed at a tiny airport, more a strip than an airport. I had to look for a Dutch woman by the name of Marianne. She spotted me immediately, the only woman travelling on her own. A big hug and she hustled me to her car. She chatted away during the short trip to her house. It gave me some time to look around, take in the smells and the warmth and take a breath – in more than one way, I had landed. She, her husband Fred and daughters Anneke and Nienke lived in a modern house on the campus of the University of Swaziland in Kwaluseni. I could stay in their servant's quarters until I had found a job and a house. I was relieved with the servant's quarter, which consisted of a small bedroom with its own shower and toilet – and I could make my own coffee. It meant that I had some privacy and did not have to spend all the time with the family. I didn't want to impose on them too much, they had their own life. I could even sit outdoors by myself. I am not somebody who opens up easily to people but Fred and Marianne made it very easy for me. They are very warm and easy going people and I could not have managed without them. The kids accepted me as a 'friend of a friend'. I don't recall exactly but I think that our story was that Marianne, a medical doctor herself, had met Tom in the Netherlands.

I knew that I had to learn how to drive a car, something I was not looking forward to since I was terrified of driving. But it made sense. Although Swaziland is a tiny country and buses were going regularly between the main centres I would need a car to be able to work and to do whatever I needed to do for the ANC. But, just as important, white people didn't use public transport and if I was to be a doctor's wife I had to behave like one and have a car. I enrolled at a driving school in Manzini and the instructor was a funny, elderly lady, always wearing a hat in the car. I wanted to have a proper, legal driving licence which could also serve me as an ID, better than my Dutch passport. It was a most peculiar experience. I was never allowed to go beyond the second gear and, although the indicators were working, I also had to give hand signals outside the car window for turning right or left. I am not sure what she thought of my driving skills (probably not much) and she had arranged for my driving test to take place all the way in Siteki. She confided in me that her uncle was the examiner and forewarned me of a particular intersection which, although there was no traffic sign, functioned as a stop street. She drove me down to Siteki and even showed me the intersection in question. She was proud of me, passing the first time.

The day I received my driving licence I got my first 'assignment' for the ANC: I had to drive a car to a certain parking lot, leave the car behind and hide the keys underneath the car. I was terrified, absolutely not in control of the car and almost crashed it; other cars were hooting at me since I was driving so slowly – I had no idea how to change the gears beyond second.

I was trying to get a feel for the place and met with neighbours and friends of Fred and Marianne. Everybody was very friendly but also very curious. For them it was so nice to have a new person in their circle. I had to get used to inventing stories about my past work experience, about Tom, about everything. It wouldn't surprise me if I had contradicted myself on several occasions. I also had to learn how to manoeuvre in political discussions and not just blurt out my support for the ANC, while at the same time staying true to myself; I just couldn't 'give up' myself. It was a fine balancing act and a slow learning process. I had never had to hide my political beliefs and a slip of the tongue was easily made. Just by showing knowledge about the situation in South Africa could raise eyebrows. And Swaziland was just a little village where everybody gossiped about each other and everybody knew each other. I was to learn that later to my distress.

I started to look around for work. In the beginning Fred or Marianne would drop me off at one of the big hotels in Ezulwini valley. We had decided that that would be a good place to work and that it would also be useful for 'the family', our cover word for the ANC. I had one beautiful tailored blue suit for interviews and I would put on my high heels only just before entering the hotel lobby. There were no pre-arranged interviews, I would just show up and ask to speak to the manager. I found this quite daunting but was surprised that I usually did manage to speak to somebody in charge – my first lessons of what it meant to be a white person in a country like Swaziland. The job market was not as good as we had hoped. I was getting nowhere with my visits to the posh hotels and I had to 'down tune' my expectations of a fancy job.

At this stage, I also started to meet my 'commander' – the ANC comrade I would work with and report to. A distinguished Indian comrade (Ebrahim Ismael Ebrahim), Conny had told me about him. I first met him at Fred and Marianne's house. He was full of questions about Conny and very concerned about my wellbeing. I also had a couple of meetings with him at one of the houses he used in Manzini. There was not really much to discuss since I was of no use until I had a place of my own and a job. The 'family visits' made me giggle. We would know in advance when to expect him and the garage door would be kept unlocked. The kids were sent off to bed. Marianne and Fred had a story ready if they had unexpected visitors. Marianne often used the story of a patient visiting or somebody else from the hospital where she worked. Between looking for jobs and getting my driving licence, there wasn't much for me to do and I started to tag along with Fred when he went into the country to visit science teachers. This was part of his job at the university. Fantastic! It not only gave me something to do but I also got to see the country.

It took quite some time before I managed to find a job and it was only in January or February of the following year that I rented my first house in Mbabane. Finally I could start with my 'job' of running a safe house.

After moving into my first house in Mbabane, I was quickly

joined by the comrade who was going to stay with me; the one I had to provide with a safe house. He was part of the underground ANC in Swaziland and needed a safe place to live and work from. I had a job during the day and in the evenings or weekends I would assist with running 'errands' such as fetching other ANC comrades from a border post and buying equipment he could not buy without raising eyebrows. But my main task was to provide housing, food and security; not very satisfactory and definitely not 'the more' I had wanted. We moved house every four months or so. Whenever he felt the security of a house had 'expired' he asked me to look for another place to stay in. It was as with my jobs, I never managed to get a legal job and moved from one job to the other the way I moved houses. I remained an illegal immigrant. It was a pity that Tom decided not to join me; he did come for a visit but had fallen in love in Holland and followed his heart.

There came an abrupt end to my stay in Swaziland in June 1988. After two warnings from people I didn't know, it became clear that the 'Boers' knew who I was and that I was working for the ANC. I also made a very stupid mistake during a telephone call I received at work and knew immediately that I'd 'blown it'. I immediately warned the comrade with whom I shared the house and I remained behind for another week or so, with plenty of whiskey to try and make me sleep, scared of what might happen. I moved to Fred and Marianne's for another week before flying back to Holland. The story I told people in Swaziland for my sudden return was the death of a family member.

I only phoned one friend in Holland (the first one I had proposed to) to inform him of my return and ask him to fetch me from the airport. He was so great, asking no questions, just the 'I'll be there'. Nobody else knew. It felt like sneaking out of the backdoor. I was so angry with myself and full of feelings of guilt towards my comrade and the ANC for failing them. I only phoned Conny once I was in Holland and met her for a debriefing session soon afterwards. Again, stories had to be invented to explain my sudden return. This time it was a lot easier: being expelled from Swaziland as an illegal immigrant. My family was happy to see me but I felt incredibly awful, not being able to explain anything. During that Dutch summer I moved around in Amsterdam, house sitting for friends who were away for their holidays, two weeks here, three weeks there. I had made it very clear to Conny that this was not 'the end' for me. If she could deploy me somewhere else, then by all means. Fairly soon after my return to Holland Conny asked me if I would be prepared to go to Lusaka, Zambia, to join Operation Vula as the communications person. I didn't need to think twice! It was a lot easier to leave this time, my cover story being that I wanted to explore more of Africa.

I went to London for training in the communication system that Vula used and left Amsterdam again in December 1988 for Lusaka. After a few weeks I moved to my own place in one of the townships of Lusaka, standing out like a white elephant. I always shared the house with another comrade for security reasons; we had all the communication equipment in our home. I was mainly involved in receiving and sending messages via our (for those days) very advanced email system: messages from London, Amsterdam and from inside the country. Most messages dealt with political briefings and discussions, requests for information and additional comrades, hardware as well as preparations for the infiltration of additional Vula people, etc. Life was not easy in Lusaka. I mainly stayed at home the whole day, waiting for messages to come in. After a fire in one of the main electricity stations, running the equipment became very difficult. I would only have power at night! The London Vula people managed to design equipment to run off a car battery to deal with this problem. The communication system was amazing, facilitating a very high level ANC operation within South Africa; without the delays and risks of the communication means of the 'old days'. In the end, we were even receiving messages from Mandela.

I stayed in Lusaka till after the unbanning of the ANC and many comrades had returned home. I went back to Holland where I worked for another two years after which I had saved enough to enable me to go to South Africa and try to find a 'new' home there.

Short biography

Born on the 17 June 1954 in the Netherlands; the youngest of 10 children. My father was a pastry baker and a very hard worker. My mother was a housewife, mother, shopkeeper, organiser and everything else and worked at least just as hard.

1976 – 1978	Volunteer in the Women's Health Centre in Amsterdam
1977 - 1979	Volunteer in the Dutch Peace Movement
1979 - 1985	Staff member Dutch Anti-Apartheid Movement
1986 - 1988	ANC Swaziland – safe house
1988 - 1991	ANC President's office, Zambia – Operation Vula.
Since 1993	South Africa where I've worked with several NGOs, currently archivist at the Centre of Memory and Dialogue of the Nelson Mandela Foundation
1996 - 1997	Volunteer Women's Café and Library, Johannesburg
2002 - Current	Trustee of the Cultural Development Trust, Johannesburg.

APPENDIX 1
Other names

There are other people whose noble efforts have either not been recorded earlier in the book, or not adequately recounted, for various reasons. It grew into too big a task. I want to mention them here. This still does not make an exhaustive list, however, because some people remain unknown to me or wish not to be mentioned in this book – Editor.

David King was the first British person recruited to go on missions for the ANC. Sadly, I am fairly sure that he is dead. He recruited Alex Moumbaris and 'James' (both of whom think they remember reading of his death). He was a member of the YCL. When he and Alex Moumbaris were working for MK they shared a flat at 335 Ley Street, Ilford, above the CPGB and YCL premises there.

Deirdre Drury, from Basingstoke, worked with Dave King on their joint missions to South Africa. I have been unable to trace her.

Jo Lewis was born in London in 1963 and became political at Ludlow College, Shropshire. In Coventry she joined the YCL and later the CPGB in the 1980s and was active in the Anti-Apartheid Movement and the National Assembly of Women. She was recruited by Laurence Harris and Mannie Brown to work for Africa Hinterland as a driver from October 1988, finishing in December 1991. Jo met Mike Harris, her future partner, while working there. She is mentioned in Stuart Round's chapter.

Mike Harris was born in 1961 in Glasgow, moving to Stockton-on Tees in 1964. He moved to London in 1982 and worked for Ford Motor Company 1983-87 where he was in the ASTMS and then the MSF union. He became active in the AAM and was recruited by Aziz Pahad in 1987 and worked for Africa Hinterland from January 1989 to December 1991, first as a 'passenger' on one trip, and then driver. There he met his future partner, Jo Lewis. He is mentioned in Stuart Round's chapter.

Menno Schreuder (Dutch) was recruited in the Netherlands and trained in Britain, going from there to South Africa. He and his partner **Sandra Duinmeyer** kept the safaris going for Africa Hinterland until around the time of the 1994 election, Sandra working in the company's Johannesburg office and Menno driving. Menno is mentioned in Stuart Round's chapter.

June and Michael Stephen were both highly committed to the ideals of the struggle against apartheid. June Stephen, a New Yorker now living in the UK, is not available to write her story for this book due to a recent health condition. She and her then husband Michael Stephen, a Scotsman hailing from Aberdeen (deceased 1999), spent eight years from 1977-1985 working with the ANC in countries across southern Africa. They worked closely with Ronnie Kasrils, Albie Sachs, Bobby Pillay, Rae and Ivan Pillay, Peter Smith, Ebrahim Ismael Ebrahim and Daniel Ahern amongst others in the struggle against apartheid.

Bob McGowan, deceased, was an electrician from London, and a CPGB member. Though not a seaman he went on the *Avventura*, so I was told by Frank Cartwright.

Gerry Wan, deceased, a black Liverpool-born seaman, was a chef on the Union Castle Line which sailed to South Africa. Roger O'Hara says he used to deliver, to 'post boxes', literature and parcels of money to places in Durban, and that he was recruited by the late **Jack Coward**, the legendary seaman's leader, communist and International Brigader.

Dr Ron Press told me that **two members of the Fire Brigades Union** – names unknown – went to South Africa in 1981 on a mission organised by Joe Slovo and 'the Doc' Yusuf Dadoo to set off leaflet bombs to celebrate the 60th anniversary of the foundation of the South African Communist Party.

Phil Greene, a member of the YCL, went to Port Elizabeth, alone, in 1970 or 1971 where he set off leaflet bombs. I could not persuade him to write his story.

Ian Beddowes, a CPGB member who volunteered to assist the ANC/SACP with underground work in Africa. Worked in Swaziland as a building constructor from 1986 and carried out reconnaissance missions in South Africa before settling in Zimbabwe and subsequently in South Africa. (Ronnie Kasrils).

'**Jack and Jill**': pseudonyms of university graduates from Oxford, CPGB members, recruited by Joe Slovo in 1974. They were deployed as teachers in Lesotho and assisted Chris Hani in his work. (Ronnie Kasrils).

This book does not name all the volunteers recruited in Europe. In addition to these persons, others have chosen to remain anonymous.

APPENDIX 2

The letter below was posted (in about 1200 copies) in Johannesburg by Ken Keable in April 1968. This description is part of a memorandum submitted by Dr Yusuf Dadoo to the United Nations Special Committee Against Apartheid, dated June 1968.

Source: http://www.sacp.org.za/docs/history/dadoo-07. html#APPENDIX%201

FREEDOM FIGHTERS ON THE MARCH
A message from Dr. Y.M. Dadoo to the Indian people

Brothers and Sisters

The struggle against apartheid and for Freedom has entered a new decisive phase. Freedom-fighters, combat units, well-trained and well-armed, are already giving battle to the oppressors with great daring, skill and determination in Rhodesia. Contrary to local press reports, they are dealing severe blows to the fascist forces of Ian Smith and Vorster. Soon they will be fighting the enemy on South African soil.

"WE ARE AT WAR" says the leaflet of the African National Congress which was widely distributed in South Africa recently. In a rousing CALL TO REVOLUTION which appears in the January 1968 issue of Sechaba, official organ of the ANC, Oliver Tambo (the Acting President-General) states that "as our forces drive deeper into the south, we have no doubt that they will be joined not by some, but by the whole African nation; by the oppressed minorities, the Indian and Coloured people; and by an increasing number of White democrats."

Period of revolutionary upheavals
Our country, South Africa, faces a period of ever-increasing revolutionary upheavals. Life can no longer go on in the same old way. The new developments call for a reappraisal of the role and the task in the coming struggle of each sector of the oppressed people, African, Indian and Coloured.

We have suffered enough

Our community, like the African and the Coloured people, has had enough of racial discrimination, apartheid and White Supremacy.

The GROUP AREAS ACT is taking a heavy toll; daily more and more families are being driven out from their hearth and home and thrown onto the garbage heap of Indian group areas; we are being robbed of our means of livelihood; the standard of education of our children is being lowered. Unemployment is rife. Once the Government succeeds in completely driving our people into Ghettos, all kinds of restrictions will be applied preventing our people from going out of the areas to seek work, carry out professional duties or to trade; prevent non-Indians from coming into our areas without permission. We shall be cooped up in a lot of hovels; cut off completely from the mainstream of the life, economy and culture of the country.

We have a proud record of struggle

From the days of Gandhiji the Indian people have resolutely and bravely offered resistance to racial discrimination and segregation. The campaigns of passive resistance and the Great March of 1913 conducted under the leadership of Gandhiji are unforgettable and historic landmarks in the history of our people. The Passive Resistance Campaign of 1946 against the Ghetto Act inspired our people and prepared them for the struggles ahead. Since the advent of the Nationalist Government in 1948 our people have marched hand-in-hand with the African people under the leadership of the African National Congress, playing our part in stay-at-homes, hartals, the great Defiance Campaign of 1952 and participating in the many demonstrations against apartheid tyranny. Our people were participants in the Congress of the People which formulated the historic FREEDOM CHARTER which guarantees freedom and democracy to all South Africans.

To the call of the Umkhonto We Sizwe, our militant youth responded without hesitation and with determination; Babla

Saloojee gave his life; and many of our brave activists like Billy Nair, Chiba, Maharaj, Indres Naidoo, Shirish Nanabhai, Reggie Vandeyar, George Naicker, Ebrahim Ismail, together with the African, Coloured and white comrades-in-arms are at this very moment serving long terms of imprisonment.

Ahmed Kathrada, together with the outstanding leaders of our country, Nelson Mandela, Walter Sisulu, Abram Fischer, Govan Mbeki, Dennis Goldberg and others, is condemned to life imprisonment.

Nana Sita, the veteran leader of our movement, men like Mohamed Bhana and those brave students who valiantly refused to participate in the Republic celebrations, continue to hold aloft with self-sacrificing courage the banner of resistance.

What now?

The terror let loose by the Government through its Special Branch has made it impossible for our national organisation, the South African Indian Congress, and its constituent bodies, to function legally. Every one of the office-bearers and prominent committee members has been banned, imprisoned or driven into exile. Every form of intimidation and blackmail is used by the Government and the Special Branch to silence criticisms of apartheid. There has arisen amongst our people a small minority of traitors, stooges and puppets who speak in the voice of their masters – Vorster and Trollip. Some of them have been cajoled, bribed or intimidated by the authorities into serving on the bogus government-appointed South African Indian Council.

Our people should have no illusion about the South African Indian Council. Remember the Judenraten (Jewish Councils) set up by the Nazis at the time of Hitler! The 'representatives' of the Jewish community on these councils were used merely as instruments to facilitate the sending of hundreds of thousands of the Jewish people into concentration camps and the gas chambers.

However, all the efforts of the Nationalist Government and its stooges will fail. Our people can never submit to the ruination and indignity imposed by white supremacy. Brave spirits will speak out and organise and fight for liberty.

Vorster cannot win

As the freedom-fighters gather strength the sound of their guns will be heard throughout the land.

All Vorster's arms and all Vorster's men will not be able to stop the onward march of the people to freedom. The struggle may be grim and protracted but it will not cease until apartheid has been overthrown and full and equal rights and opportunities ensured to all the citizens, irrespective of race, colour or creed – until the Freedom Charter is translated into reality.

Our tasks

History calls upon us to play our full part in the new phase of the struggle:

1. Heed the call of the ANC – ally yourselves with the freedom-fighters – help them in every possible way! Make their path easy!
2. Reject the government-managed South African Indian Council!
3. Maintain and intensify resistance against the Group Areas Act and against every aspect of apartheid!
3. Youth! Your place is in the forefront of the struggle. Become freedom- fighters! Carry this message far and wide among our people. Help mobilize full support for the freedom-fighters in town and country! We shall win!

Amandla Ngawethu! Jana Shakti!
Matla Ke A Rona!
Power to the people!

APPENDIX 3 – by 'JAMES'

'James' was recruited through the Communist Party of Great Britain by Dave King (see Appendix 1). 'Alice McCarthy' and 'James' went on two missions together, one in November 1969 (to Port Elizabeth) and the other in February 1970 to Cape Town, including a visit to Lesotho to warn a comrade to get out. (The second mission was for the SACP, not the ANC.) James has provided the following press cuttings and other material which he has carefully preserved over the years. – Editor.

Fig. 1. Front and back pages of the four-page leaflet, printed on airmail paper.

Fig. 2. Inside pages of the four-page leaflet.

Most of the newspapers in South Africa carried stories about the 'leaflet bombs'. The following is from the *Star* on Saturday 15 November 1969:

SHOWERS OF ILLEGAL PAMPHLETS IN CAPE

Cape Town. – The Cape Town police have collected and are examining pamphlets reported to deal with the activities of a banned organisation.

According to Det.-Sgt. J. Troost of the Cape Town Security Police the pamphlets are the same as others distributed from time to time in the past.

Outside a bank in Adderley Street last evening pamphlets fluttered into the air out of a plastic bucket in which a small charge had been detonated. Within a quarter of an hour the police had removed all the pamphlets.

A report also described one of the pamphlets as being printed on fine airmail paper with photographs, headlines and columns of text.

As the pamphlets erupted outside the bank, a tape recorder broadcast slogans of a banned organization from the roof at the entrance to the non-White section of the railway station. Railway police removed the tape-recorder from a ledge on the roof.

Hundreds of pamphlets, described by the police as subversive, were found at two points in Port Elizabeth last night – in Pinchin Lane and in Strand Street, both places near non-European bus termini.

Police seized a large number but a strong wind blew away others. Three women said they saw a plastic bag flung from a fast-moving vehicle in Strand Street. The bag burst and pamphlets scattered in the wind.

The pamphlets were reported to have come from a banned African organization. – Sapa.

The *Cape Times* carried a similar story the same day, although some details were slightly different. In Cape Town, an ex-Rhodesian police officer was driving down Strand Street and through the closed windows of his car heard "a penetrating voice over a loudspeaker speaking in an African language. I've seen excited crowds in my time, and this was one of them. I double-parked my car and called the Railway Police. On a ledge above the station entrance we found a paper carrier-bag through which ran a chain attached to something inside and locked to a pole on the ledge. The Railway Police looked in the bag and told me there was a tape-recorder inside. We had to cut the chain to remove it."

The *Cape Times* report also covered Port Elizabeth, and provided some more information about the leaflets:

"Inside are pictures of two former ANC leaders. They are Oliver Tambo, former ANC deputy president now in exile, and Nelson Mandela, former secretary-general of the ANC, now imprisoned on Robben Island.

On the same page, exact details of how to make a Molotov

cocktail are given with a diagram.

How the pamphlets were dumped in Pinchin Lane could not be ascertained.

Large numbers were then confiscated. By-standers reported that the police were searching passing pedestrians. A security branch officer said afterwards possession of the pamphlet was illegal."

The timing of these events in South Africa coincided with the Communist Party of Great Britain's congress, attended by three delegates from Southern African liberation organisations: Nelson Moyo of the Zimbabwe African People's Union, M.P. Naicker of the African National Congress, and Peter Katjavivi of the South-West African People's Organisation.

As reported in the *Morning Star* on Monday 17 November 1969, the liberation movement representatives were given a standing ovation by the delegates, who also heard a message from the South African Communist Party, which expressed "deep appreciation of the help and encouragement which we persistently received from your party."

The same day, another event took place in Cape Town. Dan van der Vat, the correspondent for *The Times* in London, reported that a protracted disturbance had taken place in the African township of Langa after a policeman had shot and killed one African and seriously wounded another.

"The security police today denied that the Langa incident was in any way connected with four simultaneous explosions in Cape Town, Johannesburg, Durban and Port Elizabeth at the weekend.

In each case, the small explosive charge was placed in a receptacle containing leaflets prepared by the banned African National Congress (ANC). When the explosive went off, leaflets were scattered all over the surrounding pavement. No one was hurt.

The 'leaflet bombs' constitute the first noticeable sign for a long time of ANC activity on any scale within South Africa. The leaflets themselves contained pictures of ANC leaders, precise instructions, with diagrams, on how to make a petrol bomb and general descriptive matter about the ANC."

Several days later, the *Morning Star* printed a transcript of the messages broadcast from tape recorders in Cape Town, Port Elizabeth, Johannesburg, East London and Durban.

Fig. 3. Cartoon from the Rand Daily Mail, 15 August 1970

Fig. 4. The two-page leaflet issued by the South African Communist Party.

Fig. 5. The front cover and inside pages of the booklet containing the Programme of the South African Communist Party, an Editorial Note entitled 'Freedom Marches South: The Fighting in Zimbabwe', and 'Partitioning South Africa' by L. Legwa.

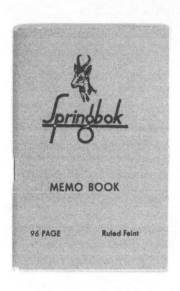

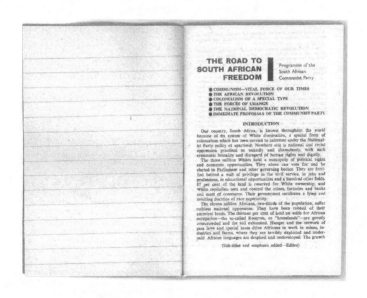

Later that year (1970), another series of 'leaflet bombings' took place in the same South African cities. In the report in the *Star* on 14 August 1970, Brigadier P.J. ("Tiny") Venter, head of the Security Police, said they were "nothing more than an attempt by the A.N.C. to get cheap publicity."

"'This is exactly what the African National Congress wants,' he said, 'and our newspapers, English as well as Afrikaans, oblige them by giving them thousands of rands worth of publicity free ... on the front page.

'When there is something good to publish it gets stuck away on one of the inside pages.'"

Brigadier Venter did not explain what he meant by 'something good'. He then added:

"'If the newspapers remained silent on this score nobody would have taken any notice of the pamphlets.

'When the so-called bombs exploded and scattered the pamphlets, people who passed by largely ignored them, and nobody read them. But since the newspapers gave them all that publicity nearly everyone wants to read them.'"

The same report referred to the previous 'leaflet bombings', saying that the police had established the leaflets had been printed in Britain and smuggled into South Africa. The Minister of Police, S.L. Muller, was reported in the *Sunday Express* as having decided not to proceed with his intention of seeking a Supreme Court interdict to prohibit newspapers from publishing photographs or extracts from the ANC leaflets. Instead, in conjunction with the Minister of Justice, he would issue a cautionary statement about the laws prohibiting the publication of banned or subversive literature.

"If the response to this statement is reasonable, I shall not proceed with any Supreme Court action. But if newspapers continue to violate the law and do not react responsibly, then I shall have no option but to enforce the law."

In a report in *Die Vaderland*, dated 14 August, it was concluded that the 'leaflet bombings' had to be seen against the background of an attack on South West Africa and the pending hearing of twenty detainees in Pretoria under the Terrorism Act. It also referred to reports that a number of people had been arrested the previous night, but they could not confirm them that morning.

The international Press also reported the events. *The Times* and *Guardian* mentioned them, and the *Guardian* carried an Editorial Comment, referring to the impending trial of Winnie Mandela and nineteen other defendants, and that the 'leaflet bombs' were a general reminder to South Africa as a whole that the ANC can still mount a well-coordinated and sophisticated publicity coup. The *National Herald* (India) and the *Hindustan Times* (New Delhi) both carried the story.

Underground broadcast

VOICE: This is the African National Congress. This is the African National Congress. This is the Voice of Freedom. The ANC speaks to You!
Africa! Africa! Mayibuye!

SINGING of the National Anthem (*Nkosi Sikele Le Afrika* and *Morena Boloke*)

VOICE: The time has come. This Government of slavery, this Government of oppression, this Apartheid monster must be removed from power and crushed by the People! It must be removed by force!

They will never stop the pass raids, the arrests, the beatings, the killings ... they will continue to drive us out of our homes like dogs and send us to rot in the so-called Bantu homelands, they will continue to pay us miserable slave wages, and treat us as their beasts of burden until the day we beat them up and crush white rule!

This land of ours was taken away by bloodshed. We will regain it by bloodshed.

Sons and daughters of Africa, you in your millions who have toiled to make this country rich, the ANC calls upon you – NEVER submit to white oppression – NEVER give up the Freedom Struggle – find ways of organising those around you – the African National Congress calls upon you to be ready – to be ready for war!

You will soon learn how to make a petrol bomb. You will also learn how to shoot a gun. You must learn how to outwit the enemy, his spies and informers, and organise those around you. We are many, they are few.

Our Coloured and Indian brothers must do the same. You must organise your people to fight the ghettoes and all the racial laws and in support of the armed struggle.

We say to the enemy that we will not be bluffed by your toy parliaments like Matazima's, like the Coloured Council and like the Indian Council.

We want freedom now! REAL FREEDOM!

But the whites will not give it to us. We want no big army. We organise ourselves into small groups. We attack the enemy suddenly when he is not expecting us. We kill them and we take their guns and we disappear.

Our brave young men have shown the way in our heroic battles in Rhodesia. Today they fight in Rhodesia, tomorrow they will fight in South Africa. All over the young men are showing the way.

They are fighting the white racist armies in Angola, in

Mozambique, in Rhodesia. Today they fight in Rhodesia, tomorrow they will fight in South Africa.

The African National Congress calls upon you to prepare for the guerrilla war, the war of liberation. The ANC calls upon you to help our young men, our freedom fighters.

We organise ourselves into small groups, we carry guns, suddenly we attack the enemy, we kill them and we take their weapons and we hide away … the forests, the mountains, the countryside, the People hide the young men. Everyone of you can help in this fight. Everyone can be a freedom fighter.

In your factory, in your school, in the land, in your church – wherever you are amongst the People – you must find a way of organising those around you. If you work carefully you will be able to cheat the enemy and his spies and informers.

You must be prepared. You must be ready to sacrifice. We refuse to live on our knees. We refuse to say "Ja Baas".

We must prepare to rise against the white oppressor. Nelson Mandela said he was prepared to die for the freedom of our People. What do you say my dear young brother, my dear young sister?

Sons of Sekhukuni, Sons of Shaka, Sons of Hintsa, Sons of Mshoeshoe … the time has come. Freedom lovers of South Africa the time to fight has come.

This is the message the African National Congress brings to you. You will soon learn how to make a petrol bomb. You will also learn how to shoot a gun. You must learn how to outwit the enemy and organise those around you. The enemy fears our organised might. We are many, the whites are few. We must find ways to organise our People.

They pay us low wages because our skins are black, whilst the whites live in luxury. At work, in the factories, the mines, the docks, the offices, the kitchens, the fields, the railways, the roads, we demand equal pay for equal work NOW!

They give our children inferior education. We demand proper education that will enable our young people to be equal to other young people in the world. Our young people must be taught how to fly jet aeroplanes and how to fly the sputniks.

In the school, our young people must organise to resist Bantu Education. We demand free and equal education for all our children NOW! The whites have taken away the land of our People in the countryside, and have forced them to give up their cattle.
We must resist the Matanzima stooges, we must resist the Bantu Authorities Act in the countryside. We want our land back. Our young men with guns will fight for it in the countryside. They will deal with the stooges and informers, the police and the white soldiers. Our People in the countryside must be told of their coming. They must hide and feed our freedom fighters, they must make their path easy and the enemy's path hard.

The African National Congress calls upon our People to prepare for guerrilla warfare, the People's War of Liberation, NOW!

Guerrilla war has brought victory to the people of Algeria, to the people of Cuba, to the people of Vietnam. Those people did not have big armies. They were like us. Guerrilla fighters organise themselves in small groups. Suddenly when the enemy is not expecting them, they attack. They kill and grab the guns and disappear.

You sons and daughters of the soil, you must consider yourselves as soldiers in the guerrilla war. There are many ways to be a freedom fighter. You will soon learn how to make a petrol bomb. You will also learn how to shoot a gun. You must learn how to outwit the enemy and organise those around you. We are many, they are few.

The African National Congress calls on all the oppressed people to organise and struggle and prepare to fight in the towns and in the countryside. Our brave men of Umkonto we Sizwe have shown the way.

They fought heroically in Zimbabwe. They will fight in South Africa. You must start to find places where you can hide the weapons you might come across. You must have secret addresses of your reliable friends who will agree to hide you or your weapons or other freedom fighters.

You must be ready to sacrifice. You must start now to find hiding places. The countryside, the bush, the forest, the mountain – these will also become your secret addresses. The time has come.

The African National Congress calls upon you to organise and to prepare.

Death to racialism!

Mayibuy' Africa! Amandla! Ke Nako! Ayi Hlome!

(Come Back Africa! Power! This is it! Close ranks!)

SINGING of FREEDOM SONGS.

APPENDIX 4
Sources of further information

"Armed and Dangerous" – my undercover struggle against apartheid by Ronnie Kasrils (Jonathan Ball, Johannesburg 2004). This was first published by Heinemann in 1993. Chapter 8 is called *London Recruits* and tells part of the story told in this book. The 2004 edition is the same as the earlier one but with added chapters covering events after July 1993.

http://www.anc.org.za/books/press1.html – *To change the world is reason enough* – the on-line autobiography of Dr Ron Press (1929 – 2009). A scientist and member of the ANC and SACP who went into exile in Britain in 1962, he played a big part in designing the leaflet bombs and loudspeaker devices.

Inside Out – Escape from Pretoria Prison by Tim Jenkin (Jakana Education, South Africa, 2003), tells the amazing story of Alex Moumbaris's escape from prison along with white ANC members Tim Jenkin and Steve Lee. An earlier version can be read online with the title *Escape from Pretoria* (see http://www.anc.org.za/books/escape0.html)

Conny Braam, *Operation Vula* (Jacana Media (Pty) Ltd (South Africa, 2004) ISBN -919931-70-8. The details surrounding Operation Vula, which was an ANC plan to have a structure in place in South Africa to forcefully overthrow the apartheid regime and that ran concurrently with the first stages of the negotiation process, are little-known, and so too are the players involved. This book tells, with emotion and humility, of her own and others' roles in what was the last and largest ANC operation against the apartheid regime.

ANC – A View from Moscow by Vladimir Shubin (Jakana, South Africa, 2008). Shubin was a high-level Soviet official who was involved for many years in aiding the ANC and its ally, the South African Communist Party, in their struggle against apartheid. It has been described as 'the most intimate and comprehensive work yet published on ANC-Soviet relations'.

http://www.anc.org.za/ancdocs/history/congress/sactu/zz1.htm
This is part of *Freedom in our Lifetime* by Archie Sibeko (Zola Zembe) with Joyce Leeson. It gives an account of solidarity shown by British trade unions to the South African trade union movement.

Roger Fieldhouse, *Anti-Apartheid: A History of the Movement in Britain, 1959-1994*, Merlin Press Ltd, Pontypool 2004. This throws no direct light on the secret activities detailed in this book, but it describes the activities of the (British) Anti-Apartheid Movement and of anti-apartheid campaigning in Britain.

Secret Safari is an award-winning educational documentary DVD about the Africa Hinterland episode described by Stuart Round in his chapter. Made in 2001 and directed by Tom Zubrycki, it is distributed by Canberra-based Donin Films. It is available in South Africa and Australia, but not in the UK.

The Will to Die, by Can Themba (David Philip, 1985) is a collection of stories (banned when first published) about black Johannesburg in the late 1950s.

The Unlikely Secret Agent by Ronnie Kasrils (Jacana, 2010) tells the remarkable story of his wife Eleanor's courage and daring in and after 1963.

117 Days: by Ruth First (re-published by Virago, in 2010) is a day-by-day account of confinement and interrogation, also in 1963. The author was assassinated by the South African police in 1982. *The ANC Underground in South Africa* by Raymond Suttner, (Jacana 2009) tells how underground networks organised within South Africa.

The Historical Roots of the ANC edited by Ben Turok, (Jacana Media, Sept 2011). This book looks at the principles and processes that led to the founding of the ANC in 1912 and examines how they have influenced policy and practice in the ANC for the century since then.

The ANC and the turn to Armed Struggle 1950-1970 edited
by Ben Turok (Jacana Media, Sept 2011). This book was first
published in the late 1960s at a time when the ANC was forced
by events to confront major ideological and policy issues.

Name Index

Also Available from the Merlin Press

ROGER FIELDHOUSE
ANTI-APARTHEID: A History of the Movement in Britain, 1959-1994

The Old Apartheid regime is dead. Campaigns, including consumer, economic and sports boycotts, the arms embargo, financial blockages and the free Mandela campaign, had a massive impact helping to change consciousness and remould linkages between Britain and South Africa.
This is the first full length study drawing on AAM archives, a full and substantial history of the Anti-Apartheid Movement from birth to death and beyond. It shows how things happened, it assesses AAM's achievements and evaluates its impact and effectiveness.

"Fieldhouse provides all the facts that the serious students needs and does so in clear, careful, concise considered English. ...It will surely be the first reference book those with a serious interest in the subject turn to" *New Statesman*

"an impressive book in size and detail". *Morning Star*

"an important study reflecting the author's personal involvement in and commitment to the anti-apartheid cause as well as six years research." *Sage Race Relations Abstracts*

234x156mm; xiv+546pp   978 0 85036549 8 Pbk   £22.50

JÜRGEN ZIMMERER & JOACHIM ZELLER, Editors
GENOCIDE IN GERMAN SOUTH-WEST AFRICA:
The Colonial War of 1904-1908 and its aftermath
Translated and introduced by E.J. Nether

Early in 1904 war broke out in German South West Africa, when the Herero tribe rose up against an oppressive colonial regime. The German army despatched to the colony brutally suppressed the uprising and set about the systematic annihilation of the Herero and Nama people.
This collection of essays considers many aspects of this war of extermination. Edward Neather adds an introduction that situates these events in the context of the great African land rush by

European powers and shows how racism, concentration camps and genocide in the German colony foreshadow the crimes committed during Hitler's Third Reich.

Reviews of the German edition:
"Anyone wishing to have a wider and comprehensive understanding of the German dimension of a conflict which was designed as a war of mass destruction is recommended to read this book" *Die Zeit*

337pp, Illus. with contemporary B/w photos.
978 0 85036 573 3 Hbk £50.00; 978 0 85036 574 0 Pbk £18.95

Life histories told to
COLIN LEYS and SUSAN BROWN
HISTORIES OF NAMIBIA: Living Through The Liberation Struggle

The stories of eleven Namibians, in their mid 30s when Namibia gained its independence, telling of how a whole generation matured in the struggle, becoming skilled, disciplined, cosmopolitan and tough.
"We need many more books like 'Histories of Namibia' in order to further illuminate this crucial chapter in recent African history".
John Saul, Emeritus Professor of Political Science

"powerful accounts of those who are now able to share their experiences with a wider audience." Journal of Modern Africa Studies
"fascinating collection of eleven life histories… these stories are inspiring testimony to the human spirit." *International Journal of African Historical Studies*

234x156mm; viii+165pp. **978 0 85036 499 6 Pbk £14.95**

V L ALLEN
THE HISTORY OF BLACK MINEWORKERS IN SOUTH AFRICA

'What Allen who has extensively researched mining in different countries adds to the literature is his excellent sense for the material conditions of mining and the meaning of the mining experience… keeps in tension the relationship between the struggles on the mines and the wider political context.' *Journal of African History*

'Invariably spot-on… Anyone who wants to understand the complex

nature of global capitalism, racism and the horrors of mining needs to read these exhaustively researched and highly readable volumes.'
Tribune

'it is unlikely that any other book will ever provide so complete an account, warts and all, of the tumultuous first twelve years in the life of South Africa's largest trade union.' *African Studies Review*

First Volume: MINING IN SOUTH AFRICA & THE GENESIS OF APARTHEID: 1871-1948
Second Volume: APARTHEID REPRESSION AND DISSENT IN THE MINES: 1948-1982
Third Volume: ORGANISE OR DIE: 1982-1994

Available as a Three Volume Hbk Set 978 0 85036 569 6 £100.00

WILF and TRISH MBANGA
SERETSE AND RUTH: The Love Story

With a Preface by Alexander McCall Smith

In 1966 a new country came into existence. The Republic of Botswana was born into a troubled region and there must have been those who were quietly pessimistic as to the prospects of this new country ever being much more than a satellite of its more powerful neighbour. How wrong such predictions were! Under the guidance of its first President, Sir Seretse Khama, the new state showed that not only would it be a truly independent member of the world community but that it would be an example to the rest of the world of what could be achieved in a country dedicated to honesty and decency in government. In the years that followed, Botswana became a beacon in Africa, with a record of achievement in every sphere, notably in health and education.
Behind this success story there is the story of one family which was called by its historical position to play a central role in the development of the new state. This is the Khama family, and in particular Seretse Khama, statesman, paramount chief, husband and father.
This book dwells on the last two aspects of this important figure, and tells, in the process, a story which I think is one of the great love stories of our times. In the face of great difficulties and opposition, Sereste and Ruth were united in a fruitful marriage which showed the

world how people from different traditions might live in harmony and happiness. In many respects, their personal story, so movingly recounted in this book, is the story of the country itself, for Botswana as a state has always stressed the importance of social harmony.
Great love stories usually reveal the nobility of the human spirit. This tale does exactly that and we who read this account have reason to be grateful to Wilf and Trish Mbanga for sharing their own particular insight into a moving and memorable story.
Alexander McCall Smith

280 x 215mm; 376pp; Green Print 978 1 85425 101 5 Pbk £ 15.95

PETER SANDERS
'THROWING DOWN WHITE MAN': Cape Rule and Misrule in Colonial Lesotho, 1871-1884

Surrounded by South Africa lies the small independent mountainous kingdom of Lesotho.

This book explores how the Basotho people came to preserve a measure of autonomy from powerful neighbours in the Gun War 1880-81. The Gun War was provoked by the determination of the Cape Colony to disarm the Basotho people.
It was not a big war, and outside Lesotho it has been eclipsed by the almost contemporaneous Zulu War. Over a period of six months' fighting the number of Basotho killed probably did not amount to more than 700-800; fewer than 200 whites were killed.
But in one all-important respect the Gun War was different, not just from the Zulu War, but from all the other wars that were fought out in southern Africa at that time: the whites were humiliatingly defeated, or at least they were decisively held at bay.
For this reason alone it calls out for close enquiry.

A word of explanation is needed for the title – *Throwing down White Man*. It is inspired by the praise poems of Chief Maama Letsie,
I struck White Man, I threw him down/ He fell before the face of my horse, /He fell before the face of my horse, Koloboi.
White Man is a translation of Lekhooa, a term of contempt. In the words of one observer, saying 'Dumela Lekho[o]a' ('Good day, white man') – was not unlike saying to a native, 'Good day, you nigger.'
The Basotho chiefs had put up resistance throughout the period of Cape rule, from 1871 to 1884. The Colony had tried to undermine

their power and to establish the rule of magistrates instead. The Basotho's victory in the Gun War had lasting significance. The Cape withdrew and imperial rule was re-established. The chiefs had won. The imperial government, for good or ill, left the running of the country largely in their hands.

This book presents oral traditions and archival sources with meticulous care. It lays bare the narrower interests and conflicting perspectives among the Basotho chiefs and the local officials, as well as the larger forces at work in the region. And at the centre of this book is a compelling and absorbing study of the Gun War itself.

'Sanders has produced a definitive work about Cape rule in Lesotho that also makes a major contribution to understanding Southern Africa history and the complexities of colonial relationships and strategies in general.' *African Studies Review*

242x164mm; 311pp, 978 0 85036 654 9 Pbk £20.00

www.merlinpress.co.uk